You're Gonna Hurt Yourself

Ben Nelson Creed

DEDICATION

"Dreams are worth fighting for."- - Langston Hughes.

Notice he didn't say anything about winning or losing.

This is for all the fighters, real and phony, winners and losers, champions and jobbers.

CONTENTS

ACKNOWLEDGMENTS

Thanks Jessica for your unending support and feedback and Louis for your patience.
Thank you Calvin Wharton for keeping me as your student.

To everyone who made wrestling what it was:

Please believe that I'm not making fun of anyone. I'm just enjoying the spectacle I was part of and fully expect my receipts.

In fact, I look forward to it.

A First in Wrestling

"Ladies and gentlemen, here he is, TJ Harley, THE JEWISH WARRIOR!" crackled a tiny voice trying to boom over the speakers.

We all chuckled at the introduction, peeking through the window. TJ loved the loosely organized clusterfuck that is pro-wrestling. Another wrestler had no-showed, so TJ Harley, the peaceful, cheery looking fellow who had never read any part of the bible suddenly became "The Jewish Warrior". It was a summer camp for Jewish teens; the promoters, two Persian twins, had promised to highlight a Jewish wrestler as inspiration for the crowd. When Ruffy Silverstein bailed last minute, someone had to save us all. It was TJ, TJ the hero.

While he soaked up the cheers, high-fiving kids and flexing his 15 inch biceps, an angry Tyson Dux paced inside the ring, growling. It was ridiculous, but the crowd bought it. That was good. In fact, the crowd was the only thing about the whole show that was good. The rest of it was typical wrestling idiocy.

We were dressing in a log cabin. There was almost no atmosphere at the event. There was no entranceway, no smoke, no lights, and long, awkward introductions. When we heard our name announced, we'd pop open the cabin door, stagger back temporarily blinded by the sun, and after about 50 delicate paces down worn-out steps covered in pine cones and gravel, we'd finally get into the ring. From there we all enjoyed the view of a swing set and a steaming basketball court littered with teens and tweens. With crowds usually smaller than a hundred people, the excited rabble of three hundred campers made this show our *Wrestlemania*. Or at least our *Monday Night Raw.*

I had already done my first match; highlights included a low-speed chase through the crowd and calling my opponent a "sloppy 400 pound pussy." I also grabbed the microphone and got the kids to chant "Puss-E, Puss-E" at him which didn't sit well with the promoters. I'd apologized, but doubted my future with Twin Towers Wrestling as I creaked across the cabin floor. I'd gotten off easier than TJ Harley though. I hadn't had to change religions. No snip for me.

"Bomber, what'd the twins say?" asked JC Owens, my 400 pound opponent from earlier.

"Meh, they're mad at me for yelling 'Pussy' into the mic." I said.

"I thought it was pretty dumb, bomb," replied JC.

"But how is that more offensive than a promotion called 'Twin Towers Wrestling' when 9-11 pretty much just happened?" I asked.

"They're the promoters, they got it all figured out" said JC.

"Well, there it is" I said, slumping against the wall.

"It's a twins' show," shot Jer, "don't worry about it. Let's figure out this match."

We started discussing the main event; I was going to take the heat (beating to get sympathy) in the six-man tag team match. It was easy to organize. We were all planning hope spots (moments of renewed vigor by the good guy) and offensive combos. Wrestling is so easy when working with talented guys; we didn't really need to talk at all. Distracted, I glanced out the window and saw Tyson slam "The Jewish Warrior" TJ Harley to the mat. He loudly clapped his hands around TJ's chin, pretending to choke him.

Deathly still, TJ sat entombed in a rear chin-lock. In a few seconds he'd be stomping his foot and shaking his fists in a blatant rip-off of Hulk Hogan. We'd all done this exact thing dozens of times. Same old shit. Meh. I turned to look at Jer sitting on a stool, the rest of the wrestlers hovering around him.

Jer was explaining how he envisioned the hot tag. We listened to his vivid painting of high spots (exciting parts) while wrestling dream fairies danced over our heads. He was great at planning a match. Suddenly, he stopped, staring blankly ahead. Stuck? He locked eyes onto me.

"Bomboid, do you hear that?" he asked.

"Yeah, I heard you, bump n feed, blind tag to me then I'll splash off the top. Why--"

"No, not that" said Jer.

"You mean what we're doing for the cut-off?" asked JC Owens.

"Shhhhhhh, not that," said Jer, pointing to the window, "that. What is that?"

We looked at each other, cocking our ears. What was the crowd yelling? I knew the words, but didn't understand the meaning. I peeked out through a dusty window.

TJ Harley, from his seated position, was fighting back and shaking his fists, while stomping his foot faster and faster. The crowd clapped along. Electric screams belted out of the audience as TJ shook with righteous fury, feeding off the excited young campers in attendance. The crowd swelled louder and louder with each stomp of his foot. I'll never forget their screams; it was a full-bodied crowd of three hundred Jewish teens chanting faster and faster;

"JEW-BOY! JEW-BOY! JEW-BOY! JEW-BOY! JEW-BOY!"

It had to be a first. TJ Harley, straight haired, devout lover of bacon, their hero, their idol, was coming back from the dead! Tyson, clasping TJ's neck loosely, shook his head in disbelief and tucked his chin into his chest to hide his laughter.

"JEW-BOY JEW-BOY, JEWBOY!" the crowd cried, united with TJ's stomping foot. Enough was enough! This Jewish warrior was not taking this sitting down!

TJ Harley began shaking his head side to side then rose from near death and began bashing the villainous Tyson Dux. First, a closeline, "Yeah!" then a running elbow-smash, "Ohhh!" followed by a springboard elbow off the ropes "YEAHHHH!" Woozily, Tyson stood and fed into The Jewish Warrior for one last blow. The crowd gasped in anticipation.

TJ Harley windmilled his arms before a last, gigantic hammer-smash that crumbled Tyson Dux into a shaking heap of humanity. To the audience, Tyson writhed on the mat, shaking with pain. To us, he was clearly shaking with laugher. TJ Harley gritted his teeth and dished out an ass-whooping while laughing and clapping along to the swelling chants. It was magical. It was pro-wrestling at its simplest. Its finest. And also its most fucked up. And all throughout his glorious comeback cheers of "JEW-BOY JEW-BOY, JEW-BOY!" echoed throughout the campground and across the lake.

"What the fuck is going?" asked Jer.

Crowded around the window, we all stared but none of us had anything to say; we just laughed. We were witnessing another first in pro wrestling. A terrible, awesome, definitive first. I don't know if it has ever gotten better than that.

The show wasn't what I dreamed life as a wrestler would be like. None of wrestling was. It was much, much shittier. Thank God for that.

You're Gonna Hurt Yourself

You're Gonna Hurt Yourself

Why Wrestle?

Me as a baby. Note the fashion sense.

You're Gonna Hurt Yourself

Hunger. That gnawing pain you get when you miss your regular meal time. You eat later, but you still feel like you're missing something. That's the unquenchable passion that all those artists and athletes speak of. You don't know why you have it, you just do and can't shake it. That's the passion I had for wrestling. As a kid, young man, and into my first years as a wrestler, it was always there.

If I hadn't seen wrestling or hadn't wrestled with my friends on my trampoline for a while, the hunger would groan and burn. I'd walk down a hallway, turn a corner, and wham! I'd wonder if Andre the Giant could bodyslam King Kong Bundy. I had to see it, I had to read about it, and I had to wrestle. From age six on, there was no other choice.

I was a skinny kid and then a fat kid, but this was intentional. In grade 4, I remember thinking that all the funny, likeable people I knew were fat- friends, John Candy, Santa Clause, etc. I decided to get fat; I ate and ate till I felt sick and I got fat. I knew getting fat would give my body a base to swell up from when I lost my extra weight; if I could run around with all that fat, I would be able to run faster without it. It wasn't hard to figure out.

Fat wasn't going to turn into muscle, but it would make room for muscle and establish strength. I began my career as a pro wrestler by getting fat in grade four, but also by staying fit and active. I owe most of it to my life on a farm and having to walk three km to the bus before school from grades one till three. And fighting my brother, Paul. That undoubtedly started my path to fitness.

I wrestled constantly on my trampoline with anyone who was around and my friends paid the price. I often bribed my brother Phil into wrestling with me; I would promise him a GI Joe figure if he would do a match, and I often justified not giving him the GI Joe because the match sucked or he hadn't finished it. I almost broke my friend Jens Jacobsen's neck once on a pile driver, so he claims; looking back it was a miracle I didn't get hurt, but I almost always erred on the side of caution.

Quinn, Jens, Joey, and I were best friends and often engaged in mercy fights where we would wrestle and try to force the other guy into submission. Poor Quinn. He was fit from riding his bike 5km to school every day, but that didn't help; he was the smallest. Since Quinn was great at annoying us, which he did intentionally and constantly, we relished beating on him.

He was a witty, slippery, smart guy, and the nonsense we got into as kids could often be traced back to him; he was a master of bad decisions. Joey was about 40 pounds heavier than me, a big Native Canadian with probably the strongest legs I've ever seen. He ran, rode his bike, worked labour jobs, and played sports. His thighs, once we got into high school, were at least 30 inches around and muscular. Our school got a leg press machine in grade 10. Every weight we had in the gym plus 2 friends went up on the machine. Joey laughed his ass off as he pressed it and we gave up on besting him. He was a 17 year old who could leg press whatever he wanted to.

Since Joey and I were the biggest, we often got to sparring with each other on the trampoline, but Joey most enjoyed beating up Quinn. Our other friend, Jens Jacobsen, was also a great athlete; he was a cross country and cycling star who eventually became a model- shirt on and off. During our middle school and early high school years, he enjoyed beating up Quinn also.

Once, Jens and Quinn engaged in a song-worthy battle at Deep Cove Elementary School. For clarity, I should state that the mercy battles weren't scheduled things like fight club. They would just erupt when we pissed each other off or a dispute arose. It was a pretty healthy way to settle differences; our energy burnt out and the conflict was mostly resolved because usually, neither of us were right, and we would both just agree to stop. Not this time. Jens and Quinn were at the school to throw around Jens' Aerobe, a flying disk that can sail a few hundred yards. Jens brought it to the school still in the package, crisp and new. He gracefully unwrapped it. Since Aerobe's can go so far, rules were required.

"Quinn, no matter what you do, don't throw it towards the forest" he said, and before he could even take a first toss with it, he went to pee, leaving the Aerobe behind.

"Don't toss it in the woods," yelled Jens as he left, "if I come back and my Aerobe is in a tree, I'm going to kill you."

Of course, when Jens returned, the Aerobe was in a tree. That's just Quinn.

"Quinn, you're such an idiot!" yelled Jens.

"I didn't think it would get stuck."

"You idiot, there's a whole field over there! Why wouldn't you just throw it that way?"

"They're supposed to curve up!"

"Why not curve it up on the field?"

"I wanted to see how high it would go."

Blood boils. Ears flap. Faces run red.

"ARGHH!"

The mercy fight began on the grassy field, miles away from anyone to judge. Only true mercy could decide a winner. Jens caught Quinn in an arm bar-headlock combo; the loser had to climb the tree to get the Aerobe (the climb, by the way, was impossible), and Jens knew Quinn was beat. There was no way out for Quinn unless he bought Jens a new Aerobe.

"Give up and get my Aerobe back!"

"No!"

"Then buy me a new one!"

"No, I need my money."

"You're so dumb! Give up!"

"No- AHH! You're breaking my arm!"

"I don't care; just say you're going to get my Aerobe or buy me a new one and we'll stop" seethed Jens. At this point, who wouldn't give up? Anybody with common sense and reason would. Not Quinn. A heave, a yell, a desperate twist to escape and "SNAP!--- AHHHHHH!" Quinn won his freedom.

"Jeez, Quinn, are you ok?"

"AHHHH! Hmmmm, hmmmmm, AHHHH" he moaned. Tears flowed, Quinn raged, spazzed, and tried to attack Jens with 1 good arm and 1 dislocated arm dangling at his side. After a few minutes of futile flapping and tears, Quinn jumped on his bike and rode home to his father, crying and alone because he had cursed Jens out and told him to get lost.

As he groaned in agony, his father looked at him then assessed us all.

"Quinn, you guys are idiots," and with a, "I'm not going to the hospital today" popped Quinn's shoulder back in. We were typical rough, dumb kids who fought for fun. No matter what happened, I always wanted to wrestle. I loved it.

"We're all going to be great when we grow up," said Jens on a bike ride a few weeks later, thinking aloud.

"Quinn will be a famous artist, Joey will make a tonne of cash working for his dad, I'll be a triathlete, and you'll be a wrestler. It's going to be awesome." Dreams. They all came true... kind of.

Fitter, Fatter, Stronger

I had a huge energy for sports due to my upbringing and inspiration at home; my father had polio in one leg, but he worked his day job, worked all day long on the farm on weekends and played squash every morning before work.

My older brother, Paul, was really into weight lifting. He filled out impressively and was probably the toughest, most feared guy in the school, although he was friends with everybody. He was a jock-artist with a long red hair and an impressive build of about 6 feet tall and 220 pounds.- a fiery Thor. I was inspired by my brother's pre-school workouts that he did every morning. Years before I lifted weights, Paul got me into my second youth passion as a sport- rugby. And rugby got me ready for wrestling.

Once grade 9 rolled around, I had a crazy desire to be the best at rugby that I could. For the whole summer, 6 days a week, I ran through the forests around my house, then lifted weights for 1 or 2 hours. I would do chest and biceps, back and triceps, or shoulders and extended abdominal workouts before hitting my heavy bag. I started lifting weights then began Judo at my high school. My sensei, Mickey Fitz, was a tough man of about 5'8 and 200lbs. Throwing him was impossible but inspiring.

I can honestly say I learned more lessons from Fitz in Judo than in most of my classes. He would laugh while

Rugby players and my coach Don Burgess.   Note the joy.

setting me up for a "Turkish ride", pinning my arms under me as he dug his knuckles into my neck, me almost screaming, and him laughing in a high pitched cackle. I learned respect, how to fall, how to throw, and how to handle pain. Fitz had shipped off from Prince Rupert to Japan in his early twenties, long before this was a common thing. He became the real deal by paying his dues. I learned from him that in life, like a judo throw, you have to commit to achieve. I wish I'd remembered that more often.

When grade 12 hit, I hit a stride. I was doing PE in school every day, and in addition to the weight training and basketball that went on, I played rugby with the local Old Boys men's club rugby team. We trained every Tuesday and Thursday evening from 6:30-8; however we also had a junior club team that would run and train from 4:30-6:00. Some days I would literally run four hours a day. My legs swelled up to 28 inches without ever doing a squat, prompting some great success in rugby. My coach Don Burgess spent tireless hours training me, coaching me, and giving me more support than a player could ask for. Without his encouragement, I probably would have spent all my time on video games or gotten into boozing. I always appreciate his contribution to my life and the positive influence he was. And rugby opened doors for me.

I was selected to play provincial representative rugby for British Columbia three years in a row. I don't know what the standing is now, but when I played, BC had won the Canadian Championships 17 years in a row. It was unbelievable; Ontario had a much larger population, but because of BC being a rugby culture, we managed to eke out wins 1996-1999. BC was the pinnacle of Canadian rugby.

In 1997 I was chosen to tour Scotland with team Canada's under 19 squad. Originally, I was a replacement player; however, since I still didn't drink and was in great shape, I moved up to the starting roster and played my first and only test match against the Under 19 Scottish National side as tight head prop. That was a disaster. After getting mauled to pieces for the first half, I went to loose head prop for the second half; you don't have to be as strong or stable in the scrums, and you get to do more running and loose play.

After the game, in which we were thoroughly trounced but I had played my guts out, I was awarded man of the match by the Canadian coaches. Did it mean anything? I think so, but it would have meant more if we had won. The next year, I was selected again to play for Canadian Nationals after we won the Canadian championships in Newfoundland. After we stripped for our victory photo, it was on.

George Street, the main strip of St. John's, was a mess of drunken rugby players and women; most of the Newfoundland men had left town to find work. It was also George Street Festival. George Street has about 20 bars on five city blocks, and during the festival, you are allowed to wander onto the street with a drink in hand. It was a scene and we had prepared by writing the name of our dorm hall in

How Rugby players celebrate a National Championship.
Note the joy.

permanent marker on our arms. We wouldn't be able to speak come 3 a.m.

The first stop was the Cotton Club, a strip bar where we all downed beers and bought $5 lap dances. The whole night was a blur; most of us got back to the dorm at 4a.m., just in time to bus to the airport for our flight. Disdain and horror mixed on the faces of passengers.

We looked awful, stunk, were obviously still drunk, but were determined to fly. At least one rugby player passed out on the bags we were trying to check in. In true rugby fashion, the coaches weren't in any better shape than the players. It really got wild when a few guys started drinking beer in line, and a friend ran up to me.

"Barnyard, give me five bucks! Five bucks!" Five bucks!" he gushed.

"What? Redbag, why?" I asked.

"That's the stripper from last night, I'm going to get a lap dance!"

The poor girl. After a few mishaps, a buddy of mine and I, the sole competitors from Vancouver Island, got our flights sorted out. I somehow got home in one piece, exhausted but unscathed; I played a game for my men's team the next day on only a few hours of sleep, did well, but realized that my passion for rugby was dying.

Despite my high school coach Don Burgess, the inventor of the rugby kicking tee, a former national player and coach, stating that I was the best rugby player he had seen in 15 years of coaching rugby, I knew I was pretty much done with the sport. I was burnt out after six years of intense training, and knew that I had always wanted to wrestle. In my career as a wrestler, I had about five great sell out moments where I gave up on my dreams for one stupid reason or another.

Somehow, with the world of rugby opening wide and a great career in rugby a possibility, this wasn't one of them. I cancelled on the national tour to Ireland, played a few more games, but resolved that, at 19 years of age, it was time to go wrestle. All I had to do was figure out how the hell to start.

The funny thing about rugby was that it actually got me my first start in pro wrestling in an indirect way. All my friends knew that I wanted to be a wrestler. Wrestling was popular with us and we constantly phoned the local sports talk show, harassing them about wrestling.

"Ok fans, we're talking the best defense in hockey today. On the line is Brandon Heatherington. Brandon, what do you say?"

"I think that the best defense has to be Bob Backlund. Nothing gets by him and his cross-face chicken wing is unstoppable."

"Ok, we've been through this. Serious calls only, please" pleaded the host. The show continued.

"Tonight our prize is dinner at Boston Pizza for two if you can answer this trivia question; who holds the record for the most wins in a single season. Caller one, go ahead."

"Uhhh, I think it was Demolition and Mr. Fuji?"

"No! No more wrestling calls, please! Next caller who hold the records for most wins in a single season?"

"Well, let me tell you somethin' brother, I've seen it all coming down the pipe, and unless you're saying your prayers, doing your training, and taking your vitamins, you're never going to beat the Hulkster." Click.

Eventually, they stopped doing live phone calls altogether. One TV host was no match for an army of adolescent boys randomly calling in to harass them. The best part of it was that there was no organization to the calls to speak of- TV sucked, there was nothing to do on a weeknight, and so people from my high school just called. We never knew if the callers were going to be legitimate or prank and had to guess who it was making the calls. This probably boosted the ratings and definitely made the show more entertaining. Wrestling was in the air.

Somebody found out that a wrestling show was happening at the Legion in Victoria. On a card featuring Greg "The Hammer" Valentine, Doink the Clown, and Tito Santana, a few friends and I headed in to see the greatest show on earth. My dad, my brother Paul, and I all drove in for one of the most exciting nights of my high school life; that's kind of sad to say, I know, but this was a step towards my dream.

I was grinning ear to ear when I walked up the steps into the legion and saw up close for the first time a professional wrestling ring. I could see right away that it was not the same as a WWF ring, but it held all the mystery and magic.

My mouth still gaping wide, we took our seats and enjoyed, as much as we could, the spectacle of professional wrestling. Paul and I loved the show, but our dad not so much. The action was interesting, and my dad had been to WWF shows with me at the Memorial Arena in Victoria (as it was known at the time) and he actually enjoyed that. He particularly enjoyed watching the lithe action of the Big Boss Man. My dad had good appreciation for wrestling, particularly Yokozuna. He thought, and I agree, that Yoko brought a bit of genuineness to the show. However, this was independent, or "indy" wrestling.

Comparing indy wrestling to WWE is, when done poorly, comparing a McBurger to a filet mignon at a fancy French restaurant. When indy wrestling is done well, it's like the best mom and pop greasy spoon meal compared to the best

French restaurant in the world; they're both delicious, but there is a reality, a love, to indy wrestling that makes it richer than the fancy stuff with the good china and immaculate plate decorations.

It is just more real, like a glazed donut burger or homemade apple-bacon pie. The character's aren't as polished and the presentation isn't as good, but there is a real love to it. Where else do you see characters like Gorilla Morilla, Toga Boy, Caveman Broda or Duke McIsaac? They all do what they feel is best for their persona, making very creative and inventive wrestling.

Unfortunately, most wrestling isn't done so well, but the simplicity of the formula makes it great. As meatloaf is best when it is a family recipe that doesn't include fois grois, indy wrestling is the simple dish of what most people like simply delivered and prepared with passion.

WCCW, as ECCW was known at the time, was exactly such a kitchen of creative flavour; it wasn't all good, but it was entertaining. There were mundane rip offs of famous stars and movies: The Power Ranger, The Bodyguard, and Steve (I think) Hart, whose gimmick was a poor duplicate of Bret Hart. Then there were big stars who came around because they were past their prime: Tito Santana, Greg Valentine, Koko B Ware, Jimmy Snuka, Doink the Clown (Matt Borne) and a few other guys who had been stars in the WWE (WWF as it was known then).

Finally there were the wrestlers who were known names on the local scene: Diamond Timothy Flowers, Gorgeous Michelle Starr, Rocky Delaserra, Buddy Wayne and the like. And then there were the beauties, the misshapen clods and creations that made me gleefully happy to see do their thing, although whatever their thing was wasn't always exactly clear.

Dancin' Dylan Powers, Marvin the Lunatic, Awesome Annie, Iron Maiden, and H and R Puff and Stuff, AKA The Magic Dragons. The Magic Dragons were feuding with S.L.A.M., the Serbian Liberated Army Movement, and their feuds were vicious.

At the second show in the legion, one that my dad for reasons of good taste had decided not to attend, The Magic

Dragons and S.L.A.M battled out a bitter feud to end all feuds. They made full use of the flotsam and jetsam floating around the Esquimalt Legion; at one point, one of the dragons was loaded onto a bussing cart and ran full speed by S.L.A.M. into the stage. Unbelievable.

The match was amazing and brutal; amazing because of how much garbage and plunder they used in the match, and brutal because of how ridiculous the characters were. The S.L.A.M. were completely dressed in camouflage, including camouflaged masks, belts, and boots. The Magic Dragons were a great creation; two fully grown men wearing head to toe dragon costumes that right out of a Halloween party or school play.

The highlight of the match for me was when one of the magic   jumped on the apron of the ring, preparing to get back into the action. As he stood up, I couldn't help but grab onto his tail. He couldn't get into the ring, so he stopped, turned and looked down at me, and as he wondered what the hell this stupid wrestling mark (fan) was doing, one of his opponents whacked him across the face with a stick.

This wrestling was weird, funny, pathetic, carnie, silly, gritty, fun to watch and even more fun to take part in; I had just learned that. I was totally hooked. But my enthusiasm paled in comparison, was a drop in a bucket, compared to the unbridled enthusiasm that was brought to the shows by the first real character in pro wrestling that I ever met: Hot Dog.

Hot Dog

"Hey, what's your name?"

"Uhh, Ben" I say, fumbling with words.

"That's my name too!"

"Cool" he says, turning to my brother.

"Hey, what's your name?"

"Paul."

"Hey, that's my name too!"

"Oh really?"

We exchange looks and looks back with the monkey taunting us. A big, brown haired, gorilla whose mouth never quite closes but always smiles, always a bit open like Pacman, square teeth that don't quite meet and a jutting lower jaw. His hair is short, cropped, his legs are bowed, and his paunchy belly leans over his fanny pack. He waddles as he walks up to us, hopping side to side, dancing like Baloo from *The Jungle Book.*

"I'm Hot Dog. I heard King Kong Bundy is going to be here! Have you seen him?"

"No, but that'll be great if he is" I say, half believing him.

"Yeah I know. Did you guys see him today?"

"No, I didn't see him on the poster either."

"I know a guy who says he seen him today. I think I could kick his ass."

Hot Dog. It's his wrestling name I guess. He scratches his butt, then the pimples or ingrown hairs on his neck, and giggles, "Ehhha, just kidding. Hey, did you guys know that I used to be friends with the wrestlers?"

His voice has a kind of inflection to it, like a bimbo voice where there is a sudden raising of the tone and emphasis, but the inflection happens randomly. His last sentence really sounds like, "I YOUsed to be FRIENDS with WRestLUURRRS". We pause, hoping for a break in the conversation but he continues.

"I seen him yesterday."

"Who?"

"Bun-dy. He's BIG, eh!"

"Yeah, King Kong Bundy sized" adds Paul.

"My dad's The Undertaker. I'm gonna kick Greg Valentine's ass later. I hate that guy! He's an asshole!"

But asshole isn't asshole, it's two words with a high pitched emphasis in the middle, and arse put in there to keep him from swearing I guess. "Arse!-Whole!" Kind of a yelped out insult, factually stated with passion.

"Calvin, we've got to go inside. The shows starting." his caretaker interrupts.

"Thanks mum. Ok, bye, I see you guys inside, eh!" he says, except it's, "Thanksmumb" in one syllable, with special emphasis to really make mom rhyme with bumb, special emphasis on the b, and his bottom lip stays stuck out, emphasizing his underbite, as if he's pouting.

A wrestling show in Victoria. Note the blurred guy in front-that's Hot Dog. He brought joy to our lives and the shows.

He turns and walks away, buzz cut hairstyle poking out of his Native American head at all angles; he starts scratching his butt again, then turns to his neck as he walks into the building and up the stairs. We follow. I grin ear to ear as I pass the wrestling ring. It's the closest I've ever been to my dream.

Yelling idiotic chants laced with profanities and peppered with spit, Hot Dog is mesmerizing. At one point, he is so mad that he stands up and threatens to fight the Atomic Punk; this prompts a, "You and what army!" from punk. Which prompts Hot Dog to put his fists on his hips, yell, then while shaking in anger, he starts taking off his belt and shout, "I'm going to kick your ass, asshole!" The crowd erupts.

"Ehhh, hae hae, YEAH!" he yells as Doink the Clown sticks his finger up Michelle Starr's butt and Starr squirms in agony. When Greg Valentine forearms Tito Santana, he stands up in his seat and yells a string of profanities in one breath, "GODAMMITSONOVABITCH!" Hotdog raises his fist, then he realizes his fist isn't effective as a taunt, so he sticks his thumb out between his pointer and middle finger and wags his thumb, as if saying to Greg Valentine, "I've got your nose!" and yells at the top of his voice, "Shut up you stupid idiot!" He hasn't sat for more than 5 seconds throughout the entire show. By the time the main event has started, everybody realizes that Hot Dog is the show.

Fans went crazy when the wrestling started, when Doink did his thing, and when Tito Santana beat "The Hammer" Greg Valentine in the main event. However, no single cheer was as loud as when Hot Dog stood up to The Hammer and told him, "Go to hell ARSEHOLE!" then turned and spanked his own ass to taunt him. Wrestler or not, Hot Dog stole the show.

* * *

Paul and I couldn't get enough of this; we quoted him all the way home, asking, "What's your name?" and answering, "My dad's The Undertaker!" far beyond it being funny. And, in a wonderful twist of fate, my dad, the proper, never swearing, respectable Mormon, ended up sitting next to Hot Dog whenever he came to a show with us. We would get there early, grab our seats, have one spare, and seconds before the first bell rang, Hot Dog would plunk down.

My father would frown and turn his shoulders away. Years later, when I was running a show in Victoria, the memory of Hot Dog was still strong, especially for my dad. I was told, "If you run, make sure that Hot Dog doesn't show up. He really ruins the whole thing." That depends greatly upon who you ask.

My dad had a break from him for a few years; we watched the shows in 1993 and 1994. I didn't attend wrestling school until 1999, so sightings of him were few and far between, but the joy and happiness Hot Dog brought me can't be contained in a book. The glee and excitement in his eyes at a wrestling show are enough of a reward to make anyone want to become a wrestler. Just as anyone will give a treat to a puppy, wrestling in front of Hotdog was a way to improve the happiness in the world. Showtime Eric Young met him, and paid homage years later: "Think of all the joy and happiness Hot Dog has brought to our lives. He's a legend."

It's true; and the weird thing is that through next years of school and college, Hot Dog appeared just enough to remind me of what I really wanted to do with my life.

After my national rugby tour, it was time to get serious about wrestling. I didn't have any money. I began working full time at Deep Cove Garage on the Saanich Peninsula. It wasn't a great job, but everybody was nice, it kept me busy, and I still had enough time to train. At $575.65 exactly every two weeks, it was more money than I had ever seen.

I also began working at my dad's office doing janitorial work, played rugby to keep fit, and spent the rest of the time working out, hanging out with my girlfriend or friends, and avoiding Mormon people trying to talk me into going on a mission. It only took me 6 months at the garage to realize I hated it and that I wasn't making enough money to save up for wrestling school. So, I gave my notice without actually having another job to fall back on.

The day before I quit, my men's league rugby coach swung by the garage and asked what I was going to do. I told him I was just leaving the garage and he offered me a job roofing. The pay was terrible, and as my coworker put it, we were expected to "Take the bad with the bad" but our boss was to get, "The good with the good." After 6 months of roofing, enough was enough and I quit. A whole year had gone by without me getting closer to my dream. I got two part-time jobs and went to college full time. It was there that I found inspiration to get started with my wrestling career.

A Second Helping

"I don't like that, it's got all that ShugaRR in it. Give me a coffee withno SUGAR!"

The cafeteria at Camosun College was a crowded, confused space that served your garden variety of semi-healthy food to semi-conscious students. Luckily for me, everyone funneled past 2 cashiers so there was no way I could miss him. Amongst the others laying claim higher learning at Camosun College was Hot Dog.

"Hey Calvin, what are you doing?"

"These aRSEholes put too much sugAR in their coffeeeee. I don't LIKE IT!"

"I think it's sugar free."

"NO. I'm going to get a Dr. PepPER!"

"That's got a lot of sugar in it" I said.

"Thanks mumb!"

I could only smile; pop in hand he went to pay.

"HOW much is IT?"

"1.95"

The cashier apparently has been through this before or is completely terrified because she barely reacts.

"Ok, I Have a NICK-el."

"That's not enough. It's ONE dollar ninety five."

"Ok. Here's a nicKEL! You're welCOME!"

"No, you need to pay me a dollar ninety more."

"OK. HAVE A GOOD DAY!" He waves and walks away, Dr. Pepper in hand; the cashier throws the nickel into the tip jar and hits the "clear" button. Life for Hot Dog is happy. Life entertaining a room full of Hot Dogs would be wonderful. What the hell am I doing if I'm not pursuing my dream? Life has shown me once again my path; time to move on it.

* * *

For the next year, Hot Dog appearances greatly enhanced what was otherwise a pointless year of random courses. Finally, in the spring of 1998, I was fed up. I was still in decent shape and I knew it was crucial to really save some money and go train. I was hired to work on the highways by a friend's father, and began making the hefty wage of $12.76 per hour. When September came, I enrolled again at college but solemnly vowed that come January I would be away at wrestling school.

I honestly felt like something was drawing me to a career in wrestling. It wasn't just all the dreams I'd had about it, it was the constant reminders of seeing people like Hot Dog, or seeing wrestlers up close and personal, and hearing my friends be excited for me. They wanted it. I wanted it. I had to do it. With no clue how, I took a leap at finding a school.

This was before the internet. Wrestling schools were found either in wrestling magazines or by word of mouth. I asked WCCW about their wrestling school in Vancouver, run by Michelle Starr, but even my dad thought I should start somewhere else.

A good friend of mine from Victoria, Wayne Paul, also told me, "You want to be a big fish; start in a big pond." Wayne knew well; he was a native or First Nations Canadian, and his uncle had been Chief Thunderbird, a huge wrestling star in Canada in the 1960's. He and my dad were both right; I picked up a phone, dialed "O", and asked for information Ontario.

Pinning Down the Dream

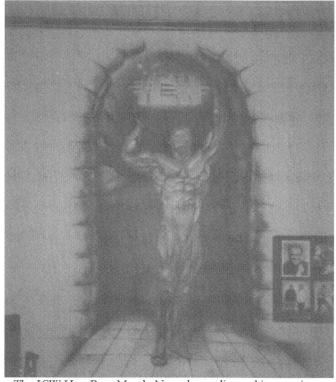

The ICW Hart Bros Mural. Note the quality sucking you in.

"**H**ow about in Toronto?"

"Hold on." The click-clack of a keyboard. Dull office ambience.

"I've got one in Toronto and one in Cambridge. Which one do you want?"

"Uhh, both I guess."

"Okay; the number for Toronto is 513--you writing this down?

"Yes, thanks"

"513- ###- ##   ##"

"Ok thanks. And the other was Cambridge-- is Cambridge in Ontario?"

"Yes, it's about 2 hours south of Toronto."

"Ok, I guess I could go there. What's the number for that one please?"

"It's 513- ###- big pause- ####."

"Got it. Thanks."

"Those are the only ones coming up. Would you like me to search for anymore?"

"No, what are the names of the schools please?"

"Oh, the Toronto one is Sully's Gym; S-U-L-L-Y-S and the one in Cambridge is The Hart Brothers School of Wrestling. Do you need me to spell that one for you?"

Some people may have. I didn't. I thanked the telephone operator, hung up, and looked at the names. I'd never heard of Sully's, or Ron Hutchinson's gym; if I had, maybe things would have turned out differently. I called Hutchinson's, heard the price, which was fair, but then realized I would have to find my own apartment and take care of my own transportation, etc. while I was there. If only I had known; a tonne of guys and gals who "made it" came out of there. I was a 20 year-old child. I suppose now, in many ways, I'm a 35 year-old child, but now I know how to catch a bus and get a job. At 20, well, knowing how to and being able to were far apart. I called The Hart Bros School.

"ICW Hart Bros" growled the phone.

"Hi, uhmm, I'm calling about the wrestling school?"

"Wait for Ike."

"Ok, thanks." A dollar a minute.

I waited a few minutes, then heard Ike take the phone.

"Ike Shaw here." Gruff and tough sounding, but not entirely unpleasant. It sounded like he'd been just awoken or bothered. It was 9p.m. Ontario time.

"Hi. I want to come to a wrestling school."

"Hmm... You think you can handle it?"

"Uhhm, I think so."

"What do you know? Are you an athlete?"

"Yes. I played rugby for Canada and was an all-star for basketball. I also play soccer and do Judo."

"Huh. Wrestling isn't like any of those."

Interesting. Professional wrestling is almost identical to a Judo demonstration- break falls, throws, cooperation. I didn't know this at the time. It still sounded odd, but I wasn't going to argue.

"Hold on" he said, muffling the phone, but I heard, "Guys, I'm not going to argue about this anymore. One of you needs to clean it up and sort it out. That's all there is to it and I'm not hearing any more of this." Interesting.

"Who are you?"

"I'm Ben Nelson. I'm in Victoria, out in BC."

"Oh, a B.C. boy. I went to Maple Ridge once."

"Cool. Was that for wrestling?"

"No, just on Vacation. I haven't wrestled in about 4 years."

"Oh. Where did you wrestle?"

"I wrestled for Stampede Wrestling, in Puerto Rico, and for the WWF. My friend, Joe, can vouch for all of this. I don't wrestle but I train the students. (Odd, I thought; how does that work?) We have amazing trainers here. Just the other day we had Davey Boy Smith come through. The number of stars we have on a monthly basis is amazing."

"Sounds great sir, I think----

"We train 5 nights a week, plus sometimes on Saturdays. The guys who really want it work out down the road at our own private gym. We offer training programs from a bodybuilder and I help all the guys from out of town get work. I suggest that when you get here you get a job otherwise you will be lazy. Some guys don't do anything all day and they are usually the ones that end up leaving. You've got to have ambition."

"Ok. I can appreciate that. I've got 2 jobs right now and--

"Do you have access to a fax machine?"

"Yes, I can get something faxed to my dad's work."

"Ok. Give me the number. The school is $3,500 for six months of training. I can't guarantee you'll make it through the training, but you can try" he stated. I hung on every word. There were a lot of numbers being thrown around and I was a bit confused. He continued, "I'll fax over an application form. Do your best with it, be honest, and if we like it, we'll give you a call back."

It sounded hard to get into this school and harder to make it through training. I was intimidated and nervous. A week later, I did a telephone interview. Ike told me he was discussing my application with several legends who were at the school; Greg Valentine, Angelo Mosca, Waldo Von Erich, and a few other names popped up. I was nervous but must have answered the questions well. I was invited to the ICW Hart Bros. School of Professional Wrestling.

I was up for a challenge but quite insecure. I knew wrestling was my dream but nothing else. I got off the phone and was on my way to becoming a wrestler. A few weeks later, I got a call asking me to pay up in full by the end of 1998 so Joe could close out the fiscal year. I didn't know any better.

In a move never recommended by anyone ever, I wired out the payment in full before I actually saw or heard anything else about the school. It sounded like the right start to an amazing school, so why not reserve my spot? Ike sounded tough and stern, but fair; Joe seemed nice enough after how long I'd spoken to him for, and the legends that came by would make it an awesome place to train. In wrestling, nothing is as it seems. But on the phone…

I left Victoria BC on January 4th, 1999. People were golfing at Ardmore golf course in Sidney because of the warm Victoria winter. I drove past them on my way to my girlfriend's house, whimpered gently the whole way to the airport, checked in for my connecting flight from Victoria to Vancouver, sat down, almost missed my flight, and then was gone. A terrifying flight- I've always hated travel and flights- but somehow reassuring. I was ready for my life to begin. It was time to leave Victoria and if I made an excuse at that point I probably would never have gone.

The plane landed in four feet of snow. I was met by Ronny, Stylin Bryan, and Greg at the airport. Greg smoked in the van on the way to the school; Ronny chatted, and Bryan and I talked a bit about rugby. I carried my suitcase up the steps, and there I was- dreamland.

I quickly met everybody (except Joe, he was asleep) and unpacked all my stuff before getting into the ring- I couldn't wait! We couldn't bump after 9 p.m., which was a bit annoying, but that kept peace with the people we shared the building with.

I smiled like an idiot as I walked the ring, climbing on the apron and bouncing a bit on the ropes. Then I got my first reality check in pro wrestling; the ropes hurt. These were just ropes covered in tape- no smoke or mirrors.

Ball gleefully showed me a few things on the ropes, made fun of the picture of Ike, and explained that he and Joe were the same fat idiot, flipping into the ring once with a thunderous bump, laughed while shushing me as we left to drink some beers with Greg down the road. We were all happy to be there. And by the end of our fourth pitcher of beer, it was home. I heard all about the school from Greg and Ball.

The cast of characters from the school is a tapestry of forgotten and unforgettable faces. Romeo, TJ, Ted, Ball, Jer, Chico, Terry, Stalker, Ike, his wife Carol-Anne, Rudy, Javhad, JC, Longo, Nerdly, TID, Vanessa, Bomber, Stylin' and Curtis. The guys there for the duration of my stay are so burned into my mind they still affect me, and not just in the ring. I am terrible with names, but somehow after only 6 months of living at the school, I still remember a lot of the guys I met once. The smell of the tarp, the icy chill of the training room and the steamy heat of the summer ring still burn my eyes when I think about where I started

Hope was as tangible a being as any of us trainees. Hope pushed through the smoky living room with the big screen TV and overcame the stench of the bathroom shared by 12 guys plus guests on a nightly basis. There was also the stench of failure, crushed dreams, misery, cigarettes, and stinky gym gear, but hope was strongest of all.

As you walked up the stairs, you turned left into a dividing hallway and then had two options; turn right and enter the wrestling home, turn left and enter the training room. The area straight ahead was for other renters on the top of the building.

The school was designed basically as an "f"; the leg of the f was the office and bathrooms. There was a shower and hot tub room off of the common area and next to the toilet; guys would soak up a shower, towel off somewhat, then drip through the TV area into their own rooms.

With a CD player and a book, it was easy enough to tune out the noise and escape into dreams. Once you got to the center junction of the f, you were in the common area; keep going ahead and you had the room of Ball, Javhad, Greg, and later Nerdly and Longo. Through that was a freezing cold alcove where Terry, the maintenance guy, slept. Back to the center "f" junction and you had the room belonging to myself, Bryan, Curtis, and for a brief while, Javhad. On the left arm of the "f" was the kitchen and laundry area in a constant crisis zone, also connected to a bedroom room. Beyond that, extending the left arm of the "f" lay Ike's room, his private residence where he had his own miniature living room and bedroom.

About halfway through my time there, all the workout and weight equipment moved to Ron's house, or Ron's Gym as he labelled it, and this was a welcome excuse to get out of the school into a somewhat normal world. We could jog through the snow or sun (Ontario has no spring, only a melt) and then pump iron in what I would call the best gym around for a pro wrestler to train at.

Ronny had been a committed weightlifter for a long time and was thick as a brick, even at 50 odd years of age. He had built custom equipment to supplement his training and owned a stellar collection of old bodybuilding books written by Arnold Strong (before Schwarzenegger [Wow! Schwarzenegger is in the dictionary!).

Ronny had tonnes of gear you couldn't find anywhere else, some of which he had crafted himself. Old plates, benches, squat racks, things drilled into walls on pulleys, things to attach to your head, your arms, your back, massage gimmicks, trees of weights, ancient machines, and a shower next to the laundry.

All this equipment hunkered down in the unfinished basement of his house. Once you realized it was filthy, you also realized it was exactly what a serious wrestler needed to grow. Dynamite Kid would have loved it.

(**Side note**: Word came down yesterday or the day before that Vanessa Valentine died. You have to look at the heart of people. Vanessa was sweet and never did anyone harm intentionally. She cared about Starr, the dog, a lot more than most people at the school did, and all she was looking for was a place to fit in and a dream to chase. While she didn't turn into a wrestler, she didn't have a bad intention in her. I think she looked at wrestling the same way she looked at life- a fun place where anyone could fit in and she didn't judge. Hopefully she's at peace.)

The details of the school and characters all come up in the stories about it; a bunch of guys lived in a crowded apartment/ training room combo with no girls or anything to do except train. It was the type of experience you can't go through when you are any older because then you wouldn't stick out the trashiness of it, but when you're a kid, you don't know any better and don't care. You still believe dreams are really worth shooting for.

Daily life was wake up, either work or sleep in, have breakfast, train at the gym lifting weights, waste some time watching TV, and then train again in the ring, eat, watch wrestling and go to bed late or extremely late. It was a lot of hurry up and wait and general BS dealing with Joe and the other guys at the school, stuff that would embarrass reality TV stars. I loved it and stuck it out because at that point, I hadn't started to sell myself out. And the illusion of what it could be kept hope alive. Plus Ike was constantly selling us on his vision of the future and our careers as wrestler, provided we did as he said. He was, after all, our trainer.

In reality, Ike only got in the ring maybe thrice the whole time I was there. The jobs he arranged were mostly just bitch work around the school that I wasn't paid for, or jobs arranged through a temp agency, not him. Experienced trainers were mostly missing in action.

But Ike sounded great, especially if you asked Joe about him. I hadn't learned that in wrestling, you should believe none of what you hear and only half of what you see. And it wasn't until I got there that I learned Ike and Joe were the same person.

This revelation became a gulf of awfulness and misery in the world of the ICW Hart Bros. wrestling school. Like so much in wrestling though, what made it awful made it work. We all discovered this as each new misadventure unfolded.

Day by Day

After a few days at the school, the other guys in the school began to trust me enough to confide that they hated Joe and that the training was bullshit except for Jer's help. I thought it out. I was there, I wasn't going home without finishing my training, so for me, it made no difference. Jeremy was a good coach. He'd backyard wrestled for years before arriving at the school and knew his stuff.

Pretty much anyone can figure out how to do most of the moves if they have wits and a TV. The real trick with wrestling is what you do between the moves and how you tell a story. Overall, the issue of training wasn't a big one because Ronnie would show us what he knew, which was limited but correct, and Waldo would get in there often enough to make us realize that we didn't want him in there because he was beyond us in some ways and out of date in others. Students don't appreciate what they have. He would be great to hear from now; with him, Jer, and Ron, we learned.

The first thing you learn when you wrestle is how to bump. Again, this is just like Judo; you learn how to get thrown and how to fall first. The number of people I've seen that have marched up to the ring, confident that the spring in the ring will make it just like a big trampoline is staggering. For me, it was pretty much the same. Jeremy got me into the ring and did a few back bumps himself.

Then he had me hold onto the middle rope, arch my hips forward so I was horizontal to the mat, and then "THUD" I fell backwards. I coughed a little, squeezing my shoulders together behind me.

"Ha, yeah, she's a stiff one" laughed Jer. I was pretty used to throws from Judo, but I still looked around at the other wrestlers sitting by the ring. They all gave me the, "Yeah, we know and know you know, ha!" look that every wrestler enjoys giving to a new or wannabe wrestler after their first bump. For the rest of the practice, I progressed to doing regular bumps and then stopped.

My head was splitting and felt cloudy. And ever since I started bumping, my voice has become nasally and cloudy, stuck somewhere in the now fluid-filled channels of my head. Like stiff necks and sore knees, it's what happens to you when you wrestle.

Learning how to wrestle isn't all that hard, especially if you've been athletic in your life and have watched a lot of wrestling. If you've watched wrestling, guaranteed you've play-wrestled with your friends. In my high school physical education class we did an entire Survivor Series one day during the wrestling/fitness unit of the course. We went out, improvised with people we didn't really know, and put each other in holds. If you've done that, you know more about wrestling than you think. The trick is being able to do it all at speed and safely. And the bigger trick is learning to tell a story, something that can take years to learn.

After the first bump, the training was, for the most part, reasonably easy. I learned the moves, about two a day, and then learned how to do the most basic spot in wrestling, the international, which lead to being able to do a match with another student. For the first few weeks, matches were nothing but me getting beaten up, but that is how you learn.

Marco, Jer, and Longo chilling. Note the enthusiasm.

As a wrestler, you go through the steps of being a trainee getting bumped around to being a jobber doing the odd bit of offense, to finally being a wrestler swapping spots and moves with your opponent. All that came with time. Day to day, we made it work.

We had access to a ring, a good group of guys, and were learning. After a week or two, I was certain the school would give me the opportunity to learn what I needed to. Once I realized this, it was clear to me and everyone else that I wasn't going anywhere till I was done, but that I wasn't one to "drink the Kool-Aid" of Joe's bullshit. The first instance of me realizing his bullshit was when I asked the guys about who was there that fateful night I was, in Joe's words "brought into the fold".

"Was Greg Valentine here?"

"We haven't seen him in months."

"Angelo Mosca?"

"No, he was only at the last show. Bulldog was here a while ago though. He had some great stories."

It was clear things were not as they seemed. One of the Hart brothers had been at the school, but had left a while before I arrived. Joe hadn't pointed this out over the phone, but JC pointed out who was who in some pictures around the school.

"That's the Gothic Nut," said JC pointing out a picture on the wall. "He's huge and shitty. Either he fucked over Joe or Joe fucked him over. If you ever see him, don't talk to him."

"Doesn't Joe get in and coach us ever?"

"Hrmckk... He can barely walk. And all he ever shows us is his stupid slider."

"Slider?"

Everyone smiled when the word slider came up; each guy had his own impression of it. Basically, it was a punch that instead of doing the typical wrestling trick of stopping short or missing, "slid" past the guys jaw and made it look, according to Joe, like you had really clocked your opponent. I've seen a few and they do look good. According to the guys however, it looked ridiculous and was accompanied by a "Brrraahhhhhh" with a shaking of the head. Everyone loved when Joe did one and would try our best not to laugh our asses of as he bragged.

"Yeah, yeah, all you little fuckers think you've got it all figured out," he'd say, "well, when you're the main event come talk to me, or better yet, come thank me for showing how it's done."

However it was with Joe and his slider, we spent 3 hours a night in the ring, and did mock matches every weekend and most nights. The matches were often terrible, but we learned the fundamentals. We learned how to call a match on the fly, how to bump, how to plan a finish (many of those terrible too) and how to have fun in the ring, what wrestling is really all about.

Despite it being ridiculous, ICW Ontario was a school and home. Couple that with rent, a gym, a room to sleep in, and Joe springing for dinner every couple of weeks, and it became pretty good. What made it great or awful was Joe, particularly two great Joe activities that snuck up on us if we weren't paying attention. One was the incredible amount of bullshit that he shoveled on us; the other, more creative one, was bitch work.

Joe's Diet

"Use each man after his own desert, and who shall (e)scape whipping?" (Hamlet) I think there is some good in Joe, like Darth Vader. Something must have happened to him to make him what he was at the school. His stories and ideas were astounding; once he went so far as to tell us that he was a certified chiropractor, giving us adjustments and screwing up Ball's neck for weeks. This type of nonsense battered our minds. But if you asked him, he'd tell you he had it all figured out. He was an expert at bullshit.

Picture "Fat Bastard" from *Austin Powers 2: The Spy Who Shagged Me*. Change his hair to brown/gray, and give him a goatee. That's Joe; I know because I saw him naked. Like seeing fat bastard naked though, I never saw his junk. This was because Joe was so fat that, even in full light, his junk was overshadowed by his gut so you couldn't see it.

We estimated he was 400 pounds, and that most of those pounds were a combination of beef and bullshit. The most amazing thing about him wasn't that he managed to maintain those pounds of beef- that alone was spectacular. The most amazing thing was that he managed to maintain that much bullshit even though he spewed it out in a non-stop river of gushing verbal diarrhea all day long every day.

It often began with, "Guys, you've got WWF, and WCW; ICW is going to come right up through the middle. How? How do you ask?" He would stop and point to his head. It was all in there, gems of great angles, brilliant booking solutions, and a business plan that Vince McMahon himself envied. So Joe said. We heard this speech with slight variations an average of twice a week. Sometimes the bullshit reached dizzying proportions. Sometimes we couldn't be sure what was true and had to play it safe. The first bullshit dose (when I got to the school and realized that Ike and Joe were the same guy) woke me up. It seemed like his proclaimed status and the reality grew further apart every day. People who had been around him a while helped to do this.

The first and last poster that you saw when you entered the wrestling room at the school was of the Taber Corn Fest 1994 or something like that. The headline of the event was Ike "The Crippler" Shaw vs Bruce Hart. It seemed like a big event and the poster was well made. I remember staring at it a week or two after I had arrived, trying to judge the significance of it.

"Duck the punch backslide!" yelled JC over my shoulder.

I cocked my head, staring at him in confusion.

"That was the finish… and the match!" he said.

"What?"

"That was the only spot they did--duck the punch, backslide. That was the opening spot and the finish," concluded JC.

Some main event. Unlike the rest of us growing into a gimmick, instead of becoming more and more "Ike Shaw", Joe was becoming less and less of Ike Shaw, and to my eyes more of a fat idiot who did a lot of talking but little else.

Wrestlers transform somewhere in their career, becoming more the name they have made for themselves than the one they were born with. Joe was going through the opposite. After the first few inconsistencies passed unchecked, the chink in his armour worsened and bullshit started seeping out.

We often giggled at the nonsense that he was selling us, although some guys were certain the house was bugged. We laughed at the idea of him doing any wrestling or anything in the ring because he seemed so clueless and couldn't walk. We said this secretly; replies came publicly and out of nowhere.

"Guys, you know I can't walk now, but it's not because I'm so fat or out of shape. It's because I used to be such a great wrestler until that son of a bitch didn't catch me when I did my finisher."

"What was your finisher, Joe?"

Someone had to ask; JC just shook his head. Not again.

"I'd climb that top rope and then do that, uuhhhh, what was that called? I'd dive to the floor."

"Splash? No wonder your knees are ruined" said Jeremy.

"Not a splash, the other one. I was the biggest god-dam luchador you ever seen. What's that move?"

"Your finisher?"

"Yeah, it was my finisher, I used it forever but can't remember what it was. JC what do you call that dive where you flip?"

"A senton, Joe?"

"Yeah, that's it. I did a senton to the floor!"

A senton is a front flip onto an opponent. It requires courage, athleticism, and a wrestler to catch another wrestler flipping with dangerous momentum. Even at a trimmer 300 pounds, Joe would never have done a senton onto anyone. What's more, a senton to the outside as a finisher made no sense- you'd have to roll your opponent back into the ring in order to win properly and get a title. What's more more is Joe didn't even know what it was called, and only a few weeks later told us his finisher was a double knee drop.

"Curtis, lie down. Now, you two guys, carry me over top of him, and when I say so, let me go."

Bryan and I looked at each other with amusement and fear. Joe had waddled into our training session and decided to start teaching us by showing his finisher. We scooped our shoulders under Joe's armpits, hoisting his near 400 pounds and walking him above Curtis. Give Joe credit, he was actually in the ring, and give Curtis credit for not fearing for his life, he played it cool. The lights were eclipsed as the Hindenburg Joe floated effortlessly- for him- above Curtis, who smiled, genuinely amused. Bryan and I groaned but bore it.

"K, when I tell you guys, I want you to let me drop. I just gotta get some forward momentum," and he began trying to rock on our shoulders, swinging his gut backwards and forwards. We all sensed the impending impact, until Joe said, "Wait a minute, I'm not wearing my knee pads." He got out of the ring, lit a cigarette, fumbled with a pair of pads, and then disappeared to the bathroom.

He came back in his sweatpants with a tiny pee spot growing through the grey cotton hiding his crotch. As he got back into the ring, the pee spot continued to grow and grow. No shame now, I pee myself at least twice a week, but at the time it was hilarious. I caught a look in Jeremy's eye, which was caught by Curtis as well; we all looked at our feet to stop from laughing. Thankfully, the pee spot was the only spot Joe showed us as he had apparently forgotten again what his finisher was and went on to show us sliders and bear claws, big open-handed mitts to the mouth. Curtis survived to hear another day of bullshit.

Other than that, Joe never showed us anything in the ring, but there were plenty of other helpings of bullshit. Like the time he told us he was a licensed chiropractor, but that he considered the professional a crock and called his chiropractic certificates his "phony tickets". It was amazing for audacity and ridiculousness. He gave us all chiropractic adjustments and screwed up Ball's neck for a week.

Joe dished up constant servings of bullshit, some of them we actually learned from.

A Brilliant Worker

Bullshit was his currency, so bullshit he spent. Joe bought a new table with a fistful of, I'm pretty sure, Bullshit.

"My friend, you weren't working that day. Terry and I came in and purchased two of these tables from your colleague." Joe. Sincere.

"We don't have a record of it."

"I'm sure I have the receipt. Can you please be patient my friend?"

"There is a bit of a line here" sighed the cashier.

"Well, allow me to take a minute. I've waited a while, but I'll be sure to be quick." Out plopped a huge, fat wallet, pulled from a huge, fat man's pants by a huge, fat hand.

"I think this is the receipt... nope. Let's keep looking."

The wallet was stuffed with notes, nonsense, and bullshit. I don't know if this was planned, but stuffed it was.

"There it is—oh, no my mistake. That's for the Canadian Tire down the road. I find it odd that I would lose my receipt- do you always issue them?"

"Yes, we do…"

"Hold on," said Joe, as his sausage fingers waddled through rows of papers. Out plopped another receipt.

"I believe this is it."

"Sir, our receipts aren't yellow" asserted the cashier, wrinkling his nose like he'd smelled a fart.

"My mistake, sorry friend. But call me Ike. My word is my bond." Mesmerizing. I sat with Javhad wondering what the fuck we had done wrong with our lives. It reminded me of shopping with my mom; she would run into the grocery store saying "I'll only be five minutes." An hour later, she would come out with 6 bags of food. Ever since then, I've hated shopping with anyone for anything. Joe's trips were no exception. The line slithered with anger.

"Here it is!" he said, squeezing out a receipt that he smoothed onto the counter.

"That only has a price on it, no store logo."

"You'll have to forgive an old man. (He was 50 tops) I don't walk or see so well, (true, he's 400lbs) and I've got my nephews (students stuck on bitch duty) here to help me out" he belched. How Javhad, obviously Iranian with dark skin, and myself, were both his nephews required imagination. The line grew.

"I've more receipts here, my friend. Hold on."

"…."

The groan in the line was audible. Maybe it was just Javhad. Maybe the cashier made it. Either way, the cashier heard it.

"How many tables did you say it was?" the cashier yielded.

"Just two, like those by the doorway yonder. I have the receipt, I remember exactly what they looked like."

"I'll walk over with you and explain it - CAN I GET HELP AT CUSTOMER SERVICE?" over the PA system; Joe waddled to the waiting tables, his new friend and us in tow. When we got home, I realized I was pretty sure Joe had been at a show the day he "purchased" the tables. Through a painfully slow load of BS, he had walked into a store empty handed, or possibly with a receipt, and walked out with a new friend and $400 worth of tables.

Bitch Work

It's not politically correct, but that's what we called our mindless slavery around the wrestling school. It is totally fair that we had to pitch in. Paying dues is part of any profession. On my first day there, Ronny told me that the guy who used to mop the ring and clean it between training sessions, maybe Julio, had just left. So the next day, I assumed it as my job to mop the ring and to clean the training area. It wasn't hard and wasn't complicated, and neither was the bitch work in general. Unlike the bitch work, however, I could clean the ring room at a reasonable time of day. Bitch work was always massively inconvenient.

The daily bitch task was taking Starr, Joe's dog, out. Keeping with the requirement of inconvenience, walking Starr usually happened at 11:00 p.m., especially during the winter. I wasn't used to the cold and figured the dog needed to walk a few blocks. I'd put on my winter coat, (which was in fact just a summer jacket over a sweater) long johns, and take Starr out to the church behind the school. Joe had no bags for picking up her poop, so I'd just kick snow over whatever she produced wherever she produced it, problem solved. It was cold, dirty, but no problem. The problem was she'd whine and I'd feel bad; the leash would come off and 20 minutes later Starr would finally return. I couldn't really be mad at her, and we'd go back into the school. I'd defrost my legs in the hot tub, one of the few perks of the school. It wasn't terrible walking Starr, but fat Joe got the dog and fat Joe should walk the dog at least sometimes, a few of us said. I was sadistically happy one morning when Joe asked me to take her out for a walk.

"Why Joe?" I asked, "She just took a dump on the carpet."

"What? STARR!! DAMNIT!"

I walked past him a few minutes later and he was lying on the floor, cleaning up her filth. I was very happy he was finally inconvenienced by his pet and had to clean up some of the shit he caused through neglect. I'm sure he had good intentions when he got her, but she was a total nuisance for us brought on by his laziness— "A chilling vision of things to come" (*Last Exit to Springfield*). The most annoying part was being told to do it while he did nothing; we were always at his beck and call. We were his bitch and had to walk his bitch. Bitch work did give some purpose or sense of accomplishment, and my duties were less disgusting than others. Teddy had to clean the showers and bathroom. We discussed his issues sitting in the hot tub one evening.

"I'm sucking that disgusting gloop out of the corners of those showers with a straw," he said.

"What? Like soap scum?"

"Soap scum if I'm lucky. I don't want to know what Javhad does when he's in here with the door locked."

"Do you think this hot tub is clean?"

"Yeah, I clean it. I dump chemicals, and skim the shit out. Just watch out if Joe has been in here."

"Why?"

"He bathes in the hot tub."

"…" I replied with an eyebrow flash as Ted continued, "Thankfully he only bathes like once a month."

I wasn't sure if that was supposed to make me feel better, but it did. Ted walked his bare, hairy ass out of the tub leaving me to ponder how the school worked. I told myself to keep my head above water. Further instruction on life at ICW came later. From Joe.

Don't Drink the Kool-Aid

Joe liked to eat. He ate and ate and ate, but usually by himself. I guess he was depressed or just found us too annoying to eat next to, which makes sense. The school didn't have a table, so we ate standing over the stove or in the living room/ common area on the couch. Once in a while, when there was a pay-per-view on TV, we'd order Chinese or Burger King. Often Joe paid; he could be very generous. His order was always a "triple whopper with double-double bacon and double-double cheese, dice the onions."

"My god. Four times the bacon and four times the cheese" I said when I first heard it.

"No, three times," corrected Terry.

"No, if you have one and you double once, you have two; double it again, four" I calculated.

We had nothing else to talk about.

"No, you add double, then add double once more. That's three."

I looked at Terry to decide between a stupid argument or sitting in silence. Why bother? Common sense meant nothing. I just sat there not caring and making sure not to order a drink. Teddy never ordered a drink, but never said why publicly; he later confided that he figured Javhad was spitting in them. Javhad later confided this was true.

I also heard complaints of food missing from the fridge; thankfully it wasn't' me. After everyone complaining about the food thief for days, Marco came out from the kitchen with a big smile on his face then sat next to me on the couch.

"Ha, I think Terry was the food thief," he half whispered.

"What makes you think that?"

"He threw out my Kool Aid saying it had gone bad. How would he know unless he drank it?"

"Was it bad?" I had to ask.

"Of course it was; I peed in it" laughed Marco.

Honesty is critical in wrestling. The most important thing I learned in the first weeks was to not get caught in the crossfire or be too chummy with Joe. I might end up drinking pee or tainted food. And I heard wrestling tales from a few guys about doing bitch work at his convenience. This following one I heard multiple times.

An Early Start

"Guys, we're getting an early start on the camp site tomorrow. Everybody up by eight, we're out of here by nine, no time for breakfast for anyone."

"But Joe, some of us have made plans" groaned one of us.

"Your only plan while you are here is to be a wrestler. Hey, if you don't want to pay your dues, don't come to the campsite, see what happens."

What would he do if we did eat breakfast before helping? Or ate breakfast and didn't help? Would that piss him off even more? How can this fat idiot interfere with basic human rights like rest and get away with it?

"Hey, I never eat breakfast and I'm fine. You don't need it. Trust me." Immortal words. From a belly of titanic proportions. Cheeks burned red. The injustice of it- since when did training to be a professional athlete have anything to do with being a slave? I don't think Lebron James or Kobe Bryant perfected their shots by polishing the floor. In fact, I'd think they probably perfected it by working on their game with experienced coaches. Since we had no experienced coach, maybe doing the opposite of what sense dictated would work, like multiplying two negatives into a positive.

"Hey, you don't want to work, don't work, but don't expect any favours from me."

We groaned. When had this sprung up? Worst of all, the campsite bitchwork session was scheduled for Saturday, so we had no other obligations; even Jer and Romeo had been drafted. Our free time and weekly practice show taken up by this fat idiot on peril of being permanently de-booked from his wrestling shows. Saturday at 8:00 am. All the guys were up.

"No *Bear Hunter* last night," said Bryan.

"Whoa, all rested up and ready for a hard day in a chair outside," said Jer.

"Haha, shitty" was Romeo's contribution.

9:00 a.m.; no Joe.

"Taking his sweet time. I'm going to get some breakfast," said Stylin' as he grabbed a bowl, filled it, and began eating. He was risking it! He had time for two, and eventually three bowls. Time drifted. *Darkwing Duck* gave way to *Mighty Morphin Power Rangers*. 10:00 a.m.

"Where is he?" Jer walked back to the kitchen, just before Joe's bedroom, and half-yelled, "Joe? You alright?"

No answer.

"Bryan, can I have some cereal?" asked JC.

"Be my guest. You'll have to wash and use this bowl though, it's my only one."

Alphabits sprinkled into a bowl, food was eaten, people were happy, a laugh was had; maybe Joe had a late night of eating burgers and pooping at the same time again, god, I think he bathed in the hot tub last night, Teddy how can you tell, why does the bathroom stink so badly when Joe goes in, I bet he can't reach his ass to wipe properly, I'm eating gross, where is he, it's 11:00 a.m., he's going to starve if he doesn't get out here soon, hahahahaha.

"Fuck it, I'm going to the gym. I'll be back in an hour, and if you've gone, I'll drive out there." Jer left. Clocks ticked. Out came the Nintendo 64 and a game of Bond 007. The multiplayer mode is a magical waste of time; we played for hours without noticing. Jer returned. Cereal was had for lunch, and peanut butter sandwiches, and some bananas. JC opened a can of Chef-Boy-R-Dee. 1:30 p.m.

"Well, fuck who wants to watch *There's Something About Mary?*" We had a pirated satellite feed at the school; hours and hours of movies and shows to watch. We watched, tensely awaiting the eruption of Joe and the dreaded bitchwork to begin. His wife worked at a factory about a half hour away, sometimes Saturdays, and yes, this Saturday. She returned at 3:30. Curious to see us all there, she crept into the Joe's room. RUMBLLLLLE!

"YOU ASSHOLES YOU GODDAMMED ASSHOLE CUNTLAPPER SONS OF BITCHES!"

We shrunk in terror.

"What?"

"I'VE BEEN STUCK IN BED. I'VE BEEN YELLING ALL DAY FOR YOU ASSHOLES TO COME AND GET ME! FUCK YOU ALL!"

"Joe, none of us heard a thing. What happened?

"I FELL INTO THE CRACK BETWEEN MY BED AND THE WALL! YOU ASSHOLES! YOU ASSHOLES, NONE OF YOU WILL EVER BE ON ONE OF MY SHOWS, EVER!"

He stumbled into the bathroom. As he walked away, Bryan had to ask, "So, no campsite today then Joe?"

"FUCK YOU." Click.

Smiles and silent laughs erupted as we hit each other and fell out of our seats. "Ha, well, I woulda just been sleeping till now anyways," said Romeo.

And with that, we got up and went outside to enjoy our day in the great outdoors, almost wishing we had gone to the campsite to get away from school.

Getting the Gravel

"Guys, we gotta do some work on the camp site" announced Joe. This was a few months after I had been at the school, during the yearly thaw that Ontario residents call spring. Also a few months after memory of the first no-go at campsite cleaning was no longer a fresh wound for Joe.

Thermostats rose. Outdoors baked. Soon the scorching summer would be full throttle; we would be breathing in fire and out ashes. Joe wanted to be ready, so he employed the free labour of his students in readying his family camp site. What Joe's campsite had to do with the school or any of us was a mystery. We never saw it except for when we had to work on it. Joe would disappear for the weekend though, so it had benefit. But the amount of bitch work we did on it was unbelievable.

"Gentlemen," sneered Dave Stocker, (or Joe Junior as we called him), "we've got to work quickly or it will be dark before we get done. Some of us have to work in the morning." No kidding, Dave. Most of us have to work in the morning. You probably just want to get home and have phone sex with one of your 1-800 lines again. Even Joe had laughed when he had busted him the night before.

"Dave," Joe Barked, "why was your phone busy? What the hell were you doing? I've been calling for 20 minutes."

"Huh, whew, uh, uh, I was just outside."

"Bullshit you were. Doing what?"

"Uhhhh, I was uh, getting a truck ready for tomorrow."

"Bullshit, you were having phone sex. Why was your phone busy if you were outside?" Joe knew bullshit better than anyone- experientia docet- so he didn't fall for it. No answer from Dave.

"Well, if you've done wanking and cleaned yourself up, we gotta talk business. Catch your breath."

"I'm done, I mean, what's up?" asked Dave.

Nobody respected Dave ever; he looked like Gene Shalit except much fatter, far less articulate, and no glasses. He knew nothing about wrestling, so his being in charge was annoying. He wasn't as big as Joe but we all thought him a much bigger idiot.

We arrived at the campsite well after sunset; picking up a load of gravel and shovels isn't as quickly done as you would think. Joe had to haggle with the guy about the price; after the umpteenth refusal Joe grunted and agreed to pay full price then left us with Dave. We made the best of the situation by jumping up and down on the trailer as it wove through the site; if we fell, one of us would be seriously hurt. Laughs peppered the air until we arrived.

"Gentlemen," sneered Dave through his nose, "we need to get this gravel off the truck and around the camper to keep out the mice and cold. It's very important that we do an excellent job."

As a teacher, I can tell you the look we were all giving Dave. It's the look students give when teachers are wasting their time, supposedly to build character, but know it won't-- busywork through forced obligation, not fraternity.

A few snide comments ran through us; we may as well get it done, we all want to get home, where should I pee, I can't believe I'm missing raw for this, just go in the bushes who'll care, better yet go on the actual camper steps, hahahaha.

"Gentlemen, keep your voices down to a quiet whisper," said Dave in a non-whispered whine.

It was impossible to keep quiet. We were shoveling gravel into a giant hole; Dave bitched about the noise the whole time; we pointed out his noise was far more annoying than the gravel, and for god's sake we're shovelling gravel; he pouted, threatened to tell Joe about our attitudes; we grumbled how our attitude was the only thing getting the job done; he bitched and threatened again, we told him to get Joe so Joe would send us all home. He shut up and let us finish the work while he stood there sneering like a miserable idiot.

This was the first instance of many where we did ridiculous things that had nothing to do with wrestling in order to please Joe so that he would keep us involved in wrestling. If we pissed him off too much, we'd be gone from the school and in his words, "Never wrestle again." We put up with a tonne of nonsense because we weren't sure what would really happen, just that we wanted to wrestle; to his credit, the one thing Joe knew well was psychology, though not in your typical sense. To us, it was a mess of manipulation, of confusion, of questioning the reality of our lives; basic life was a complete mystery. To him though, it was simple Psy-Col-Oh-G.

Psychology

Joe, owner of the school and "head trainer", was constantly using his warped "psychology" to confound us. His psychology was his understanding of how people thought, and how to make people think the way he did. We struggled to match him wit for wit, always submitting angrily. In the ring, in the house, on a shopping trip, on the way to an event, Joe dumbfounded us with his psychology. A mentality where he would "turn around" and divide a mattress that was two inches thick into two one inch halves, then double them up for more effectiveness. Nonsense was reason. Bit by bit we became brainwashed into thinking like him.

One amazing lesson came on the set of the *Jesse Ventura Story Movie.* On the outskirts of Toronto, we spent days rehearsing and filming in an old army barracks, the location for the film. We had a ring stationed a flight of stairs away from the cameras, in a dusty, cloudy windowed room. We were enjoying our break from Joe's complete control. Then he called a meeting for us. We boys heeded and came. His boys slumped onto the floor and crash pads; he polluted the dusty air, his voice trailing out of the secluded room, down the stairs, and onto the rest of the set. For the outside world, his voice was diluted and ignored. For us, it was potent wormwood.

"Guys, why do people come to wrestling shows?"

A hushed silence fell. We pawed with his words. The answer of why people came to a wrestling show was blatantly obvious. Why would you go to a basketball game? Basketball. Baseball game? Baseball. Hockey game? Hockey. You get the idea, we got the idea, but we knew it wasn't as obvious as that. His psychology made us doubt reality and ourselves. Certain defeat loomed, but we still wanted to try. Like a child trying to wrest control from a parent while still in the crib, oh god, we had to try! If not for honesty, for sanity! There had to be some truth not controlled by Joe. He was not God; we had to fight him, truth or psychology, or not. Why did people come to wrestling shows? Anyone knows that! ANYONE!

"Wrestling, Joe?" said Jeremy. Irrefutable. From Joe, silence. Then...

"Nope" he scorned, puffing out his cheeks.

Our best weapon, commons sense, died.

"High flying?" asked Romeo.

"Nope" puffed Joe.

"Good storylines, Joe?" My contribution.

"Nope" accompanied by scorn and disparaging look.

"Hardcore wrestling?" came another voice.

"Nope."

"Stars?" asked Rudy.

"Nope" he scoffed.

"Action?" pleaded another.

"Nope." His puffing picked up pace.

"Excitement?" Bryan tried.

"Nope. Nope. Nope. No, Guys, no! OH MY GOD!"

Defeated and broken, our minds splintered from the unbelievable stupidity of it. It was like trying to reason with a baby, an all-powerful, dim-witted, baby. There was no

reason to it! But Joe knew, he held the secrets, as he so often told us, and the secret here was again, psychology.
"Jeez, guys, no wonder your wrestling is so awful; they come for the Pyro!"

Ashamed and confused, we hung our heads. If we had daggers, we would have used them; not on Caesar's body, but on our own. This turmoil, this purgatory of nonsense was more than anyone with a reasonable mind could bear. No wonder we went nuts. Give me honesty or give me death; our training was bad, but Joe was the head trainer. Our psychology was bad sure, but Joe was the guru who was to teach us. If we were bad, it had to have something to do with the trainer and guide in the school, namely Joe.

None of us had real daggers, just the ones in our eyes that stabbed into the miserable ground that supported his immense weight. We stared at the floor by the ring, a floor already rotten, outdated, and nearly useless. How could a floor hold up so much fat? So much stupid, ignorant fat? 400lbs of wasted food and my wasted money straddling a beam in the floor, a beam that if God or decency existed anywhere, would break, letting those pestilent portly jowls fall to certain death. Damn him, damn his psychology, damn this floor, damn the beam that didn't break, and damn life. We sat stupefied as Joe leashed our minds.

"Wrestling fans want to see pyro. They come for the fireworks. The WWF has it, WCW has it, everyone knows that the number one reason wrestling fans come to a wrestling show is that they want to see fireworks. We are going to give them the best god-dammed fireworks show they ever seen since the fourth of July. They'll tell everyone. We'll show them why we're number 1."

Never mind that we're in Canada and the 4th of July is an American holiday, or that I'd been breaking my body for months trying become a good wrestler. All that time I should have just focused on choosing a good theme for the pyrotechnics before my match.

The devastating psychology of Joe defeated any and all of us; it dammed not only what we were doing do to achieve our dream, but everything we had done so far. We felt defeated. Hopeless. If only there were some objective standard, something that couldn't be argued with, that no reasonable person could deny! A truth such as "snow is white" where everyone based on common witness would have to admit, agree, and concede that truth was indeed, truth, would be a god-send. We were surrounded by snow in Ontario but we still needed a saviour.

Time passed; desperation grew. Once the movie finished, we were confined again to the school. But we had our dreams. We pushed ourselves, hoping that beyond the insanity of ICW Hart Bros School, our wrestling skills would give life to those dreams. Normalcy returned... somewhat. We went back to training. Our minds healed when we avoided Joe, hope revived, and then, when we least expected it...

"Guys, do you smell gas?" Joe puffed, walking in, and making a big show by sniffing at the air, flaring his nostrils.

This was in the training ring, weeks later, back at the school. I was mid-headlock, a high spot away from the finish of the match I was taping for my promo video. The match was ruined. Never mind that, I was told, you're not ready anyways. Just listen and later, Joe said, I'll show you how to *really* work.

"I smell it sometimes guys, and I'm really worried about carbon monoxide killing you. Terry is going to come in here and put in a gas detector; we gotta make sure you guys are safe while in here."

Never mind that he smoked while watching us train, or that carbon monoxide was undetectable by the human nose-those were foolhardy volleys of logic batted away as gnats by an elephant; he could smell it, doctors were wrong about cigarette smoke since it never harmed him, and gas was a worry, especially while we were training. If the gas killed us across the hall in our bedrooms, it wasn't such a big deal apparently. But to die in the ring, well, that was not for fate to decide.

Terry (or as Joe labelled him on posters throughout the school, Terry "Lipshits" Norris) put the "smoke detector" above the ring in the training room, pointing directly at the vending machine; the vending machine was a bitter point of anger. For Joe, it angered him because it was being stolen from. From us, it typified the whole psychology of the school.

Joe had a car, we didn't. He bought cans of pop at Zehrs, $2 for a dozen, then sold them through the machine to his prisoners at a dollar each. I suppose it was theft to take them, but when you pay $3,500 to go learn how to wrestle at the ICW Hart Bros School of Wrestling and not one of the Hart Brothers is there (they had left long and Joe hadn't changed the name; we all figured it was being fought over. Legal things take forever to sort out, no discredit to the Harts but we really wished they were there), you feel entitled to a bag of chips or free pop now and then.

Nobody was fooled by the "detector" above the ring, but there was enough of a bluff zone between us knowing what it really was and Joe knowing if we knew for us to play with ambiguity. He would never come out and admit that he had lied to us; he would just accept later that it was known, and never mention that it was supposed to be a secret. He'd say he knew we were going to find out, he was just testing us. We took the little draws as very real victories and took this opportunity to load his back with our blitheness. I ran the ropes in a thong, fingering the smoke detector while calling it such, daring him to expose himself. If it was just a smoke detector, we were innocently making fun of it, not him. And nobody would be stupid enough to steal in front of it. We should not have doubted the master. Days later, as we loafed around the TV, a decree came down.

"Guys, we're having a meeting. Everyone in my office."

The vending machine was still being stolen from. So what? We were all being stolen from, just in a different way. Pop was physically disappearing; dreams are seldom tangible enough to say someone has stolen them from you. You can hardly ever grasp them, so how can you blame someone else for losing them? We marched into the office. Time for one of our pointless meetings; perhaps tonight it would only be an hour. No, I don't have anything better to do at 11:30 p.m. I'm happy to be here, Joe.

We sat around a human smoke stack popping and spewing bullshit into the air.

Myself and Sean Cross; note the porn on the TV and my thong for tanning. What's wrong with me?

"Guys, it's not the guys from the outside that are stealing from me, it's the guys living here on the inside. You come into my house and steal from me. But I'm a forgiving man. I'm going to give you a chance to come clean. Someone in this room has stolen pop from me. They've stolen from each of you too, by doing that. So, if that person wants to come clean, now's his chance."

We couldn't be right or win, so why beat around the bush? Someone from the inside, not the outside; stealing from this man in his own house. I glanced around at the hodge-podge crew of misfits, all of us exhausted, ready to sleep, pissed-off -at-having-this-stupid-meeting, students.

"His chance". That narrowed it down; there were 9 students, only 1 female. Vanessa probably hadn't gotten desperate enough to steal yet; plus her coordination was suspect. It would take planning and a coordination to manipulate the machine. Down to eight. I could count myself out, since I had come with some money prepared for the school and didn't drink pop. That left 7. Jeremy had a job and lived away from the school, as did Romeo; that left 5. By default there could be only--

"Guys, I'm going to give you one more chance; does anyone have anything to say, or apologize for as far as theft goes; does anyone want to admit to stealing? If you're honest, I'll give you a second chance."

Silence. Still down to 5; Ball, Rudy, Ted, Javad, and Marco. Marco worked like a madman, and was never at the school since he was always out chasing girls and sleeping over at their houses. That left 4.

Rudy wasn't fool enough to steal, or was too lazy; he spent the whole day smoking and only drank chocolate milk anyways. He wouldn't jeopardize himself for a can of coke. That left 3. Ted would probably not steal from you, but would kill you if you called him a thief and were wrong. He would probably kill you if you were right too. Joe understood this. He knew our minds, and Teddy's. Joe proceeded carefully; the "Dirty Dutchman" sat there sucking on his filthy handlebar moustache- FSSSTP- staring at his fingers curling a twist of his hair in front of his eyes. Once in a while he looked at Joe. If he had stolen, he would soon explode with anger at the ambiguity of it; he hated incoherence.

"Yeah, I heard ya Joe" shot Teddy.

That ruled Ted out. Or did it? Could we be about to see a showdown? Teddy just sat there in his chair shaking his leg, and he had one hand in the pocket of his pajama pants, which he wore almost all day when not working at Sears Auto. He even wore them grocery shopping, an odd match to his full bomber jacket- FSSSSTP. He could match Joe with Psychology, but it would end real ugly, like how the cold war could have ended. I looked for the exit. Teddy just sucked on his 'stache, nodding a little bit, shaking that leg of his and fumbling in his pocket, either with his member or a knife. What the hell was going on in his head?

"Ok guys, I'm going to tell you, I've got someone on tape stealing from me. Does anyone have anything to say? Anyone? Anyone at all?"

I was pretty sure we were down to two, and who would steal from the stupid Vending machine at this point? We all knew it was a camera. Then I remembered; Ball was stoned and Javad was away when the whole "I smell gas" performance happened.

Javad and Ball sat there, two bored 4 year-olds being preached at for chewing gum in church. Everything was going in Javad's left ear and out Ball's right, but Javad had his 'face' on. I'd seen that face before. It was the face that said "I know something, and you probably know it too. In fact, I'm certain you know what I know, but I won't say what I know because I'll be damned if I'm going to call my bluff for you." It was the same face he would make in a car after somebody had farted, it wasn't you, and he was the only other person there.

You'd look at Javad, wretch a bit, and he would say nothing, like you'd imagined it; he'd lie to your face and make you feel stupid for it. Every time Joe ordered fast food, Javad volunteered to pick it up so he could spit in Joe's shake and rev the van to max before slamming it into gear, trying to kill it but not suspiciously. The van squealed and complained, and only Javad knew what other liberties he had taken at the school. He had his own psychology. Revenge was in his thick Iranian blood. Maybe he could out-psychology Joe. Maybe.

The other candidate was Ball. Aaron was always a likely candidate for theft- no job, always hungry from the munchies, and a little slow. He barely talked, never really had anything funny to say, and spent his time stoned, laughing at TV on the big screen. We called him Ball because Aaron (his real name) sounded too lofty. He liked green things, and once on a tour he sat for hours saying nothing, then when he saw a kid playing soccer with a green ball, Aaron just spouted out "ball," and that was it; from then on he was Ball. Once he watched a wildlife show about Zebra's. When the Zebras finished mating, the male pulled out and ball saw that horses probably envied Zebras. Ball's comment was "Zebras are cool" and that was all there really was to know about Ball. Although he could solve a Rubix cube in 30 seconds, he was not a match for Joe in a battle of psychology. Poor ball. If he had stolen, he was doomed.

"Guys, last chance. Is there anything you want to say? Anything at all? AARON, I'm looking at you. Anything to say? About stealing? AAIRR-RUN?" Joe whined.

"Nope" with trilling, punchy n, and a finish like a popping bubble.

"You didn't?"

"Nnnnope."

"You're sure?"

"Yyyyep" said Ball as he looked at Joe, too stoned, or too scared to respond.

"Erry (Terry) " big inhale for dramatic effect, "rollllllllll the tape." Terry "Lipshits" Norris put in the tape, pushed play and Javad, Ball, and Teddy all took a deep breath in. So did I. We had all been outdone! It wasn't of the training ring as we all thought, no! It was Terry's room! The camera that protected the precious Van that Javad repeatedly violated was now focused on Terry's messy den of toilet paper, greasy clothes, uncovered mattress, and few cases of pop. We had been so easily duped. Who would it be? We watched in horror at the still filth of Terry's musty room. The tape rolled. Then the victim entered.

Ball walked in, looking side to side as though he knew something was up, then walked to the pop. He took one, opened it on the spot, and took a long swig. He drank probably half that pop and picked up another one, pocketing it. Another sip. Again he looked side to side, one side being directly at the camera, and then walked out of the shot, one pop in hand and one in pocket. I noticed Javad's gut extend a bit further over his belt, and his mouth opened slightly as he exhaled; his expression didn't change, but he had survived. Teddy sat there still curling his hair - FSSSSSTP- his leg still twitching. Apparently game not over for T. For Ball though, the writing was on the wall.

Truth. The camera had seen it. We had seen it. Joe had seen it. Ball had seen it. Hell, even the silence hanging in the room had seen as plain as day; Ball had stolen pop. Undeniably, on camera, without even a hat to offer some hope of a plea of "not me," Ball had taken a pop, opened it, drank it, and left with it all on Camera. We looked at Aaron with sympathy and awe at the obstinacy of his "Nope." The grand inquisitor had done his part, now only the confession had to come. Joe paused for dramatic effect and pursed his lips together. Twiddling his fingers together above his gut, he inhaled as he got ready to impale the traitor. Ball was in the stocks but we were all going to lose-- again. Psychology match over, victory to the master.

"Aaron, I'm going to ask you one final time. Did. You. Steal. My. Pop?"

Ball looked right at him, then looked nervously around at all of us exhausted, ready to sleep, pissed off at having this stupid meeting, mentally exasperated, no trainer, out $3,500 for nothing, students. Theft.

He looked at Joe. Square in the eye.

"Nope."

You're Gonna Hurt Yourself

Pork Brothers and Purgatory

Bryan's morning routine. Note the small mirror and annoying time of day.

Bryan was a good storyteller. Great in fact. Thank god, because the hours driving to bitch work in the van (which had no heater) were miserably cold. Bryan filled the space with tangible warmth. Some people you listen to, some you don't. If Bryan spoke, you listened, well, unless you were Curtis. He would only listen to his brother sometimes. When Bryan preached, no. When Bryan and Curtis made fun of something, yes. When Bryan was saying something that would piss Curtis off or being too much of a little brother, or trying to be a big brother to Curtis, Curt listened especially well so he could set him straight. The two tough brothers came from a family of pork farmers and had sharp wits for dealing with stupidity.

Curtis was still in Saskatchewan, so for my first three months at school, it was Bryan and myself sharing a room; even with just the two of us in there, I still couldn't remember his name for the first two weeks.

Bryan had an infectious smile, straight hockey hair, and big glasses. He wore his contact lenses only when he had to; too much work otherwise. I knew this because we shared a room and every morning I suffered his routine of getting ready. In five months at the school I worked a total of 20 days; I made money doing the *Jesse Ventura Story Movie*, (a movie so bad it isn't even on Netflix) so I figured I didn't need to work again till midsummer, and that's exactly what I did, or didn't do. Bryan however, worked every day at a different temp job at a different factory, often for long hours and minimum wage.

He would awake with 25 minutes to get ready; first a shower, then he would stand for ten minutes holding a mirror the size of a deck of cards in his hand combing his long hair straight backwards, which was how he dried it. He'd dress in thirty seconds, then look through his coin jar for the next ten minutes trying to find the largest pieces of change possible; it was a plastic jar and he would shake, shake, shake it, the noise of gravel in a plastic bucket, grab a nickel or dime, then shake shake shake it again until a few more appeared. Once he had two dollars or once Ronnie got to the school, he go work at the Toyota factory or Cambridge Towel for the day, happy if he had enough money for a pop *and* a snack. I think the average time of coin shaking was seven minutes, which felt like an eternal hell at 5:45 a.m., which also explains why I hated him every morning. But I loved him again every afternoon, and that is easy to understand, too. Bryan kept me sane.

Joe ripped off Curtis and Bryan for an extra $10,000 each, and was a pain in a lot of ways. But he was funny as hell and genuinely brought a lot of cheer to the school. It was often at his expense, but not always. But with Bryan around...

Dodgin' and Weavin'

"That was bullshit, tell me it isn't fixed."

The Evander Holyfield - Lennox Lewis fight had just finished to a chorus of boos from the crowd. If you watch the fight, you'll see it's clearly a fix or the judges have been bought off.

"Well, it was still impressive. They are pretty good athletes."

"Bullshit, I could go 5 round with either of those guys. It's a work!" Mocked Joe; Bryan's ears perked up.

"Joe, do you really think you could fight Evander Holyfield for 5 rounds and not get knocked out?" he asked.

"No problem. I know how to cover. I'd put up my hands and let him go to town."

"Yeah, but he's the heavyweight champion of the world. He would knock you out in thirty seconds."

"Bullshit, I'd just cover, stand there and take it."

"You'd still be exhausted. Wait, do you mean now, or back in your day?" posed Bryan, sneaking in a jab at Joe's age.

"Now! Those guys aren't anything!" Shouted Joe. Jer had the wisdom to just roll his eyes and stay out of the fight.

"Joe, have you ever even boxed? It's tough." I had to pipe in. I guess I wanted a piece of the action.

"I'm fuckin' tougher than you" volleyed Joe.

"That's not the question; the question is have you ever even boxed?" asked Bryan, sticking to his guns.

"Look, guys, there's nothing to it. I'd block my face and he wouldn't be able to do anything. Like this." Joe nimbly covered his face with his hands, putting up his dukes and readying to face Evander Holyfield, the best boxer in the world; he exposed a weakness, and Bryan exploited it.

"Uhhh, Joe, wouldn't he just punch you in the gut, and when your hands dropped, punch you in the face?"

"That's a lot of padding," said Terry, "I don't think it would have an effect."

The bullshitters had multiplied, but Bryan had backup too.

"Joe, you couldn't last 5 rounds with me. Come on, you can't be serious" I said.

"Ben, are you a boxer?" pushed Joe.

"I've done boxing, lots of rounds hitting my heavy bag. It'd be pretty much the same as hitting you."

"Let's get in the ring then. You get the first shot. I'll close my eyes, you can square off and hit me, and then I'll return the favour."

Great strategy by Joe; play up to fairness and stubbornness, avoiding skill. Full-on clocking someone in the face with no real provocation isn't something I'm comfortable with. I debated. Today, for Bryan and Curtis, I would probably hit him and not stop for their $20,000 and Ronny's $30,000 +.

"Joe, you'd never have a chance. Holyfield would knock you down in 30 seconds" countered Bryan.

"I'd get up" Joe bluffed.

"Before you said you'd never get knocked down."

"I never said that; I said he'd never knock me out."

"You think that Evander Holyfield hitting you full in the face wouldn't knock you out?" said Bryan wielding his logic.

"It's not like he's Tyson."

"He beat Tyson!" we all shouted.

"You get the gloves, and I'll do the fight."

We laughed, Joe cursed, left, then came back in.

"Just you wait, I'm keeping track of who is laughing. You'll see, boys, you'll see. Just wait till I get Johnny Canine in here and then we'll see."

Johnny Canine was a legitimately tough, burly man who had wrestled in Japan and the WWE. He was about 6 foot 2,

280 pounds, and would be tough to knock out with a baseball bat, let alone fists. He also had made it clear that, while he worked with Joe, he would happily knock out anyone who mocked him, Joe included.

"Oooh, ooh, can I be the first to knock him out after you knock him out Joe?" begged Brian.

"What?"

"You can take Holyfield, so I'll tell Johnny Canine you said you could knock him out no problem!" Bryan laughed. He was nutty and fearless enough to actually tell Canine this. Joe knew this as well as we did.

"I never said I'd fight Johnny Canine..."

"Well, it won't be a problem if you do."

"Ha ha, Bryan," said a shaken Joe.

Bryan winked at me; Joe was on the ropes and ready to dive outta there. One more shot was all he needed.

"Don't forget to say your prayers, train, and take your vitamins!"

"Who are you, Hulk Hogan? Fuckin' pork farmers."

With that, Joe wandered out the door to his private bathroom. If I said anything like what Bryan said, I would have had to legitimately fight Joe or gotten into a yelling match. For Bryan? Nothing. He was master of calling bullshit without calling the actual bullshit, bullshit. The only person who tolerated bullshit less was Curtis, Bryan's brother. He arrived a few weeks later, and he and Bryan fought like brothers, but if someone else interfered, they honed in on the new target quickly. And they found plenty of targets at the school. But they were also entertained, especially Bryan.

The wrestling school was above a Scotiabank and a coffee shop. It was just one floor off the main street in Cambridge, Ontario. We couldn't do any training during the day because of the bank. During the days, especially ones like this, time in the school was a neurotic mixture of minutes spent avoiding Joe, trying to get out the door before you were roped into bitch work, but trying to milk out your semi-privacy in the school to enjoy a few hours alone. We were always on edge. We never knew what was going to happen next.

Waldo Von Erich was officially the head trainer at the school, but Jer was the one doing it all. Ronnie had taught us all he could, but his back was messed up and he wasn't in a good frame of mind to be training us. If you want to picture Ronnie, imagine Bubbles from The Trailer Park boys with slightly weaker glasses and a better heart. He had a totally justified hatred for Joe boiling under the surface, and had to deal with idiot kids like me coming in to the school. Ronnie bore the brunt of our stupidity. And he had to bear with Waldo correcting him.

Waldo was well known and justifiably so. He had an impressive build, even as a 74 year old at the school, and he had a presence about him. He once wrestled Bruno Sammartino for close to two hours in Madison Square Garden and is a justifiable legend in wrestling. However, his wrestling was so different from anything I had ever seen that it was confusing. He would tell us to shoulder tackle guys by ramming our shoulders into their guts for real, he was used to pacing a much, much slower match, and he didn't really show us anything because he couldn't bump.

Waldo was smart though; his psychology made sense, especially his statement of, "Never give them two apples if you can give them one." (Think of apples as things that are interesting in a match). It's a true tenet of wrestling I've personally heard repeated by Les Thatcher, Harley Race, Bruce Hart, Tom Pritchard, and a bunch of other guys. Of course, and I'm sure they would all admit, if you have to give them 5 apples to get yourself over, do it. We were all shown another reason why Waldo was over. Waldo had ab control.

Waldo could make his abs ripple up and down, even at his advanced age. He showed us this, and we sat there watching, kind of hypnotized, kind of scared, during a training session where both Joe and Waldo actually showed up. This ab control, of course, made Joe jealous, so one day he tried showing us his "pec control". He waddled into the training room, told us, "Guys, I know I'm fat now, but you can tell I was a legit athlete because I still have pec control," and then proceeded to jiggle his pecs at us by waving his shoulders like a burlesque dancer. Yeah, his pecs jiggled and undulated, but not from muscular control; as soon as he left, we exploded, laughing. Waldo had a much better physique, and Bryan new this especially.

Waldo trained every day and he ended up sharing a room with Stylin' Bryan while they did promotions in Toronto. Bryan vividly remembers Waldo waking him up early in the morning and telling him he was out of shape. "You've got a belly and weak abs. You need to start doing conditioning." Waldo got Bryan to hold onto his ankles and do some leg raises, then swapped positions so that Waldo too could do the exercises, saying, "Watch my abs while I do these." He was in shape, said Bryan, but it was hard to notice with his dick flopping all over the place; Waldo had done the whole morning workout naked.

In addition to Ab Control, Waldo had a genuine Nazi WWII helmet, which he wore to the ring for his matches. He also wore a complete Nazi outfit, goose stepped, spoke German, and did the "Zig Heil!"Nazi salute. Yes, in the 1950's, Waldo was a Nazi for his gimmick. Do you think this got him just a little bit of heat? It did not take a lot of skill or creativity. But it took balls, huge balls, (balls which Bryan can verify) and no wonder he was booed out of buildings everywhere. I'm sure an ISIS terrorist would get a little bit of a reaction these days, too. Wrestlers love forcing reality on people when they least expect it. When you're not ready for reality, reality hurts. Joe taught us that. He also taught us about god.

There is No God

When Joe ran a show, he ran a show. When I was in BC I saw a TV ad during Monday Night Raw for one of his shows; it featured The Bushwackers, The Wild Samoans, King Kong Bundy and Tatanka. It was a stacked card and drew close to 5,000 people. He was successful. In fact, he was so successful on that front that he decided the next time he ran a show, he didn't need to advertise… until 3 days before it ran.

A crew of us drove to Oshawa from Cambridge and postered the hell out of the town; it was obvious because on the way to the arena, every single pole had a Johnny Canine poster on it. But that was it; thousands of dollars on the hook, and only three days' notice for the show, so thousands of dollars in the hole.

No blame on Canine or Greg Valentine or Typhoon, the stars advertised; nobody knew they were coming so why would anyone show up? Joe had dug his own hole and naturally the students would help dig him out of it (not that you can dig yourself out of a hole.)

"Guys, you're here at the school getting all of this training and not giving anything back. I need all of you to come with me tonight. Terry's rented a truck, we're going to move the travel agency" he declared.

So much for our training session. Clearly, we were getting too much out of him by getting what we paid for; tonight would even it out because we wouldn't train. Joe would be treated fairly for once.

"What? When?" someone asked.

"Never mind that, we'll go when we go. But don't start training. I don't want to wait for you."

So we waited for him. It was five thirty at night, and training started at six. This was a bad sign. Jeremy and Romeo both got out of it because a) they had jobs to go to in the morning and b) lived at Ronny's. They hadn't arrived yet and someone tipped them off. Joe didn't notice.

After we had been sitting around for another two and a half hours not training, which made sense because we weren't there to learn to wrestle we were there to do bitchwork, Joe finally got his ass together and we headed out. Joe. Big, fat, taking the steps like an eighty year old woman, Joe. We arrived at the travel agency at 8:30 p.m. and Joe barked orders as we hauled out heavy office file cabinets, supplies, organizers, desks, dividers, and everything else.

I remember sweating bullets despite the cool weather; the trips up and down the ramp were exhausting and it had already been a long day before this nonsense began. By midnight we were all grumpy and sore. There was no end in sight.

"Joe, what time are we going to work until?"

"You young guys shouldn't be bitching already. I used to load the ring, drive to the show, set up the ring, do a match, another match under a hood, sell programs, tear down the ring, then drive home and unpack the ring before going to work my day job. I never slept, you don't need sleep. Jeez guys toughen up" he spouted from his chair.

"It's easy to sit there and boss people around. We're doing all the labour," said Bryan. Bryan always knew how to call a spade a spade but avoid retaliation. Curtis mumbled, "Don't sleep my ass, you slept all day" but only I heard it. We started to laugh, but even that was interrupted.

"Listen, you guys want to learn the wrestling business, this is the biz." Grumbles all around.

I was there till 3 a.m. I finally had enough and got Ronny to give me a ride back to the school. Bryan, Terry, and Curtis all stayed behind. Joe promised all that we would be back there the next day, threatened that he knew who were "the real prospects" and grunted as we left. That was no small threat; he was the one who was going to book us in all our matches and help us to get booked elsewhere. I was too tired and pissed off to care. The agency would take a week; no training till it was done, Joe commanded. No training, hardly time for the gym, too tired to work, bank accounts dwindling, nothing getting learned, and he was the one who, as he always liked to point out, "held our careers in our hands". He controlled every aspect of our lives, and none of us could handle that idea. There was no god. Life was too unjust.

Joe is God

After 2 nights, I was sick of the damned travel agency. Exhausted. I wanted to train and learn to wrestle, not move furniture around or paint walls or remove wallpaper in a stupid office. What the hell was I doing? What the hell was Joe doing? I never got to sleep, I couldn't lift weights with good intensity, I had to nap in the afternoon because life was miserable and I was exhausted. Joe had changed from cancelling practice to moving duties after practice. If you practiced, you had to go help. If you didn't go help, you didn't practice, and vice versa.

Hostage to his whims, we arrived at the travel agency when all decent people were fast asleep. We labored to the groaning whims of a beast we couldn't defy without killing our dreams of wrestling. In movies, in songs, in every Disney film ever made, you learn that dreams are worth fighting for. You learn that dreams are true and will come to life if you keep working at them.

The harder we pursued, the further away Joe took us. The more we wanted our dream, the more we had to succumb to his manipulation that lead us further into frustration. Our days were a mix of misery, sweat, and hopelessness. We got further and further away from wanting to be wrestlers every day we spent with Joe.

Wrestling was the point of life. Wrestling made us bitches and slaves for Joe. Joe was causing nothing but misery and pain, so we started to hate wrestling. The second night I left at 2 a.m. utterly exhausted. I was mentally and physically defeated. Life at the school was run at the whim of Joe. It was not that god didn't exist; Joe was god, and god, like life, sucked. Then… at seven in the morning…

"Ahhhh, sometimes, just when you are ready to give up on everything, life comes through for you. I have never believed so much in God as I do right now." Bryan was always chipper, but that seemed a bit much, even for him.

"My God, I've never seen anybody that fat move that fast. I believe in miracles."

Curtis too? What had I missed?

"Hahaha, the look on that fat asshole's face. I would move a dozen travel agencies to see that again!" Such hyperbole.

"What happened?" I had to ask. Cheerfulness at 7 a.m. means something worth hearing about has happened. None of us were morning people. I barely got the question out before Curtis gleefully explained the "miracle" while trying not to offend the "fat cripple" that might overhear him, either through the door or through a microphone in our room. Joe, he reminded us, had eyes and ears everywhere. Curtis began:

* * *

Joe is Proof of God

It was no accident. There is a god, even in professional wrestling. My faith has never been stronger.

For starters, there's no electricity in this hellhole of a travel agency that Froglegs (Joe) is making us move. What's worse, Errrry (Terry) plugged up the toilet with one of his king-sized dumps of McDonald's and cigarette butts. It stinks, we can't flush the toilet, and there's no electricity except for the extension cord running out the heavy-as-hell fire door at the back of the building.

Froglegs figures we still can work, toilet or no, so away we slave into the early hours of the morning while he sits there smoking. And bitching and farting. We took a break around 4:00 a.m. to eat, guess what, Burger King, "Dice the onions" and then for the next two hours Joe bitches at us to hurry up and work faster while not doing anything himself, clutching at his gut and balls the whole time. Finally, I figure out why.

After drinking about a dozen Cokes, he has to piss too. I figured he didn't actually defecate or piss but just swelled more and more with shit and piss every day- I mean, how else could he get so fat? Anyway, he has to go, but I've added a massive loaf to the pile mounding out of the toilet already and it stinks to high heaven. I was going to take a dump out in the woods bear-style, but I didn't think a charge of criminal indecency would sit well with my parents or my future. There's a major roadway in front and houses behind.

We did all take pisses on the back wall of that godforsaken hellhole, but a dump is special. Well, after bitching for another 20 minutes, Joe gives up and decides that he will indeed have to pee outside too. Keep in mind that we've been going in and out of the back door all night.

I'm busy sanding some paint off the front wall as I watch him waddle to the back door to do his business. I realize the fat bastard isn't even going all the way outside because that would mean going down a step. His laziness of making everyone else do his bitchwork extends to his bathroom habits- surprise, surprise. He goes, props open the fire door with his huge gut, and starts fiddling his hands around where his dick must be. I can't watch.

The fat asshole is going to pee all over the door and his hands then pull the door shut. We're going to handle his pee for the rest of the night. I look at the drywall in front of me and curse my life one more time. Then, "BZZZZZTTT!" and then, "OW OW WHOO! WHOOOOOO! TERRY TERRY TERRY! JESUSFUCKCUNTLAPPERSONOVABITCH!"

I've never seen someone so fat move so fast! Joe bounced off the walls into the hall and past me, running and yelping like a dog that's bitten a porcupine. His fat ass waddles and scoots as he hops and belts out, "HAAA, HAAA OHHH GOD THAT SONOVABITCH FUCKIN TERRRY! OH GOD! TERRRRRRRRYYY!" Terry comes bolting in, looks at him, and says, "What's the matter Joe?" like he thought one of us was killing him. Joe just keeps jumping around, biting his lip as tears form in his eyes, pointing at the growing pee spot in his pants.

What happened was the cord had been frayed by the heavy fire door slamming open and shut on it all night for three nights. Joe had peed right onto it! He burnt a hole the size of a loony on his dick-- he showed it to us and made us look so we'd stop laughing at him- but that just made us laugh more. He wanted to ice it, but we didn't have any, and he's too fat to rinse it in the sink, so we came home.

We laughed the whole ride while he moaned and whimpered, saying stuff like, "Fuckin pork farmers. I hope one day you burn off your tiny peckers then you'll see what it's like". That too made us laugh more. And now we're home. And I'm never going to doubt God again."

* * *

Just before Joe's burn, I had my first match at the aforementioned show in Oshawa, Ontario. I was lucky enough to work Jer. "The Mad Bomber" made his professional debut in a loss to "The Director" Eric Young. It was a great match for me, but really just an average match, which is good for a pro debut. I hit a spinebuster, did a dive to the floor as did Jer, and my dad flew out to tape the match.

If it hadn't been for Romeo Adams, I would have been much more nervous.

Romeo was the brunt of bad luck that day. True to his word, Joe helped give the greatest pyro-technics show on earth, a key component of the ICW wrestling show. Give Terry Norris credit, he knows just about everything about anything mechanical. I don't know where he learned it, but he had the skill and knowledge to put together a solid pyrotechnics show that, given him being the only one putting it together, was amazing.

Terry stayed up all night getting the pyro ready. Safety first, he made sure everything was cued and put together properly. These weren't just Roman Candles from your local party store, these were the big guns. Things that are usually reserved for state fairs or provincial celebrations were unloaded and exploded inside the Oshawa arena. I don't know how they even got them. Terry took care of everything, but neglected to mention how far away each of us should be when the pyro went off.

In the opening match, a sneering Romeo Adams strutted out to the ring preparing to kick ass and looking tough, then "WHOOOOSH!" Romeo Adams jumped 4 feet in the air, eyes as wide as saucers, his mouth stretched wide, terrified, one arm pinned to his chest in terror, cringing.

Sticking tightly to the path clearly marked with black duct tape in a blacked out arena, Romeo pumped both his fists in the air in triumph, sneered once again and told the fans to shut up.

Maybe it was what gave Karma the idea of burning Joe at the travel agency, which was a "be careful what you're putting people in risk of when you don't know what you're doing" lesson. Maybe it was just wrestling. We all laughed, and between Romeo's bad luck and my great opponent, I had a good pro debut. I was getting closer to my dream, the boys were bonding, and things were coming together.

I actually felt like the school had more or less worked itself out; we all got along, Joe was infuriating at times but we had learned how to avoid most of his idiocy, and the idiocy we did have to put up with, other than the travel agency, was entertaining fodder for our conversations.

We trained. We honed our gimmicks. Joe got us hired as stunt doubles for the *Jesse Ventura Story* TV Movie, and he deserves a lot of credit for that. He, when he put his mind genuinely to it, delivered amazing things. He didn't do that often enough, but things were going...well. Things couldn't run so smoothly for long.

Enter a Dragon

Miles using his talent of drawing. Note the cross-legged pose. I haven't been able to do that since I was nine.

Whenever I'm exhausted I think of Miles. How can you not find him inspirational? He's a source of strength and hope. He tried when any sensible person would have given up. It's not uncommon in pro wrestling. But Miles had to have been especially delusional, at least that was how we saw him. How he saw himself, well, no one could believe. Miles was doomed the moment he came to wrestling school because he was Miles.

A lot of wrestlers want to get away from reality; Miles was no exception. However, he couldn't escape the gimmick life had given him. When he arrived he was Miles, but he donned his gimmick within days, only it was not chosen by himself but by god. "I tried-- "Oh **LORD**, how I did try!" (*The Otto Show)*-- to like him, to know him, but we just couldn't connect. His gimmick overpowered us all. In only a few days, to almost everyone, he was no longer Miles. Like all gimmicks, his most well-known came about organically.

Miles: Student and Teacher

Miles spent the whole day with Godzilla. Drawing Godzilla, reading about Godzilla in his giant Godzilla encyclopedia, and watching Golden Girls on TV. That's right, he was a 23 year old boy watching a TV series about menopausal women. He would sit cross-legged on the floor, doodling in his sketch book and giggling to himself while we all wondered what the hell he was. None of us could handle Miles in any large amount, not just because he was beyond hideous in the ring, but also because he thought he should lord it over us as he trained at the school months before. Joe had sent him packing then; he realized he was pissing everybody off. However, Miles had paid up beforehand, and to his credit, Joe let him back into the school.

When I say Miles was hopeless in the ring, I'm not exaggerating. In wrestling one of the most basic things you do, no, the most basic thing you do, is circle an opponent in the ring. You face them and they face you, and while you do this, you stalk each other getting ready to lock up, pretty much what you would do in a real fight or what fighters do in the UFC. The two combatants look at each other, prepare to fight, and walk in a circle. Miles couldn't do this. I know because once I took him into the ring with aspirations of making him into a worker disirregardlessly of what everyone else thought of him. He could do it, he could be a wrestler, I was convinced, and I would be so proud when I had taken this sow's ear and turned it into a silk purse. Or any type of purse for that matter. That dream faded quickly. As we paced around, getting ready to lock up, I noticed Miles didn't seem at all threated by me. He was duck-waddling around the ring, his hands down by his love handles, feet barely shuffling off of the mat, a grandfather in loafers. What was more, he wasn't even really looking at me; he was looking ahead and turning his head slightly to look at me as though we were out for a Sunday stroll together; we just needed to hold hands.

"Miles, face me and step sideways. We're getting ready to fight."

"I can't do that."

"Why not?"

"I'll get blown up (tired)."

I thought he was joking and laughed, then caught my laugh and realized he was serious. This guy wanting to be a pro wrestler couldn't pace sideways in a circle because he got too tired. Getting tired in the ring is part of wrestling. Strike one and two just like that- where could he possibly go from here? Maybe he would get motivated to try getting blown up if we did something fun. I got him warm enough to try something else. I asked, "What's your favourite move?"

"I like dropkicks."

I didn't laugh on the outside this time. I looked at the red-headed comic book keener with pudgy legs, pudgy arms, a pudgy face and no muscle tone to speak of. He was wearing his swimsuit, a black swimsuit with one giant pink wave and one giant blue stripe. It was the kind of swimsuit I wore all summer when I was 11 years old because it had a liner and I didn't like wearing underwear. I was sure he wore it for the same reason.

"Sure, let's do those." I had nothing to lose.

83

I told him the technique, explaining that to do a pretty decent dropkick you only need to pick up one foot as high as you can, and then to bring up the other foot next to it, then turn to face the mat and guide your way down with your hands. I had taught myself dropkicks in my basement when I was 16, dropkicking my boxing bag then landing on the carpeted floor, which unlike his swimsuit had no liner underneath, only concrete. This quickly taught me to control my fall with my arms. In the ring was a hundred times easier, but I showed him one more time for good measure. I demonstrated the steps a few times. Then I asked him to pick his leg up as far as he could, which was barely above hip level.   I explained the dynamics of it, how you can turn your hips a little and bend your leg to cheat your foot up, and after a while he sort of got it.

I taught him the whole dropkick. I did one, then got Miles to hold out his hand. I did another one against his hand, then got him to move it a little higher. I did another one and then told him to start at the bottom, and work his way up. He did one and I realized two things. 1) He was so stiff it actually hurt my hand for him to dropkick it and 2) I couldn't see what he was doing so I couldn't help him. I remedied these two ways. 1) I got him to dropkick the turnbuckle instead of my hand and 2) I started the camera so we could record and replay the video later.

Miles's first attempt missed the turnbuckle completely, so I encouraged him to do a second one. His second missed the buckle but tangled his feet in the ropes so that he ended up bumping a little high on his chest and shoulders, crying out "Ughhheee." With that, our training session ended.

Thankfully, the video was preserved; when Marco went to see if he could record over the video we had made, I told him what was on it and his eyes grew wide. "Let me see, let me see" he said. He took enough time to watch the video, laugh, say "Huh, oh, show me again, ha, show me again," and laugh again. He then very seriously said, "Don't ever erase that' and then, "ha, Keef sucks."

Miles did suck, but you had to feel like there was something else at play. You felt he had just been given a bad hand or didn't know what was expected, so, you'd hang out with him, even if it was a grating experience. I played video games with him once; I have a mean Streetfighter 2 game, so I whooped him, which must have been painful for someone so obviously a gamer. I say that without any judgment; I'm a big nerd and love video games, too. Well, I beat him about 11 times in a row and felt bad so I let him win; when he beat me in round 12, he gloated my, "lucky streak is over." I beat him twice more then went to the gym.

He also knew everything, which didn't help his cause. Curtis, Romeo, Stylin' and I were sitting watching *Willy Wonka and The Chocolate Factory* one day. When Augustus Gloop falls in the chocolate river, his mother screams out "Augustus, my darling." When we all saw it we laughed, especially a high on mushrooms Romeo.

The Oompa-Loompas came out, and Romeo slapped himself in the forehead, laughed as hard as a human being could, rolled onto the floor, and then went out the door to wander the streets high as a kite. (It was 4 in the afternoon and Romeo had done mushrooms just because and all by himself. That was Romeo, but he's got his own section. Hell, he could have his own book). Mrs. Gloop said "Augustus" one more time. Nerdly piped in with his wisdom.

"Hey, Augustus. That's where the name of the month August comes from. It's Roman."

Curtis hated Miles with a deep passion, so he stood up, slapped himself in his forehead and said, "My god, all this time we've been living with a fucking genius." I laughed, Bryan laughed, but Miles sneered and groaned.

"Well, I just thought you guys would benefit from it."

"Why the fuck are you trying to tell me anything?" Seemed like a fair response. Curtis had been working for a living for the last 5 years; Miles still lived with his mom.

"Well, I don't know what you guys know and don't know. I went to college for 2 semesters."

"My god, you're a college man. Thank god I never went because I woulda probably killed myself if I did and you were there." Curtis left, then Bryan smiled and left. It was Miles and I. Unbelievably, the lesson continued.

"So yeah, Augustus Caesar was a Roman Emperor who they named August after. All the months are named after Romans or Roman names."

"Ya Miles, I know. I was valedictorian and went to college for a couple years."

"Oh, well nice to know there's a fellow college man here. These other guys just don't get it. Why is Curtis so mad? I was doing him a favour" said a wrinkled Miles.

"Miles, maybe you shouldn't teach people things."

"What? It's good for people to listen when someone knows more than them. I'm helping them learn."

"OK." These days I would lose my mind at the audacity of it; that day, I just smiled and walked into the training room to play video games with Curtis. He paused from playing *Command and Conquer* just long enough to say, "I'm going to kill Miles. What a moron. God, he's more condescending than my old man."

Miles never had a chance; he was Miles, and that was the problem. He did try to make it up to Curtis, however. Curtis wrestled under the name "Insane" Wayne Silver. A crazy gimmick, but Curtis had the crazy smile to pull it off. It seemed decent to tag him up with Bryan. The Silver Brothers would work well. We called Curtis Insane Wayne, and Miles liked to draw. So, with about 12 hours a day of free time, Miles decided to draw Curtis.

He spent hours first sketching the frame in pencil, then inking it, then finally adding some color and a bit of shade. The picture was good. It had weight, it had personality, it looked great, a bit like Mankind but more muscular, with nicely coordinated colors that were a bit similar to the colors of Jason from *Friday the Thirteenth.*

He was so proud that when he finished the picture, he showed it to "Fatboy" JC Owens and myself. JC looked at him with his version of the "duckface" (a good 15 years before the duckface became prominent in society) which, combined with a scowl, sent Miles over to me. I looked it up and down, saw that it was good, and said as much. Miles smiled, kinda wiggled his head side to side, pinned it up to the noticeboard in the common area, then went shopping for groceries at the 7-11.

We ached watching him head out the door in his white tank top, swimming suit, and ridiculously huge cataract sunglasses, the costume he always wore shopping. He stuck out like a sore thumb. You couldn't miss him. And you couldn't miss the picture. When Bryan saw it, he stopped, looked, cocked his head sideways, and said, "What the hell?"

"He's a fuckin moron but he can draw," said JC, "but I could draw too if I spent 12 hours a day doing it."

JC was right; Miles had spent about 12 hours doing it, and he could draw.

"Yeah, but he's a moron," said Bryan, "and Curtis doesn't look a thing like that."

Killing any hope of Miles making amends with Curtis or Bryan, Bryan wrote on the picture, "Hey Moron, he doesn't look a thing like that" and left. Miles just couldn't get over with the boys.

I Dub Thee ... Nerdly

You need a gimmick to succeed in wrestling. It isn't just a cool name- a gimmick empowers you with a new identity. You get stronger. You take on new being. Your gimmick is what you really want to become in wrestling business and in life. It is no less potent than donning a cape and becoming Batman as opposed to Bruce Wayne. Miles had come to the school with a gimmick in mind (we all did), but was given a different one. When he wasn't Miles, he was Nerdly Mcfatty, as nicknamed by Notorious TID, and after a few events, his gimmick was over and never to be forgotten. Some wrestlers can claim fame by giving another wrestler a gimmick that takes them far. TID accomplished as much by keeping Miles from going anywhere and out of the business. This may sound cruel, but keeping Miles out not only did a favour to his opponents, but also Miles.

Miles, if he ever did a match, would probably have hurt himself or his opponent. When you're a competent athlete and well trained, you still run the risk of nerves causing an accident. If you are poorly trained, the risk multiplies. Besides these, there was a good chance that someone would have taken liberties with Miles in a real match, and that would have ended up with Miles injured, maybe seriously. You have to be cruel to be kind. TID was good at that. He kept Miles out of the ring; Miles still had a belt, but avoided real life physical battles which he would definitely lose. And Miles was busy losing another battle of being Miles and not being Nerdly Mcfatty; it was just time until the title became official. Meanwhile, he fought to open our eyes to his greatness.

Miles had come to wrestling school with his own homemade belt, his own pretend version of a WWE belt. I bet Joe Montana brought his own super bowl cup to training camp, too. Miles's hope laid in not being Miles, and in being a character so awesome, so amazing, so awe-inspiring that he could permanently escape the daily insults of "Nerdly" and rise above it all to his true potential. He believed his gimmick was just that good; not surprisingly, we didn't. But he had hope. Not everyone called him Nerdly... yet.

The Great Green Hope

Miles had an ultimate, go-to gimmick; he believed it was the one that would make his career and save wrestling—at least, that was the impression you got from him. The gimmick was, wait for it... The Psycho Dragon. The Psycho Dragon was a dragon that had magical powers. Yes, magical powers. If it sounds intimidating, it wasn't.

First, it wasn't intimidating because under the psycho dragon costume was a pudgy 23 year-old who would get blown up waddling around the ring and couldn't do a headlock. Second, the costume was beyond ridiculous, and the tongue-in-cheek era of wrestling making fun of itself as a means to success was still a few years away. A crappy costume wasn't seen as a funny take on professional wrestling. It was just seen as a crappy costume worn to hide the fact that nobody could believe in Miles as a wrestler. Wrestling requires substance in either your gimmick or the reality behind it; Miles had neither, especially not in the costume.

The costume consisted of, if I remember correctly, a green bathrobe for its foundation. The green bathrobe wound snugly around the portly frame of Miles, but the loose sleeves allowed room for his hands to maneuver, presumably so they could circle and cast magical spells. The hands were definitely important, and Miles had spent meticulous hours crafting his two green gloves, which were actually oven mitts with yellow bits of pleather glued to them.

The yellow pleather triangles were the dragon's nails. The pants I really don't remember; I'm picturing green sweatpants, but this was a long time ago. I do remember the feet though; they were eggshell foam, like the stuff you find when you buy a giant carton of eggs, only made of soft foam spray painted green and with big yellow triangles of pleather for toenails. These had straps on the back of them that wrapped around his leg, so he could wear shoes or boots. All this ensemble was capped by the mask of a dragon, something Godzilla-like, only pathetic looking and totally impossible to see out of. The costume was good for a 10 year-old in a homemade costume contest; it was not good for a 23 year-old to wear while wrestling.

When we were privileged enough to see Miles parade around in it, we couldn't contain our laughter.

Sitting in the common area, next to Jer, watching some wrestling, Miles felt inspired to show us his gimmick. As I tried my darndest to keep a straight face, Jer's cheeks lit up in pure delight. His eyes were wide as saucers and his infectious grin stretched out his face with a look of shock, awe, and pure bliss while he repeatedly chopped me -- The Pyscho Dragon had arrived!

Miles waddled out, did a turn in front of the TV, and whoever else was there must have also laughed their ass off because Miles only did the one turn and then went back into his room, slamming the door behind him. He muttered under his breath and swore at us through the door, noting that we didn't get the biz and we were "stupid marks".

"It's pro wrestling, not Halloween" Jer astutely noted. That was true for the rest of us, but not for Miles. His other gimmick was to be "The Sun King" a character all other wrestlers would bow down to as their actual king, although no reason for this bowing was given. His persona was to be an asshole, or as Joe astutely pointed out one day, "Just like you, eh, Nerdly?" Joe also liked poking fun at Miles.

One day we were all sitting around in the gym, just kinda talking about training and getting ready to workout, when Joe entered and asked each of us, "What's your gimmick?" and we answered. He kind of grunted after each, and then repeated whatever we had just said. "Hmm, The Mad Bomber. Huh." And on around the circle. When he got to Miles (why Miles was anywhere near the ring I forget) Joe paused for an extra-long time, chewing over Miles's chosen name.

"The Psych-oo drag-uunn. Huh. Got a gimmick?"

"Yes sir." He actually said sir. Hope.

"Well, go get it. Let's see."

In a flash Miles was out and back with the whole ensemble. He passed it to Joe who took a long look at it and, poker-faced, stared at us, then looked back down at the costume and donned the robe. He tried putting on the hood (wrestler terminology for mask), but it didn't fit around his head, so he squeezed it halfway on while he stuffed his fat hands into the mitts.

Joe was a worker at one point, and he understood dramatic pauses, so he employed one as he overlooked the gloves. Surely he was assessing the great craftsmanship involved in their creation. The fine stitching, the dimpled pattern of the fabric, the acutely detailed grain of the yellow pleather fingernails; truly, it was worthy.

Miles leaned forward from the edge of the ring, close to falling onto his face. His eyes were wide with excitement and a faint smile was spread across his face. His mouth smiled with anticipation as he awaited the verdict from the grand poo-bah.

His tail wagging, surely, surely this would be the moment when Miles's genius was acknowledged and appreciated. All of the stupid marks would have to eat their words and accept that Miles, the senior student because he was the oldest and had been at the school months earlier before getting kicked out, was truly the veteran we all had to respect. All the tails in the room wagged out of excitement for what was next, and even the workers knew something great was coming down from the throne of Joe.

"Hmmm-mm" he chewed. A pause. A shift in his eyes. Anyone who paid attention knew what was coming. Miles held his breath and perked up. Our eyes grew wide with excitement; Curtis bore the gleeful expression that he only gets when something truly awesome is about to happen, and Bryan saw the look in Curtis' eyes. Infected. Jer bore the same look; he knew what going to come, and I of course had the same look as well, because I had seen it in all three of their eyes', plus the gleam in Miles's eye and the slight shift in Joe's eyes. We were all about to burst.

"Welllll, loookeeee here, I'm the Psycho Draaag-Unnnn," spewed Joe, "I've got mystical powersssss!" There was a giant collective spit.

"Bwahh-haaaa haaa!" Laughed Curtis.

"Ha, stupid Nerdly!" Laughed Bryan.

"Dahhahahahhahhaaaa, ehhhhh, yeahhhh!" Spat Jer.

"Yesirr, I've got Pysss-chooooo MAGICAL POW-URRRSSS!!!" Laughed Joe as he waddled in a circle, clamping the oven mitts open and shut like a fat green lobster.

"Standdd backkkk mommmm, I'm bringing home the BELT!!!!"

The laughter boomed in the room, each gaf a slap in the face of Miles, or Nerdly, who had to smile and laugh through his swollen, red cheeks. He laughed so hard that long after, as he was hiding away the Psycho Dragon never to be seen again, his eyes were still wet.

Miles Meets Destiny

Miles liked sitting cross-legged. When I started writing these stories, I showed one to TJ Harley. He replied, "Great, but you left out how Miles sat cross legged. How can all these fat guys sit cross legged so easily?"

It's still a mystery how Miles, with his pudgy white legs could sit cross legged like a tranquil Buddha without even having to limber up. And it wasn't just the basic cross-legged format either; he sometimes went full on and locked each foot over the opposite thigh. I haven't been able to sit cross-legged comfortably since grade 3, despite stretching, exercising, and doing hot yoga. Even when seats were available, Miles would plunk himself down cross-legged on the floor and enjoy a nice hot bowl of ramen noodles or Chef Boyardee, grinning. It was one of those phenomena that irked us for no reason; you'd think we'd be happy just not have him next to us.

One day I was fighting a particularly huge load of laundry and kept it in place by leaning waaaayyyy back. Of course I wasn't watching the ground, but I knew the path to the laundry off by heart- it was no more than 8 steps, which I intended on covering as quickly as possible. I shoved open the door with my foot, stomped out, turned a sharp corner and began hustle-strutting to the laundry. Stupid Starr, the "family" dog, was underfoot. Not moving out of the way, I upped the ante of dropping the laundry by standing on one foot and shoving Starr with the other. I felt my foot on her furry butt and said "Outta the way, Dummy." I was surprised when Starr said in a whiney tone, "Jesus Christ man." Turning sideways, I was shocked to see Nerdly, not Starr, bearing the brunt of my clumsiness. A Nerdly covered in pasta and stuck cross legged on the floor, fork in hand, pasta sauce on face and staining his t-shirt. I couldn't help but laugh, but said, "Sorry Miles."

"Jesus man, watch where you're going!"

"What are you sitting in the middle of floor for? There's a whole couch over there," I asked.

"I can sit wherever I want."

"Sure. But if people can't see you, you're going to get stepped on. Why didn't you say anything?"

"My mouth was full" he snapped.

I laughed again because the picture was too funny. A gleeful Miles sitting there, enjoying his noodles and sauce, taking in another episode of Monday Night Raw and stuffing his cheeks with Chef Boyardee's finest. Out swings the door, which almost hit him, and as his mouth raced to mash down the food, out lumbers a cloud of laundry, pushed by a stumbling ogre.

He didn't have time to swallow, which is why I had time to push him with my foot, and he didn't have time to get out of the way because he was cross legged and just couldn't move that quickly. Without meaning to, I had given Miles a perfect Kitchen Sink (running knee) only instead of him catching it in the gut, he caught it in his face, which was cramming food into his gut. Terror seized him when he realized that I would just keep pushing or kicking until he said something, but he couldn't say anything because his mouth was full. "There you go, tubby" (*Bart's Friend Falls in Love*) I thought to myself. What a way to ruin his dinner; poor Nerdly.

Worst of all, about 4 other wrestlers were sitting within a few feet and could easily have prevented the whole thing. But they didn't; they would all rather watch the show. I couldn't blame them.

Side by Side

The only way to really gauge someone, to really understand if your reaction to them is fair or not, is to gauge how they react with other people, although even that has flaws. I don't suppose the 40 hands that murdered Caesar were a good group to judge with. Then again, maybe Caesar deserved it. Whatever the truth of that, Miles took on proportions of Hitler and a gnat, of annoying fleas and a bumbling oaf; he was terrifyingly pitiful which made our feelings all the more biting. We all knew his annoyingness was as much on us as on him. I only burst out once in a while and it seems I was the norm. Even Longo got annoyed. Not Roberto Luongo of the Vancouver Canucks, the real original Longo, Mikey Zel.

Longo was a fiery, good natured little man with curly hair and a wiry build. I don't remember all his details, but I do remember hitting the gym with him. I was 6'1, 235lbs; not shredded but with faint abs for the first time

Longo working out. Note the fiery attitude and great smile.

in my life. He was 5'8 and maybe 160lbs with a tummy full of poop. At this point, we actually trained a lot, and because of the hot Ontario sun, I was tanned. But not Zel. He didn't tan. He had dark, curly hair and pasty white skin. I suppose you would have thought he was a little Jewish warrior, (a gimmick TJ Harley knew about) or a ginger who dyed his hair. We looked very different, but that didn't stop comparisons.

"Bomber, don't you think we kind of have the same build?" Longo would comment.

"Yeah?" I had to ask.

"Yeah you know you've got arms that kinda look like mine and kinda the same frame" he prodded.

"Yeah? Like we both have the same type of body?"

"Yeah, and like we look the same kind of, you know?.

Me working out. Note the similarities in builds,
douchebaginess, and cave-man weights.

Like the shape of your shoulders and whatnot is the same as
mine" he noted, pointing to my shoulders and his
"Yeah, even though I'm a foot taller and weight a hundred
pounds more, we're basically the same."

"Uh-huh. Look, I'm not saying we're the same, but we
kind of have the same build."

"Yeah, like my muscles look just like you're muscles,
only bigger. And my hair is like your hair, only short,
blonde, and not curly."

"Listen you idiot, I'm not saying the same build, I'm
saying we kind of look the same."

"Like our hairstyles."

"Uh-huh" he snarled through his clenched teeth.

"Yeah, and we both train together so we probably have
the same type of muscles and build. And we probably look

the same and have the same body compositions, abs or not, or tans, or whatever" I continued.

"Mmmm, hmmmm."

Lips pursed shut, a slight snarl crept onto his face.

"Totally Mikey Zel. We totally look the same. I think we should have the same wrestling name too; I'll be Bomber Zel and you can be Mikey Zel. And everyone will believe we're brothers cause we look so much alike! It'll be rad!"

My ribs hurt looking at his boiling, hateful gaze.

"Mmmm-hmmm. K. You know what? You know what, Bomber?" he hissed, getting right in face and staring up at me, "I'm just trying to be a nice guy. I thought you were a nice guy. But it's obvious now that you're just a frrrrrrrickin' idiot and I'm wasting my time. So you can go to heck!"

Longo was so nice he wouldn't even swear. I sound like a dick in this conversation and I was being a dick, but we had this conversation nearly every time we went to the gym. Zel was so nice; all the rest of the time spent together must have outweighed this conversation. Did we have the same build? I dunno, look at the pictures.

Nerdly Annoys Longo

It goes without saying that Longo was the nicest, most patient person at the school. It should follow that if Miles managed to piss Longo off, he was causing problems. For a few weeks, after Longo had gotten back from helping with the harvest at the family farm, he had a plethora of farm fresh steaks. I remember the afternoon Longo got home to the school; I was excited to see him and he was excited to be back. It was a blissful reunion, well, I was happy to have a good buddy back, but it was not blissful for Miles or Longo. As I remember it, when Longo left, Miles wasn't at the school. There was a fair bit of space in his room since Ball had left to live across the road with Romeo, Jer, and Marco. Patient as he was, it didn't take long for Nerdly to start pissing off Longo.

"Bomber, does Miles annoy you?" he asked one day.

"Yeah, he does. I tried not to let him, but gave up, I just avoid him."

Longo went on to explain an issue he was having with Miles. I can't remember exactly what it was, just that he was slowly pissing off Longo. Overall, Longo was still his chipper self, happy with his time at the school and how things were turning out. He was becoming a pretty good wrestler and we were talking about teaming up; we even had figured out a finishing move. I could apply my rugby prowess and boost him on a leap, making for a super high impact leg-drop that would definitely be worthy of a finish in the year 1999. It seemed like it would be a good marriage. And every night Longo would enjoy his farm-fresh-frozen pork steaks, which he grilled and I would bitch at him for ruining.

"Longo, what did you do? That doesn't look good."

"Listen Bomber, I enjoy my steaks like this. It seals in the juice and adds good flavor."

"I think you'd get better flavor by eating a wild boar steak. Those look like they would be good. Why doesn't your dad shoot a wild boar instead of farming pigs?"

"Mmmmm-hmmm. You ever eat a boar, Bomber?"

"No, but I read about it in *Call it Courage*. Sounds delicious" I countered.

"Mmmmm-hmmm. Sounds stupid to me. Boar is gamey and tough. This steak, this, this is tender and juicy. There's no way I could even cut a boar steak" Longo parried.

"Sure you could, you've got that sweet survival knife you're sawing your meat with right there."

"Does my knife bother you?" he asked, holding it up, and turning it slowly in the light, staring at me.

"No, it's great for survival, or for cutting up a wild boar steak plus wild boar ribs, baby back ribs, loin, bacon—you're missing out."

"Mmmmmm-hmmmm. Well, anyone who isn't a friiiiiiiiickin' idiot would know that whatever way you cut it, wild boar isn't as tender as farm fed pig from Longo farms, ok idiot? So you just go back to eating your peanut butter sandwich or whatever you have there and I'll enjoy my juicy, tender steak."

"Tender steak, but it's gotta be cut with a survival knife," I mocked.

"Yeah? Yeah Bomber? You know what else I can cut with this steak knife? You want to find out how sharp it is Bomber? I don't have to cut through the thick hide of a boar, just your friiiiiiiickin' stupid butt!" Longo threatened.

"Jeez you two are annoying" Miles cut in. We froze. A pork cutlet dangled limply on Longo's fork.

"Everybody knows that pork steaks aren't as good as beef steaks. My mom only makes beef steaks" he asserted.

Silence. Eyes lowered and lips pursed.

"Really, it's a dumb argument you guys are having. I challenge you to try a beef steak and see if that compares to your pork steaks" he lectured.

It was a good thing neither Bryan nor Curtis were in the room; they would have relished putting Nerdly in his place about the redeeming qualities of pork. As it was, I just looked at Longo, he looked at me, and I said "Well, there it is" or some other pointless comment you make when there's nothing to say but feel you should, like "Take's one to know one" (*Lisa's First Word*) or "Leaves of four eat some more" (*Kamp Krusy)*. Longo went back to his steak, knife busy at work. It was a nice knife with a wooden handle, long straight blade and pretty useful when it came down to it. But it was definitely not useful for cutting up wrestling mats. Which is what Miles tried to use it for.

The School had gotten some new ring mats; Joe's great idea was to split them in half and then double them up, or at least that's what we kept joking about. I can't remember if we made that up or just thought it was what he would say, but that's what we said was going to happen. "You see, if you cut them in half and then double them up, you get twice the cushion effect."

Joe's psychology had lost effect on us, and we didn't care. Miles did care though. The mats didn't fit in the training ring properly, which wasn't really a problem as Joe was going to use the mats for the show ring anyways. For whatever reason, Miles didn't know this.

He waddled his way into the ring, knife in hand, and began cutting the corners of the new mats, trying to split them. I can still see him sitting cross-legged in the ring, half the mat hanging out of the ring, holding a corner in one hand and the knife in the other. No one said anything. Either we all knew Joe didn't really want to split the mats or we wanted to get Miles in trouble. JC was in the office, Longo was at the campsite, and I was wandering around bored. Miles asked me to help but I said no.

"Come on man, do something for once."

This coming from the guy who sat watching *Golden Girls* all day, drawing doodles, reading a book with the stats of all of Godzilla's battles in it, and hadn't worked a day since he arrived. I wasn't working; the movie had paid enough for me to coast till I got home, so I spent trhee hours a day at the gym and three in the ring for my last months there. The rest was tanning, hanging with my buddies, working the odd day, but I had already done tonnes of bitch work. One snide word from Miles was enough to get me outta there before I lost it; I still didn't call him Nerdly to his face, but man I was getting close.

"No."

I looked at the pool table and the *Pinbot* pinball machine, trying to decide which one to kill time with. The phone rang. It stopped, then JC came bounding gleefully into the gym.

"Kief! Nerdly! Joe wants to talk to you!"

Out waddled Nerdly. JC danced and ran back in to listen on the other line. A minute later, redder than usual, Miles came back in, dejected, pouty and kicking his feet. He picked up the mat, angrily shoved it back on the pile with the rest of them, grabbed the knife and headed back to his room. JC came in a minute later laughing and jolly saying, "Joe just tore a strip off of Nerdly- 'listen here cuntlapper, who told you to touch the mats? Leave them the fuck alone!'"

Monday, after he returned from being at the campsite with Joe, Longo was more pissy than he should have been. Bitch work was the usual sentence being passed down to anyone nice or patient; Longo was both. The camp site was torture for us and heaven for Joe. He left to take a break from us, but that's understandable. Hey, the man got sick of us too; you can't blame him.

As he usually dragged one or two poor souls along for a miserable weekend of bitchwork, our goal was to annoy him enough to avoid being drafted. Cleaning up shit, painting, weed eating, mowing the lawn, cutting branches down from the trees, you name it; if it was physical and Joe wouldn't do it (pretty much all yard work) you were conscripted. The only perk was Joe left and something funny almost always happened; however, this Monday, a surprisingly low number of laughs were shared.

Longo was pissed beyond normal and didn't have anything funny to say. In fact, I remember him snapping a bit at Miles and saying as many harsh words as he ever spoke to anyone. Hmmmm. I pondered. Later. Jogging to the gym.

"You know what, Bomber? I don't like Miles."

"Yeah? How come?"

"You don't know what he did?"

"No, what?" I genuinely didn't know.

"You know that knife I have? My dad gave it to me."

"Yeah."

"Well, he broke it. I went to use it the other day and there's tape on the back of the handle. I was like 'what the hell is this?' and then Miles said 'Oh, it broke while I was fixing the mats.'"

"Damn."

"Yeah, there's some things you don't do. I can look past him annoying me and being stupid, but you don't touch other people's stuff, you know? That's just disrespectful and one thing my parents always told me not to do. I don't know why he did that and the worst part is he didn't even apologize or seem to think it was a big deal."

Well, this pissed me off and I kept it in the back of my mind; something had to be done. Beautifully, I didn't have to do anything. Nobody did. Pinbot had seen enough.

Miles Loses a Belt & Gains a Title

If boredom got a hold of you, you would go batty in days. To fight against it we often turned on each other, usually mildly. If you knew a weakness however, you opened that up until it was well beyond a joke. As I write this, I have to think about what I was poked fun at for. I can't remember. I think it was probably how I was late all the time or how I was just an idiot a lot of the time; I'd do stupid stuff and say stupid things, sometimes for a laugh, a lot of time because I didn't have a clue what was going on. I'm especially bad at names; I'm sure I had a conversation with Ronny about Ronny at least twice during my first weeks at the school. Not too bright. I guess I probably didn't even notice half the ribs coming my way. Hell, I'm probably being ribbed right now by the guys as I send them stories. Well, there it is.

What brought us together at the school and kept us from going crazy was ribbing each other. Joe was good at ribbing, but had to space it out as he was in charge and didn't want everyone to hate him. We all did hate him because we felt ripped off and tired of his BS, but his ribs were funny. Once Nerdly arrived, I noticed something and most of the other guys did too; we didn't see Joe around as much. He spent most of his time alone in his room or up all night playing *Bear Hunter*. That was a highlight.

Bear Hunter is a video game where you, that's right, hunt bears. The game was shitty, even for its day, which made it even better that Joe loved it so much. We'd be sitting in the common area, and Joe would be hunting bears in his office, usually from the hours of 12:00 a.m. till 6a.m..

"Tuck-tuck-tuck." The simulated sound of footsteps in the forest, bleeping out from the speakers.

"Tuck.... Tuck.... Tuck." Something ahead in the bushes...

"Ca-chitch." The gun was loaded. You felt the tension as Joe aimed his gun.

"Blam! Blam!"

"Ru-owr."

"Blam!"

"RUOWR"

"Blam, blam blam!"

"RUOWR RUOWR RUOWR!!!!"

"dee-doo..."

"CUNTLAPPER!!! I SHOT THAT SONOFABITCH TWELVE TIMES AND HE DIDN'T DIE! WHAT THE FUCK! BULL-SHHHHHIT!"

We would burst out laughing, staying in earshot, until finally it got too annoying to bear with. Other than that, the interactions with Joe mostly disappeared. And because they were, in a way, funny, they didn't seem nearly as bad as dealing with Nerdly. Joe was a worker.

Joe understood the psychology of having a common hatred in order to have common haters come together. With Nerdly around, Joe was no longer the main heel in the school. Joe was almost one of the boys. Of course, there is also the other theory that we didn't see Joe as much because he just found Nerdly too annoying. That's a simpler story and just as likely. Either way, things were reaching a boiling point at the school, at least in regards to Miles. He'd been there for about four weeks, not many more, when he had broken Longo's knife. It was no more than a week after that when fate stepped in.

We were bored, playing a video game in the training room, and Stylin' was bored in particular. He had taken a job working under the school at Pita Wrap, a restaurant like Subway. It was busy enough but Bryan was feeling the pressure of his investment with Joe. Joe had talked Bryan, Curtis, and a few other guys into investing $10,000 each into the school, on top of the $3,500 they already paid to train and live there. It was, as Stylin later called it, "A magic bean loan" with all of the expectation implied but only more bitchwork as the payoff. Bryan was starting to boil.

As we played videogames, championship belts came up, and Nerdly as well. Bryan noted that Nerdly was terrible in the ring. Hell, he was worse than a table or a chair- either of those had more charisma AND ability than Nerdly did. If Nerdly was a wrestler, the floor should be main event on Raw. If you had the option of watching a table or Nerdly wrestle, 90% of fans would choose the table. Hell, Pinbot would make a better wrestler than Nerdly. In fact, Pinbot was a hundred times better than Nerdly and deserved his belt more than Nerdly did. Pinbot was already champion, we just didn't recognize it! Fired up by this conversation with himself, Bryan walked out of the room, across the hall into Miles's room, to the shelf where Nerdly kept his homemade belt. He grabbed it, walked back into the training room, and put the championship on Pinbot, the pinball machine that Joe had bought to keep us entertained and away from the public. The belt looked good there, but only Bryan, JC, and I were around to appreciate it. We quickly ran out of things to say, so we forgot about it and went off to do whatever for the rest of the day. Probably nothing.

Later that evening we sat watching Monday Night Raw.

"Hey, I'm surprised that Austin still has the belt. I could have sworn that Pinbot was the new champion" shared Bryan. Our eyes opened wide in remembrance of the earlier events of the day. At this point, everyone but Nerdly had seen it. A few chuckles washed through the room.

"I heard Pinbot beat Mankind in a falls-count-anywhere match in Leftovers, Indiana. I think that's why you're confused. Mankind isn't the champion anymore."

A good contribution by Curtis. A few more chuckles, and a quick, curious glance around the room by Miles to see if anyone else was confused. Everyone played it cool- what didn't he understand?

"No, no, he didn't beat Mankind. He's not that good. He beat Bob Holly in that match" I shared.

"Oh, what am I thinking of?" Curtis probed.

"You're probably confusing Pinbot with the Undertaker. They're both really good and tough."

Ball didn't have anything to say but did look around with enthusiasm. All the workers who had moved out usually came back to watch raw on the big screen at the school, probably because they missed the exact idiocy that they were witnessing now. Nerdly looked around with enthusiasm but a lot of confusion, feeling like he should be in on the joke if he wanted to be one of the boys. Any worker knows if you're not part of the rib, play it cool because the rib is probably on you or you're going to spoil it. Nerdly was not a worker.

"Do you think Pinbot could pin the undertaker?"

Bryan's performance was Oscar worthy.

"Ohh, tough one, I don't know."

We quieted down as raw continued.

"Morons," spat JC, "he's already beaten Undertaker a bunch of times. Pinbot IS the world champion."

"Pinbot is the world champion—I knew it!" shouted Bryan.

Nerdly still lagged behind; Bryan flogged him on. "Just when you think they can't throw any more curve balls or swerve you with another angle, they come up with some brilliant booking and surprise you."

Our sides hurt from holding in our laughs. Bryan's infectious smile and child-like enthusiasm for entertainment never waned. He danced on. Miles was becoming curious. "I always believed in him, and now I'm happy; all my years as a Pinbot fan have paid off in spades!"

The smiles grew on the faces of the crowd in front of the TV. Concern started to seep onto Nerdly's face. Almost there…

"Yep, thank god. I never thought I'd see the day."

Waves of bubbling laughter began to trickle out and splash into the room. Miles was picking up on the trail we were leaving behind and could smell what we were cooking.

"In fact, I know I saw Pinbot proudly wearing his new championship belt just this afternoon. I should go ask him for an autograph." As we soaked up the laughs and joy of this brilliant pantomime, our delight slapped Nerdly in the face and stung his eyes. His face was now in full-blown terror as he ran out of the room and across the hall in a panic. One door slammed shut as another thudded against the wall, then it thudded against the wall and another thudded against the wall as it flew open. Miles was pissed.

"Stay the hell away from my stuff!"

"HA HAAAAAA HA HAAAAA!!!"

Nothing but laughter and scores of jeers at the pouty monster invading the room.

"Yeah, Nerdly! NERD-LY! NERD-LY! NERD-LY!" someone chanted. His gimmick had come to life.

"It's not funny!" shouted Nerdly.

None of us could do anything but laugh and cheer.

"You guys are idiots and need to learn respect for other people's stuff!" whined Nerdly.

"Miles, didn't you just take Longo's knife without asking and break it?" I shot.

"That was different, it's not the same," he begged.

"Why?"

"Because this is my belt. Nobody else can touch it. It's mine."

He held the tin frame plated with golden macaroni in both hands and looked down at it.

"How is that different than Longo's knife?"

"Just stay away from other people's stuff. I mean it" he poked back.

"You too."

Sometimes I wish I could say he broke down and cried, or spazzed out, or exploded in a fit of misery as we danced around Piggy. Sometimes I wish there was some great reckoning that we all witnessed. There is a chance that like Don Quixote, Miles finally became aware of the character he was to us and that from there he grew more into just Miles the artist. He left the business shortly afterwards, so there is hope. But Miles had hope too, the hope of being a wrestler. There didn't seem to be room in reality for his dream.

The only reckoning I saw for Miles was a few hours later. Raw was over and almost everybody had left. Longo and Miles were in the common area, watching TV, two ships passing in the night.

"Are you mad that I broke your knife?" Miles asked, summoning his courage.

"Well, kind of" said Longo.

"Well, should I replace it?"

"Nah, it's ok."

"I'm sorry."

"Don't worry about it," said Longo. He meant it.

We were cruel, like a bunch of teens teasing our little brother's friend. We did what the business told us to do; rib a guy until he quit or became one of the boys. When you learn to love the pain of being ribbed, you are no longer a threat. But until you realize we are all the butt end of someone's joke, you never fit in. You have to be able to make fun of yourself so all the wrestlers know you'll do the right then when they take you seriously.

Miles couldn't accept that. Until he was happy to be laughed at, he couldn't be trusted to laugh at anyone else. His gimmick had been chosen by life and we wouldn't let it go; Nerdly was the reality.

It was shortly after this that I went home and received an email from JC Owens; you can hear the excitement in his voice and because of this excitement, it's easy to excuse the typos. It was sent under the title "Open First! Excellent News! I tell the truth!"

* * *

Heer-y Heer-y Come one Come all! The day of the lord is here (I'm not actually trying to preach!) But the one known as "Nerdly McFatty" is gone! He leaves tomorrow morning. The royal boot of JDF has come down! Ans struckitf him in the rear end! As he revals in the pain of the fatness jiggles in side his rump! This pour individual has tried to fight it out with JDF. Well as I and the bodyguard sat as bistanders, we listened to the words of wisdom he spewed forth. "Pack your bags you dumb cunt lapppppper, and don't come back until you have a job!!!" So there is a thin slice a very, very, thin slice that he will be back! But we all doubt that! as I sit here, having to stay up all night and watch out for his master mind techniques to come in to the office and erase the files he has on them! Well to get in the good books I offered to stay up all night and protect the sacred Bear Hunting game from Nerdly's destructive key strokes! So I'll be alive sometime tomorrow! Hopefully! Well that is all for the news bulletin!

* * *

There was nothing more in life that Miles wanted than to be a professional wrestler. He had the desire. After seeing recent wrestlers pull off awful gimmicks that are pure comedy, I have to admit that maybe he could have had the ability. Despite not being in shape when he started, he could have trained enough to do it. I have never seen anyone show up to a wrestling school who can't, without dedication, get fit enough to wrestle.

What it came down to was the wrestlers, the students, me included, wouldn't let it happen. We protected the biz, something that we felt made us part of the exclusive club of professional wrestlers.

Maybe it kept Miles from getting hurt. He got hurt emotionally by the wrestling business and we all took part in that. Why? Because we feared that once we got to a big enough pond, we too would be Miles in one way or another. We all wanted to fit in. We all wanted to succeed. We just didn't want him around to remind us how there was a very real chance none of us would.

There it is.

You're Gonna Hurt Yourself

Go West

Jer and I on a tour of British Columbia. Note the enthusiasm.

After my debut match, I had one more match at a fairground against Insane Wayne Silver, known to me as Curtis, my roommate. In the words of his brother, Stylin' Bryan, I was clearly "the most over babyface" at the time and so I should stick around. I would have loved to, but after 6 months of not seeing my girlfriend and almost no other prospects for wrestling shows lined up by ICW, I had to make a call.

I emailed all the promoters in and across Canada that I could find contact information for three weeks prior to my departure. It seemed like leaving would never happen, and then it came. I recalled the story of the man sentenced to execution; as he rolls past all the houses and buildings he grew up by and thinks to himself, "My execution will never come, I have so far to go." He keeps thinking that until he's at the gallows.

To really celebrate my departure and time there in Ontario, we went to 69 pickups, sang karaoke and drank as much beer as possible. Suddenly it was the last song of the night. I always hated Pearl Jam; a friend of mine thought Pearl Jam were the best thing ever throughout high school, forcing them on me constantly. Naturally, I hated them more.

In a twist that really shows the power of friendship, the last song at Karaoke that night was Pearl Jam's Daughter. Before that night, I hated it. Ever since, it has filled me with dreams and intangible feelings of being swept away into something beyond ordinary life. Even now it takes me back to the moment on stage, with my arms around Bryan, Ball, Curtis, and Jer, us belting our hearts out. Some of us knew the words, some didn't, but we figured them out on the way. As each next verse sprung up on the monitor, I realized the unknown would be ok and we would never be back the same way again. I swelled with hope, a spiritual bastard flying away so I could return again quicker than I left. Some days now I can handle hearing the song, some I can't. It depends.

I returned to BC, moved back home, enrolled in college again, worked at a gas station, and began the struggle of trying to be a wrestler, a college student, a rugby player, gas attendant, janitor, and a boyfriend. It was all very conflicting. Being a full-time wrestler was nearly impossible in the late 90's, especially in Vancouver, and I wasn't going to sit around waiting for something to happen when I could be building a backup plan. Frustratingly, wrestling was all I wanted to do.

There were glimmers of hope. I began wrestling with ECCW and it seemed like maybe, just maybe, I might make a go of this wrestling thing after all. Helpfully, everyone I knew offered advice on wrestling. It's amazing how many people are experts at something they have never done. A fan told me to be "'French Fry Man' because everyone loves French Fries." There had been "The Burgermeister", so maybe it was ok.

When people at college learned I was a wrestler, they offered suggestions and support in unique ways. In my Biology 101 class, a fellow student had a brainstorm, a flash of brilliance for what I should do for my new gimmick.

It remains a highlight of my time at college, which shows where my head was at and what was really important. I don't need to say anything about it other than it was bizarre but totally undoable. Still, men can dream, even about having 4 cocks...

God Ribs Us All

A Wrestling tour of British Columbia! As usual, the wrestlers were heading up in The Yellow Submarine, Michelle Starr's yellow van. Once you were inside, there was no way to see out because all the windows had been boarded up on the inside. It obviously couldn't pass any roadside safety inspection, especially once you crammed 12 wrestlers into it, but nobody seemed to care... until the snow started.

It was March and snow was common along the road to Prince George, but disconcerting for Stu Kemp. He had slid off the road a few weeks before while in Portland. He still had serious issues with driving in snow.

A gimmick imagined by a fellow biology 101 student. Note the four cocks. Yes, he passed the course.

"I'm not OK Mad, I'm not Ok," Stu said over and over as he pulled off to the side, rocking in his seat. Juggernaut didn't feel like driving, and Weasel, the name given to the ref, didn't have a license, so it was up to me. The snow was pretty much all on the roadside anyways so it wasn't really a big deal in Stu's car. However, God had a lot of ribs in store for Starr and the yellow submarine.

The first rib was that it was snowing-- not really a problem for a crappy old van with 400,000 km on it carrying a dozen guys weighing 200 pounds on average and towing an overloaded trailer. The fear of sliding into a fiery death wasn't on the wrestlers' minds because they couldn't see out the front of the Van and had no idea what was going on. The flakes were big but brushed off. The real issue was the wipers died. They weren't ineffective or in a poor state. The whole mechanism that worked the wipers quit. Whoever was driving, probably Starr, realized safety was an issue and pulled over to the side of the road.

After a brief conference and a look under the hood, with everybody offering their two bits, everyone realized that nobody knew anything at all about cars or vans or wipers. They did know what they had in the Van, however, so about 28 feet of yellow nylon rope was mined from the tunnel of bags and gear in the truck.

The wrestlers sped off down the road making up for lost time, all taking turns pulling on the ropes stretching out the front windows and latched onto the wipers. It was a good team building activity. "Left... Right... Left... Right... Heave.... Ho.... Heave....Ho." Some of the boys actually started singing as they rowed on the rope. After a guy's arms tired, he would pass it off behind him. Overall, it was an ingenious solution until. They made it to the show, a dismal event in front of 45 people in William's Lake, British Columbia, and to the hotel without any more issues. But the wrestlers were too proud of their rope mechanism to put it away. The next morning after the show, the snow died down.

"Shouldn't we put the rope back inside the van? It's probably going to get us heat."

"Ha, right. After Coffee" said whoever was driving.

About 3 minutes later sirens blared and lights whirred, bringing the yellow submarine to the side of the road. After a completely unsuccessful plea, the Van and Trailer were both impounded—the van was no longer roadworthy and the trailer was overloaded and without working lights. 7 hours from Vancouver, no Mechanics open Saturday, and at least a day of work to be done on the yellow submarine. The only solution was the most obvious- rent a U-haul truck to move the ring. But what about the wrestlers? Well, this was another occasion I was glad I had chosen the car over the van.

All the wrestlers who were in the van squatted in the back of the truck on dirty ring mats, metal pipes, and moldy wood. "Good luck, see you guys in 3 hours" said Starr as he and Ladies choice jumped into the front of the truck-- "Enjoy your deathtrap, ladies!" (*Fear of Flying*) I thought. As the truck raced down the snowy Canadian roads, the boys laughed, farted, tried to avoid thinking about what would happen if the truck crashed because they couldn't open the rear door, and really tried to avoid the spool of barbed wire slamming around the back of the van. Bumps in the ring are bad, but paying dues is worst.

The rest of the tour was no fun for me; Gigolo Steve Rizzono, my opponent for the tour and a few shows before, was drinking before our matches, so the matches sucked. I finally had enough and broke his nose with a punch in our second match of the tour, and by the third one, he had completely changed his tone. Instead of being a lousy partner, he said before our match, "Tonight is all about you, whatever you want to do we'll do."

It was an ok match, nothing special, but marked the night as important because it was the first championship I won. In a bizarre stipulation, I won the Vancouver Island Championship (which was just a trophy) in Quesnel, BC. It meant something to me, and I was still mark enough to enjoy my championship, although it was just a plan to get local fans out in Victoria. After I got home from the tour, I did a few newspaper interviews and a few TV interviews in Victoria to hype up some shows, then fate stepped in.

During a match in Victoria, I gave Lumberjack Bubba an inverted monkey flip. I launched him, and he didn't get over all the way. The move had started with my feet too high on his chest, and so he ended up bumping high on his neck, actually cracking a vertebrae. I've never felt so bad about anything that has happened in a ring, and this was the only time I could be blamed for some of a major injury. It wasn't a huge mix up; my feet were a little high, and he was a little unready to bump. It was a combo of things, but most fans and marks in the back, the ECCW workers, put the blame on me although you take a lot of your own bump on a monkey flip. I wasn't supposed to have control of him as he took his bump, so it didn't make any sense to blame me for any of it, let alone all of it. Blamed I was though, and after having to put up with a lot of bullshit on the ECCW fan message forums, I was getting ready to leave the company. Wrestling for ECCW was not what I believed it was supposed to be. ECCW was carny, petty, and focused a lot of their energy on garbage wrestling, something I couldn't stand or endorse.

Garbage wrestling is when two fat guys hit each other with random pieces of plunder and bleed all over the place. It is not when two hard workers do an anything goes match, build a story, and use props such as tables, ladders, and chairs to build excitement and tell a story.

If two guys drag a baseball bat covered in barbed wire up to the ring and start hitting each other with it only looking to mark out fans through pointless violence, you've got garbage wrestling. If one guy grabs said bat at the very end of a match and hits a guy with it to avoid losing, it's debatable, but still has a touch of garbage to it. When a guy uses a chair to steal a victory, it's not garbage wrestling, just a way to build heat, and maybe lead to a hard core wrestling match that is built on psychology first, weapons second.

Garbage wrestling is weapons first, psychology an afterthought or no thought at all. In ECCW at the time, many of the matches were just garbage for the sake of garbage. Main event matches are tough to pull off in talented areas, for sure, but in Vancouver and British Columbia at the time, the main event matches were almost entirely garbage matches. Tables covered in barbed wire, flaming tables, baseball bats covered in barbed wire, etc. for no real reason were the norm.

I was heavily involved in this garbage wrestling and booking in my hometown of Victoria. I hyped the show and sold tickets to rugby friends, school friends, teachers, and everyone I knew. It was a solid crowd of almost three hundred people. And, to add to the excitement, the show featured a steel cage. Note that it wasn't a steel cage match, it was a steel cage show. Every single match in a steel cage since nobody could organize putting up the cage during intermission. Call me a cynic, but I believe this took away from the significance of the cage. I don't call cage matches garbage matches, but this night the cage was a meaningless piece of plunder. It was garbage.

By the time the main event happened, a 3 way between myself, Juggernaut, and Steve Rizzono, the crowd had seen every spot possible. To counter this, Juggernaut and Rizzono both got color and bled all over the place.

As most fans were already aware, the blood comes from cutting one's own forehead with a razorblade. It didn't add drama, it just added a sense of stupidity. And a feeling like the whole wrestling thing was a bit unorganized and juvenile. The reaction was either, "Gross, those guys are going to get Hepatitis or HIV," or, "Why would full-grown men be so stupid as to cut themselves with a razorblade for 250 fans?"

Women who had come out were completely disgusted, parents who brought their kids were repulsed, and the average fan saw the company for a circus of idiocy. To make the match even worse, Rizzono convinced me I should heel and team up with him, albeit briefly, during the match. I don't know why I did.

Heeling, or turning on a crowd and being the villain or heel, takes skill and can add a lot when done well. When it's just something thrown in, and then the babyface who turns heel gets turned on by the other heel, it is pointless and hurts all involved. Somehow, as the hometown boy and guy responsible for the newspaper press, papering the town, and selling a lot of the tickets to friends, I was picked to heel at the show. Basically, I told all the people who I had sold tickets to and the newspaper press who had come out "Haha, you suck" and then had to ask them to buy tickets next time. If we had planned to do it worse, we couldn't have. A month later, the guys in the back wondered why the house was down to under 100 people.

Never mind that the show was scheduled for 2:00 p.m. on Grey Cup Sunday, or that most of the fans from last time had been turned off by the matches and blood, or that the venue owner was pissed because fans had clogged a toilet with beer cans last show, or that the venue owner was pissed at ECCW over the resulting dispute about the damage deposit from last show, or that ECCW booker Dave Republic embarrassed the owner on public TV instead of just apologizing (not really fair but probably the best thing to do), or that the press turned on ECCW in support of the owners and the building; I couldn't sell a ticket with a clear conscience.

There was a lot of talent but a lot of garbage. I didn't want friends or family to come to the show. I didn't support the content being promoted.

Victoria had fallen victim to ECCW's long track record of running a show, drawing a fair-sized crowd, then ruining the town with poor angles and bad publicity. Wrestlers call this "killing a town" and ECCW was especially good at it.

If a show drew a crowd, you could be fairly certain that the fans wouldn't want to come back because of how awful or tasteless the main event was. It was basically, "Goodnight Springdon, there will be no encores" (*The Otto Show*), leaving the crowd repulsed by hardcore wrestling or feeling ripped off. If they drew only a moderate crowd, the next show would use trainees who couldn't work and were the equivalent of The Psycho Dragon, only they had done a bit more training.

Cactus Jackson, Rockin' Vengeance, Chi Town Gangster Mike Lee, Average Joe, Moondog Manson, Count Monsterod Von Hugenstein- mostly decent people, but not respectable as performers or worth admission. One or two joke wrestlers, and ok, it was kind of fun and interesting- a little different flavor. All of them on a card capped by a hard core match full of senseless blood, or a boring battle royal as a special event, and you've got an awful show that 1 in 10 people might want to see again. This far overshadowed the legitimate guys and outstanding talents on the show. So after two shows, you've got a town of people who have either seen a) hard-core, tasteless wrestling or b) awful joke wrestlers not worth the price of admission. Even with a few hard-core fans in any area, you're not going to draw enough to make it a good show.

Town after town was killed by the company, and when it happened in my hometown, the mirror held no secrets. Wrestling was going through an obsession with "hardcore" wrestling, and ECCW was riding the wave. It was what some fans wanted, but not what I wanted to do. I was embarrassed to be part of ECCW and knew it was time to leave. All I needed was an excuse. Fate provided.

Showing up for a match just outside of Vancouver, I heard that Randy Tyler and Mike Roselli, two mainstays and former champions, had left ECCW to start their own promotion. All the ECCW guys were walking around like they'd been mortally betrayed and the two guys were never to be mentioned by name.

I later heard the reason they had left was that Starr had a dispute with Randy Tyler regarding training a huge student with potential. Dru Drastic had been actually drafted in the CFL and was a man, not a kid in pajamas. He would be legitimate and add to the shows, but Rocket wanted to be in charge of the training so Drastic wouldn't suck. Starr and he disagreed about some of the details, and Rocket left, figuring since he had to train one guy, he might as well train a bunch of them.

At the time, I had no idea about any of that. All I knew was I'd met Mike Roselli and Randy Tyler and trusted them. Roselli was a legitimate Olympic wrestler and for a while the best in Canada in his weight class. He had played provincial rugby for some of the same as I did. Randy Tyler was studying to become a lawyer and brought class to wrestling.

My father always said, "You know, Randy is the best, ask him about it." They were both head and shoulders above many guys on the ECCW roster because they a) had jobs b) had builds and c) could actually wrestle.

A voice was buzzing in my ear to just turn and leave when I arrived at the venue and heard this news; I should have listened. As it was, I did a tag match with Mr. Gillis against Starr and someone else. In a brilliant angle, Gillis turned on me for no reason and dropped an elbow on me from the top rope. I thought he'd broken my ribs as I gasped for air and grimaced as I replayed in my mind the feeling of my ribs bending into my lungs. I survived, but was not enthused; Gillis was freakishly strong and more than a little stiff in the ring. We were set up to do a match at the next show.

The next show was a taping for the ECCW: INSANITY show that apparently was going to be picked up by TSN. It was a huge moment for the company and one that they were sure to capitalize on... or not.

They diluted the elements that made the shows exciting, and skimped on the essentials of the show in order to make sure they saved a few bucks. I don't know a lot about business, but have heard that you can't be penny wise and dollar foolish if you want to survive. ECCW had never heard of that, and their track record should have warned all involved.

The high tech lights around the entrance were left over Christmas lights; the tables that were so integral a part of the show were replaced with doors that had legs attached to them- the doorknob whole in the door disguised as a table gave it away. The table legs were a clever disguise, but not enough people were fooled.

More troublesome, guys who had been building their characters were suddenly thrust into hastily conceived gimmicks with little payoff. For example, The High Fivin' White Guys was composed of Chance Beckett and Havoc, two good workers who had to play roles that didn't suit them and neither seemed engaged in. They were stuck doing a chore they couldn't enjoy.

Perhaps worst, the audience was commanded when to cheer and when to boo, taking out the genuine emotion that crowds always brought to the show. They weren't watching the show, they were working as an audience.

On the first TV taping, in a match that is still painful to consider in detail, Gillis and I wrestled a horrible match. I was scared stiff of being stiffed by him; he wasn't too bad, but when we did the finish, it couldn't have been worse. The finish was a tombstone piledriver, and instead of a pile driver, Gillis gave me the cage roll. In wrestling, safety often comes down to a matter of inches.

A Tombstone piledriver is one of the most dangerous maneuvers in the sport. You are held upside-down in 69 position while your opponent drops to his knees, making it look like he's driven your head directly into the mat from two feet in the air. This can go wrong, but there's an even more dangerous option.

You're Gonna Hurt Yourself

The cage roll is a piledriver where your opponent sits down with you in the same prone position as a tombstone-your face is buried in his crotch and you really have nowhere to escape to if it goes wrong. The inches are even less forgiving. Owen Hart broke Steve Austin's neck doing one in the late 90's, amongst other injuries that have come from it. When Gillis changed the move from tombstone to cage roll, instead of my head having an inch or two to spare, it was a good foot out of position.

I was wary, scared, and had tucked my face right into his balls against the suggestion of a chiropractor that the lockjaw position of looking up was the strongest posture. Good thing. If I hadn't, I would have definitely broken my neck. As it was, the full weight of Gillis and myself crashed onto the back of my neck and base vertebrae of my shoulders.

An announcer said, "I wanted to throw up" when he saw it. I very nearly broke my neck and ruined my life for good. I was lucky; I had some nerve damage and stenosis of my vertebrae, but that was all. After x-rays immediately following it I had massage and physiotherapy for months but I was just happy be walking. But I was also pissed off. The only comment I remember clearly was from some stupid fan saying, "Serves you right for hurting Bubba." The comment didn't account for any of the technical side of wrestling.

These were two completely different injuries- one where a guy takes mostly his own bump versus one where you are completely responsible for the safety of your partner. Ignorance swam not just through the fans, but through the wrestlers, with rumours and trash talk circulating but not coming to me directly. When I spoke with Randy Tyler about it, he said, "Your treatment by the fans and workers is just totally disrespectful and unjustified."

I agreed.

Months later, after another show in Nanaimo (home of the famous dessert bars) and one more terrible show in Victoria, I quit working for ECCW. I told the fans and the promotion that ECCW was disgusting, and left to work for All Star Wrestling. I was certain I would have far less matches, but didn't care; I wanted nothing to do with it any more.

The Mad Bomber circa 2000. Note the shocker.

I gave my notice and began working for All-Star Wrestling ran by Rocket Randy Tyler. For a guy new to the biz, it's always gutsy or stupid to burn a bridge and quit a promotion on bad terms. The way I saw it, I either had to quit ECCW as it was run at the time or quit wrestling altogether. There was something else that I had to deal with as well, equally abusive, and much more difficult to let go of.

* * *

Pussy Control

The tears swelled but died, she ignored them, and they slept as best they could. The next morning they put as much effort into saying goodbye as they could muster given the fact that neither really cared, but neither really wanted it to happen. It was utterly confusing, uncomfortable, and painful trying to make a perfect kiss happen. Hours loomed over them and minutes ticked by with desperation. A 9 a.m. departure left little time for dawdling.

Pushkin hissed at her kennel, but got in. No scratches or biting this time. The road had less rush hour than it would on a weekday, but that lagging Sunday driver feel that made things more retarded than they should have been. She reached the outskirts of Hope in 2 hours, a half hour late, and reached Williams Lake in four more. 8 to go. She couldn't hold it anymore.

After a veggie sandwich, she pulled over on the outskirts of town to let Pushkin scratch in the bushes and defecate. Pushkin walked a few feet, kicked at the loose gravel on the side of the road, squatted, peed quickly, then turned and looked at her owner. In half a second, Adrienne read the look on the cat's face; and in the next half, the cat dashed into the bushes.

-   -   -

"Is it true?"

"What do you mean?"

"Did you kiss him? Eryn said she saw you and Dagan making out. Is it true?"

New Year's eve, 6 months before the decisive trip up North would begin. A bustling party full of young adult stupidity and temptations.

"We were hugging."

"Were you kissing him?"

"It's New Year's, we kissed once, I don't know what she's imagining, she must be way too drunk."

"She's at least as sober as you. Why would she say that?"

"She can't hold her liquor-- trust me, I know her pretty well. I wouldn't make out with her boyfriend, and I wouldn't trust what she says. She's drunk."

"She's your best friend, 30 pounds heavier than you and had the same amount to drink; she knows what she saw."

"Don't call my friend fat! I'm not a bad person and neither is she! Stop bugging me, stop making me think I've done something wrong. I'm not a bad person, I'm not a cheater, you're insecure. Why do you have to ruin nights like this when I'm out having fun?"

"...."

"You always do this. I'm sick of it! I'm sick of you thinking I'm cheating on you or that I slept with whoever or that I'm making out with people. I don't cheat!"

"..."

"What? How many times have I been on the spot for cheating on you? It makes no sense! Stop it!"

"...well..."

"Well what? You're ruining another perfect night for me. Stop it!"

Pauses. Adrienne looked into his eyes, tried to see how her words came across, what he was thinking.
"Well?"

"...I never said you cheated on me. I said Eryn saw you and Dagan making out."

-    -   -

"Pushkin! PUSHKIN! Here kitty kitty! Pushy!" The top of her lungs at the edge of the forest. Her placement began at 9:00 a.m. sharp Monday morning. Anyone who showed up late was dismissed from the program and sent directly home, and the next placement was a year later. It was another 8 hours to Terrace from where she was, and that was driving non-stop. 3:30. She glanced back into the woods and stepped in, trying desperately to find some sign of where she had gone, a trace or a track to find the footsteps of her friend running without aim away from her, maybe trying to get back home, where they started, so long ago. But a hopeless run nonetheless. Cats are hard to hold down until they needed something, a well-wishing best friend that had to push everything to its limits. Who can endure the fickle friendship of a cat?

-    -   -

The dark woods hung over Adrienne as she stared up at the sky. Summer solstice had not yet come, the sun was high and bright. The shimmered glow of evening sun pressed in. Swollen clouds hung over her while she sat and watched for Pushkin, pulling at her hair. 7:30 p.m. Four hours gone. A 9:00 a.m. start and site orientation, learning where to sift, where to dig, where to cast the dross that didn't reveal anything. It was an indigenous sight of a village, where people had lived their lives in their way. It seemed ordinary in its day but a mystery now. A simple past where people lived, hunted, hung in the village, and left from one encampment to the next following the food migration. Her hands fumbled with her Swiss army knife as she opened a can of tuna. She couldn't yell anymore.

Taking the tuna in her hands, she walked as far into the woods as she could without getting lost, keeping ears and eyes open for signs of bears. She stopped, scooped some tuna out and plopped it onto a log. She scattered a mess of flakes into the surrounding moss and ferns, then walked back a few yards dripping the juice of the tuna lightly along the way. Another stop, and a repeat of the same, sewing hope into the huge dark forest, throwing tiny specs of tuna in a huge wood, praying the lingering smell would attract only her cat; bears, coyote's, raccoons, all would pick up on the scent as easily as a cat. Adult eagles have been known to prey on bear cubs weighing up to 40lbs. Pushkin weighed 5.

-    -   -

"I don't understand why you can't come all the way."

"I'm working. I can't afford two days off just to drive up 12 hours one day and down 12 hours the next day in my own car tailing you. I'll be exhausted" he explained, but without sympathy.

"So I've got to drive up 12 hours by myself?"

"Yeah, and you get to stay there. It's a lot easier for you. If I drive up in your car, how do I get back down?"

"You can take a bus."

"From Terrace to here? That's 16 hours if I'm lucky. So, I start work on Monday, I helped you move and sort everything out, I'm storing your stuff while you're gone for 9 weeks minimum, unless you find a job up there permanently, and you want me to drive up with you 12 hours one day, then take a bus down for 16 hours the next day, so we can spend the hours in a car together, and all this because you want to take your car up instead of driving up with your friends?"

"They're not my friends, I hardly know them, and it'll be fun for us. We can talk and stuff, hang out... We get no time together. You and Kenny are always wrestling and training and working together and I hardly ever see you and it's not fair and I want some time together."

"Then why did you take a placement up there for 9 weeks? It's not my fault Adrienne, and it's too much for me to come up 12 hours one day and 16 hours down the next just because you don't want to travel with some people you don't know so well. How do you not see that? I know what I want to do. It's exactly what happened with Blacky."

His cat, how could bring that up? Yes, he had wanted to stay in Victoria and not to come over to Vancouver, and he had made it clear, but she had pushed him to do it so she wouldn't be alone with her family. It was Halloween. When they had come home, his father had told him "Blacky the cat is dead. Probably scared by Halloween kids or out in the driveway as usual. Someone ran him over."

Blacky had always wandered the driveway; her boyfriend had always locked him up on Halloween because he knew how terrifying the fireworks were. He had left on the 9 a.m. ferry; his brother hadn't locked up the cat. She knew he had always blamed her, he'd said so when it first happened, but later he wrote it off as an outburst. It wasn't. She could tell. He never really listened to her again. He never liked being told what to do, and hadn't been so easy to guilt after that. Wrapped around her finger? Only loosely, a relationship strained by resentment, growing suspicion, and flashes of contempt.

-    -   -

Adrienne grabbed her keys, thumbing them between her fingers, then putting them into the ignition. She stared at the forest, at the woods, and thumbed her keys again. 12:00 a.m.. No sign. No noise. Her yelling and crying for her cat rescued nothing. One hour left. One hour for Pushkin to show up or to for her to accept the loss. No other possibility.

- - -

"I'm reaching for a dream here, it's all I ever wanted to do with my life. Why is that so hard to understand? I quit rugby, something I could have played professionally, to wrestle. I'm going to make it happen, why does it matter if you like it or not?"

She'd never had dreams, just an often absent father and cold mother who adored her brother though he treated her like shit. Adrienne was left alone wishing for a family with no deception and cattiness between them. That was a dream itself.

"You're mad at me for not supporting your dream?" she said.

It was his fault for being a god-dammed wrestler anyhow. How could she respect that nonsense, his life-long dream or not? How could anyone enjoy play fighting, celebrating violence, and getting covered in blood? She'd seen him in that cage, covered in blood from other people. Of course she didn't support him, who could? So of course she cheated on him. But he didn't know. And if he didn't know, he couldn't care, and if he couldn't come up to do the trip with her, long as it was...

When he finally caught her, she hadn't argued or protested. She just read the email message over and over.

"I know what you are and what you've done. I hate you. When you get back, your stuff will be sitting waiting for you. I won't put it out until you call and say you're on your way, but I never want to see you again. You're a slut and I hate you."

- - -

She sat on the gravel at the edge of the road. If she pushed hard, she could make it. Her career depended on being there. Her future and all the misses from the past that had depended on her loomed in the sullen glow of a summer moon. Whispering inside her head she passed the next ten minutes as a lifetime playing out infinite possibilities of what could happen- did it matter or not? Was the placement important or not? What would they say? Was this her career, or did it even matter, would she land on her feet somewhere else? Was "there" so important compared to her "here"? Every scenario spilled out onto the highway bitterly.

Blubbering eyes and wailing were muffled by her hands, small and fragile. The same hands that as a young girl held her daddy so tight before he left to sea for months on end. Her eyes, the same eyes that saw too much and loved birds, her first word, when she was a child, cried. The same eyes that witnessed the slaughterhouses, that made her cry in fear for her fellow animals. Her ears perked up, miserable ears that had burned when friends told her to get help, stung her heart when a boy called her "monkey-girl" at the waterslides. And her nose dripped out, flushing the abuse of days gone by out in gobs and gods of shape and scent. Her hands retreated into her sleeves, rubber her shoulders, hugged her knees, patted her ears, smudged the tears on her eyes, and finally wiped her nose. Filthy. For minutes she wailed silently. She gave over to desperation, to misery, to faithlessness, then the sober resolve that replaces hope when reality speaks up.

Her cat was lost and never coming back. Freedom and death loomed over Pushkin in the endless green forest. Cats are just cats. A domestic cat in a wild jungle, a sweetheart in a war, a princess in a pile. She straightened her back, stared into the forest, and took a deep breath. Her cat was gone. Between more tears, more misery, through poles of hopelessness and hate, both tempered by desperation, she sat, staring. She could see nothing. She looked at her watch but didn't notice or care about the time. She looked at the car, the road going off into the distance in two directions, ahead and behind, infinite. Long, gray, and bleak. She looked into the woods, then at the road, then back at the woods. Sighing, she surrendered; we give up so much and can do so little. Some things we can never get back. Sometimes trying is all you can do, impossible or not.

She stared at the road, then at the woods. She grabbed a blanket from her car, standing on the gravel edge between the path laid out and the distant unknown. She sat down to wait till hope, till reason, till faith all died completely. She would sit, cry, and wait. What else could she do?

* * *

All that really happened; you can decide about the cat as you see fit (go read *The Lady or The Tiger)*. Fairytale or no, life sometimes takes turns we can't see our way out of. I couldn't see any way to get ahead in wrestling, and Adrienne couldn't see her cat. We both lost at times.

Disirregardlessly Adrienne and I split. A four year relationship down the drain for a dream that seemed impossible to achieve. I had no prospects in BC for wrestling, but few indy wrestlers did anywhere. There really was no reason not to go back east, other than some insecurities financially and being closer to my family. But I hesitated.

In what turned out to be fate, I won a coin toss that got me off the wait list and into a creative writing course at college, and Kenny Lush landed me a job serving coffee in Vancouver's West End. Vancouver had more non-wrestling opportunities at the time and Jer told me it was hell trying to break in to the Ontario scene.

Lush and I moved into a house in Vancouver that we rented from Randy Tyler just before the break up with Adrienne. After a while living together, Lush broke up with his girlfriend too. It gave me the chance to train in the ring twice a week, wrestle once a month, earn some money, and finish an English degree. It seemed like the logical thing to do, but my heart was only in one of all those things-wrestling. Highlights came; it was just a matter of surviving the daily nonsense to enjoy them.

Everyday Superstar

Thursday at Delany's Coffee House. 10:30 a.m. Four hours into my shift. Four more hours away from leaving for Portland and a wrestling dream come true. I just had to survive till then, to wait for my gasp of air above the drowning of surface of day to day life. The smell of coffee, of peaceful mornings, with the gentle buzz of hushed morning conversation was broken by foaming milk. After waking up at 5:00, I still squinted while looking out from behind the espresso machine. The sun peeked out from behind the clouds, through the big bay windows, and onto the wooden seats of Delany's.

"Tall latte no foam extra shot" I called.

"Is this skim milk? I asked for skim."

"Uh, let me look at the chit. No, it's not," I sighed.

"I have a tough time with milk fat, can you make me another one?"

"Sure…. Dawson, when you write on the papers, make sure you specify if it's non-fat" I coached in the direction of the till..

"Oh, I thought I did. Well, I said non-fat when I punched it in. Doesn't that work?"

"No, it doesn't. I'm already making another drink when you do that. I'm busy concentrating elsewhere. That's why we write them down. You know that, you've been here three weeks."

Three weeks in hell. For both of us.

"Oh, well I just figured it was okay."

"Well it's not, so write it down."

"Yeah yeah."

He and I both found our odd-couple work relationship frustrating. He had no idea what he was doing; I had no idea why he had no idea about everything.

"Here you go sir, tall latte, no foam, extra shot, non-fat," I beamed.

"Oh great-- is it half decaf like I asked?"

I glanced at the paper in front of me. I looked at the customer then shook my head. He nodded, handing it back to

129

me, and I began the order again. Once he was gone, I had a moment. He had a promo coming. If I could explain it in wrestling, or even Joe terms, it would be "Pack your bags, you're bloody awful and get the hell out of here." But, I had to speak like a manager, not a pro wrestler. If only.

".... Dawson..."

"What?"

"When you take a drink order, write down all the information that the customer tells you."

"I thought I did."

He was genuinely lost or the greatest undiscovered actor on planet earth.

"You didn't. It should say non-fat, half-caf on it."

"Well Jeez, excuse me. You'd think nobody ever had to remake a drink before."

There is a smart-assed impunity in the generation of entitlement that comes from having no shame. Give me twenty seconds as a wrestler, please! Let me heel on him, be the Mad Bomber, and absolutely thrash him with milk jugs and cookie sheets. It sounds vindictive, but Dawson, in all fairness, was a complete tool, and had no idea that getting catty in front of customers is unprofessional and embarrassing. Neither did he realize that the person who supervises him at work, at this time me, had a lot better things to deal with.

Dawson had ADHD, had quit school in grade 11 because he felt "constricted" by it, and was only a few degrees below flaming in his personality. I stared at his blond hair and lost, beaky face with a sparkling earring. If I spoke right then, the wrestler would really come out. I was grumpy. Dawson was a special case. Overall, I enjoyed working with gay guys. I didn't have a problem with the flaming side of Dawson's personality unless he used it to become a whiny bitch to work with, which he often did.

The rest of the boys were fun, happy, and easy to get along with. A few customers wanted to get into my pants, which made them great tippers. They knew I was straight but hoped for a moment of "indiscretion". I admired their persistence, but only when polite. Dawson was basically the worst of all there had to be with a fake personality- nice and entertaining at first, a real bitch and whiny as hell when things didn't go his way, and ready to cry foul or "hate crime" at the first opportunity. He would turn Gandhi into a violent bigot. A justified violent bigot. Especially after another 25 minutes of idiocy.

"Dawson, don't talk to the customers for so long when you're on cash."

"I'm just being social" he quipped.

"And you're holding up the line while people want to get a coffee and go to work or catch a bus. Keep it moving; talk to one customer and serve the next."

"Fiiine."

"Dawson, don't eat in front of the customers. Go do it in the back room."

"But I'm hungry."

"Yeah, but people don't like seeing someone who's serving them food eat it first. Do it in the back."

"Fiiiine..."

After another thirty minutes of this, I hid in the back, making cookies, praying for the end of his shift... and mine. One last hurdle to jump.

"Dawson, you've got to restock the front fridge before you leave."

"Uh, I think it's ok" he asserted, not really knowing since he never looked in it.

"Go look at it and make sure it's ok before you leave."

"But I'm off in 2 minutes."

"It'll take you two minutes to do it."

"Nobody'll notice if I don't."

"No, only the next person on will. Do it."

Out to the front fridge and back again twenty seconds later.

"K, it's fine. Anything else for my last minute here?"

The words "hate crime" hung heavy in the air above my head. My forehead would make such a perfect dent in his nose, and his collared shirt had such tempting handles. It would be a great way to quit...

"Just go already. Let's just call it a day."

"Bye. Enjoy" he waved.

You're Gonna Hurt Yourself

In tromped Jolene, store manager; 50 years old, a bob haircut, and reasonably good to look at, all things considered. She sometimes even seemed sexy with her southern drawl.

"Hon, I just went to make a latte and there are only 2 jugs of milk up there. It holds 14. Why didn't Dawson stock it up?"

"Oh god... he said he did" I groaned.

"Well, you need to check up on him. Make sure."

"I need to check on him, or he needs to do his job properly? Honestly Jolene, it's just easier if I do it. I'm tired of fighting for competence around here and he's an idiot."

I searched around for an escape from this nonsense. If only I was a wrestler, not just a pretend, weekend warrior.

"Hun, your job is to make sure Dawson does his job. The point is that you tell him to do it, not that you can do it quicker or better."

"Jolene, don't hire idiots."

"Hun, he's not an idiot. He just needs some help sorting his life out."

My eyes wandered to a length of rope dangling from the hole in the ceiling. It was about 20 feet long and could make a good lasso. Huns were notorious for killing people by lassoing them and dragging them behind a horse. I would've loved to have really been a "Hun." Is killing an idiot because they're an idiot a hate crime?

"Look, I'm going to restock the front fridge then take my break. I need some air. Sherri just got in and can help you for the next bit."

"Well, don't take too long, it's almost time for lunch rush."

"I'm going to take my 15 minutes that I'm entitled to - I've been on since 5:30 and I can't leave Dawson alone to run the store cause he's an idiot, so I'm taking 15. You and Sherri can handle it."

"Well, if I have to buzz you to come up, you come up. You can't just hide in the back."

Doc Bruce Banner,
Belted by gamma rays,
Turned into the Hulk.

You're Gonna Hurt Yourself

Ain't he unglamor-ous!

Wreckin' the town
With the power of a bull,
Ain't no monster clown
Who is as lovable.
As ever-lovin' Hulk! HULK!! HULK!!"

In a faraway voice my head started to hum as my eyes turned green. I could feel my skin stretching, bulging. If I stayed any longer, I'd split into a monster. The Hulk always was my favourite comic character- there's a certain orgasmic release in completely losing one's temper and thrashing everything in sight; I would really enjoy it. Funnily enough, one of my Halloween costume at Delany's was the Hulk. The symbolism is an essay unto itself, not just for Freud. But this day the good doctor and desperation for a dream kept the Hulk under wraps. Too bad, but bills had to be paid while I waited to become a star. I sighed...

"I'm going across the street for Shawarma. I'll come back and eat here in case there's a problem."

It was the best I could do without snapping. Why does society get mad at nice people if they don't cover for morons, yet never gets frustrated with the morons who caused the problem in the first place? Usually because morons are in charge- Jolene had sympathy for Dawson, and that said all I needed to know about that. This dilemma haunted me everywhere in life, even in my WWE tryouts.

Of course I ate lunch across the road over a leisurely twenty minutes, not ten or fifteen; I had a few hours until I could free the beast in the ring. A few hours until Kenny, Roselli, and I drove down to Eugene, Oregon for one of the biggest nights of my life as a professional wrestler, working for Roddy Piper in front of a crowd of 5,000. For the moment, I was still a barista being harassed and earning $8.75 an hour plus tips while going to college and training to wrestle 3 times a week, but hardly actually doing matches because of the local politics. If you worked for one company, you couldn't work for the other. I had almost broken my neck working for one, and they were a garbage fed that was embarrassing to bring friends to, so I worked for the other, which never ran shows.

"You and Kenny are going to get yourselves killed doing that stupid wrestling. You should grow up and get a career."

Who says that to a 20 year old? What gives a 50 year old woman who has to manage a coffee shop full of morons the right to talk to anyone like that? Apparently $8.75 an hour does because I put up with her attitude to keep that $8.75 an hour coming in.

"I'm going to school, I'll have a career. Wrestling is my passion."

"Well, you guys are just asking for trouble."

"Should I quit and work here the rest of my life?"

"It's so violent and stupid, I could never do that."

"You don't have to, but thanks for the support. See you in three days."

"Don't be late Monday."

We did the trip, rented a Durrango, a 10-seater and a pig on gas, but Roselli insisted he would pay for it. Kenny slept the whole way because he never got a driver's license. Luckily, we didn't have any problems with border guards and didn't need to come up with any lies. The trip down was easy. And the night before the show was fantastic.

Two of my favourite wrestlers of all time were Mr. Perfect and Dan "The Beast" Severn. They both were in Roddy Piper's hotel room the night before as the boys hung out, ate pizza, crushed beers, and a few of the guys took turns wandering into the back room, coming out with crossed eyes and dilated pupils. I had partied and drank with wrestlers before, but nothing like this.

Jim Duggan, Greg Valentine, Piper, Perfect, Severn, Roselli, Kenny, Bart Sawyer, and I all in one room-- a huge step for an unknown like myself. Only 4 local guys were in actual matches, the rest were established "names" in the business, guys who could draw a crowd wherever they went and they had been major players in the WWF of the 80's and 90's. All the other local wrestlers had been piled into a battle royal to be cannon fodder for the big names. There were a lot of jealous eyes shooting daggers at Lush and me, and as much as we wanted to succeed, every other local wrestler wanted us to fail in a fiery ball of a clusterfuck match. Roddy told us he wanted us to go out there and "kick the show into high gear" by having a fast paced, stiff match. It was time for a gut check.

5,000 fans? Check.

Legends in the back critiquing our every move? Check.

Every other wrestler jinxing us? Check.

The usual nerves that makes you shake before you get out in front of crowd? Check

Extra worry because of a fear of injury in the states when you don't have health insurance? Check

Possibly a way out of the daily misery that is sucking the life out of you every second you are away from the ring, and a huge hope to escape the aimless sea of unknown local wrestling? Check.

And a "What the fuck is your gimmick anyways?" speech by Bart Sawyer just before I walked out to do the biggest match of my life, stabbing at my confidence as a wrestler? Check.

Did I know my gimmick? Hell no, but I knew that I was more "The Mad Bomber" than Ben Nelson at that point in my life. I didn't have a clue who either one was, only that "The Mad Bomber" was a damn good wrestler, from Canada, and he would get a hell of a lot of heat and show all the jealous assholes in the back and at home that he was one of the best local guys around, and that was why he got the match for Piper.

I can honestly say, in the highest stakes match of my life, I went out there with Kenny and tore the roof down. We stiffed each other with slaps, ran great high spots, and popped the crowd with an awesome swerve finish. 5,000 people yelled their lungs out at me, swearing, cursing, throwing stuff, and hating me; 5,000 yelled even harder for Kenny, deafening the arena with chants of "U-S-A" and exploding when he pinned me. Pro wrestling is a team effort, and he and I both earned the heat and the pop. His cheer was my cheer, his victory my victory. Job well done.

To celebrate, I journeyed into the bowels of the stadium, got undressed, and began showering in a dingy, tiled locker-room shower. Soap smell mixed with mildew. I was pondering the meaning of all this wrestling when in walked Mr. Perfect in all his man made and god given glory; 6'4", blonde, criminally tanned, built like a Greek god, and completely naked. I was too nervous to speak; he could care less.

"You got any shampoo dude?"

"Uhh, no, but I got a whole bunch of soap in my hands from the dispenser."

"Can I have some?"

"Uhh sure."

And I poured the liquid soap from my hands into his while we stood in the University of Oregon shower, alone and naked. It was a scene dripping with homoeroticism, and I have to say that naturally I checked out his package. What else could I do? He was my idol, so I had to see if he measured up. He did. Life as a professional wrestler continued to amaze me. I spent the rest of my shower staring at the wall as we made small talk. My mind was a whir. On one hand, I didn't want to weird Mr. Perfect out and was pretty much just standing there, hosing off, barely going through the motions of showering. On the other hand, how often do you get to shower with Mr. Perfect? If it was a rugby shower, ten other guys would have walked in and we would have had a naked football game, cirques against toques. That wasn't an option. There were only two of us. After what felt like was a reasonable amount of time pretending to clean myself, I abruptly turned off the shower, then dried and dressed. I grabbed my unsold T-shirts, went upstairs and sold a few more, doubling my pay to $300 for one day's work.

I couldn't have gotten any higher- except I did when I picked up a ring rat after the show and hooked up with her in the Durrango, putting the reclining seats to good use. It was a fumbling, messy affair, but I loved every second of it. When she went her way, I ran into Roddy who gave me a congratulatory rub on the back of my neck, thrust a beer into my hand and said "Son, glad you guys are in the business. Thank you for coming down and working for me."

"Any time sir, the pleasure is all mine"

"Call me Roddy, you're a worker."

Lush and I with Rowdy Roddy Piper in 2001. Note the joy.

In the words of Roddy Piper, I was a worker, a good wrestler, not a pretend wrestler who only did this on weekends and was working a day job, but a real wrestler. I could go anywhere, I could do anything, I could actually be a professional wrestler doing this for a living, having parties every night, sowing my wild oats across the world and living the dream. Forget the local scene of jealous wrestlers, forget the assholes at work who told me I couldn't do it, and to hell with the parents, girlfriends, and forget everyone else who ever told me it was stupid to try or that I was gonna hurt myself. I was living my dream.

I tried, and I succeeded. I was good enough; dreams do come true. Sell out yourself and miss out on your dream all you want but I love wrestling and I have done it. I am a pro wrestler and I can go anywhere. Mexico, Japan, to the WWE, anywhere that Roddy had been was now open to me as a wrestler with his endorsement. I could go anywhere! When no magic opportunity came up immediately, I went back to Delany's Coffee House. The next day at work came too quickly.

"Grande Latte, extra shot, extra hot for Dwayne. Hey Dwayne." I beamed.

"Hey, you look great. Good weekend?"

"The best, went down to Portland with Kenny, wrestled a show, had a crazy party afterwards."

"Oh cool, how much fun! Let's hear it."

"Well, first we got--"

"Ben, I need a hand bringing in the milk delivery from the back," cawed Jolene, "and we've got to make it snappy. It's hot out and I don't want the milk to spoil."

"K, I'll get it in a second"

"Hon, it's going to spoil. It's hot out."

"Dawson's in the back, get him to do it."

"He's on a break, and he's not strong enough."

"I'm just talking to Dwayne I'll do it in a minute."

"Now."

"…Okay."

Dwayne shrugged sympathetically, turning away. 5,000 cheering fans couldn't drown out one rude lady in a shitty coffee shop. Wrestling be dammed. I was nobody once again.

Pepper Spray

Every Thursday became a blur of nonsense for Lush and I; what started out as having the odd drink here or there turned into a weekly debacle made affordable by Dollar High-Ball Night and funded by my student loans. Any drink- gin, vodka, whiskey- was $1 for the house label at The Stone Temple. It was the messiest I've been besides the time I was a Barnyard Cock. For $20 each we seemed like high rollers and got loaded. Word spread, and soon enough, the crew from Delany's started to come with us once a week, even when we had a 5 a.m. start time at work. There were a ton of hangovers, but more laughs and fun.

One typical Thursday, about 25 minutes before the bar closed, I finally made a move and kissed Colleen, the hot 28 year-old Aussie cougar that I had been eyeing and flirting with for weeks. To my surprise, she kissed me back. A smile lit my face; I hadn't really dated anyone since breaking up with Adrienne; I needed some affection and a boost in confidence. We carried on, and before I knew what was happening, the lights were on at the bar, it was closing time, and Lush and I were stumbling outside, Colleen in tow. Then things got interesting.

"Watch it Pinner!" yelled Lush.

"What'd you call me?"

"He called you a pinner; what are you going to do about it?" I got in some stranger's face and was completely out of control; I didn't think he would actually do anything. I thought for a second, "Is this idiot going to hit me?" No surprise, he did. I deserved it.

It wasn't hard enough to even ring my bell, but did swell up my lip. I was totally hammered and realized I had better do something to shift things to my favour, so I took him over in a headlock and started feeding him shots on the ground. "Cops, Cops!" someone yelled. I got up just in time to get blasted with pepper spray. If you've been lucky enough to avoid pepper spray, let me explain; I've never encountered something so aptly named.

When you get hit with it, the burning starts, you taste and smell hot pepper sauce, and try as you might, you can't open your eyes. You don't want to open them but feel you have to. The spray was mostly in my left eye and over my face, and I could see enough to walk away from the mob and cops. As I stood at the door of a pizza shop, Colleen poured a bottle of water on my face, and as my eyes cleared, I saw Lush handcuffed, face down in a muddy puddle.

"Don't throw me in the drunk tank, I give you free coffee at Delany's," he yelled, then, "argh, the handcuffs aren't so bad but the concrete is cold and wet. Why'd you throw me in a puddle? Argh, cold and wet."

He shook his head side to side, trying to keep his face out of the murky water. The cops were actually smiling when they walked over to him and hoisted him up.

"I know Tarrell and Handy—they're regulars-- I give you free coffee at Delany's. Be nice!" his plea continued.

They loaded him up into a paddy wagon, loaded up the guy who hit me into the other side of it, the crowd dispersed, and I found myself standing there with a swollen lip, pepper spray on my face, Colleen, and no more cops in sight. I was a free man.

"Well, I guess your night's over, huh?" I said fingering my face while examining it in a window; I looked like a sunburnt idiot with angry, swollen, Jar-Jar Binks lip.

"Idaknow, what you goin to do?" Colleen asked.

I had already thrown in the towel, but since I'd already been punched in the face, anything less was a positive...

"Uhh, I'm just heading home; want to come over?"

"Sounds good ta mei" she said with a smile.

We got home, started making out on the couch, and before things got very far, Lush came walking in.

"How come you didn't get arrested and I did?" he asked, laughing.

"How'd you get here so fast? Didn't they take you to the drunk tank?" I asked back.

"No, I told them I knew Tarrell and Handy. They told me to keep it down, Handy showed up, asked me what happened, I said the guy sucker punched you, then they dropped me off around the corner, making me swear to get the next cab home. So I did."

It probably wasn't worth the hassle of the cops to drag him to the station, but you still had to admire the ability of Lush to get out of trouble. He sat down, started watching TV, then at some nudging, Colleen got me to take her downstairs to my bedroom. The kissing started again; the clothes came off; the passion picked up and before long, we were consummating our new relationship. I'm well put together, and sure enough, she started moaning while the bed springs squeaked. "Ohhhh" Squeak. "OHHHHHHHH" Squeak, squeak, "OHHHH OHHH MY!" I was kind of confused; I wasn't doing anything particularly adept, just thrusting, thinking about math problems to buy time.

"OHH, AHHHH, AHHH!!!!! STOP!!! STOP!!!" I figured it was a hot stop request, like, it felt good, so I kept going. She piped in with her adorable Aussie accent. "Sumin's wrong, AHHHAA Sumin, OOHHH, Sumin's burnin'…. YOU GUT PEPPA SPRAY IN MEI!"

I leaned back a bit and looked at her, clueless.

"AHHHHH! IT'S BURNIN!"

"Uhhh, what do we do?" I asked, stunned.

"We gotta get meilk, meilk will get rid of the burnin-AHHHHEH!'"

"UHH, I think we've got milk in the fridge."

I pulled out, moved back, and sat at the edge of the bed while she panicked and fumbled to find some clothes. Watching her bend over, I realized that a) I only had one condom b) she had a fantastic ass and c) I hadn't had sex in about 4 months. In the dim light, bent over, panicking for clothes, her cookie shop was waving me in; she was not getting away. I prowled up behind her, grabbed her hips, and did my best to finish as quickly as possible.

To her credit, she not only gave in, but pushed back harder and harder. Her moaning got louder, more pained, and began bursting out in "AHHHHH!! AHHHHH!" until finally mother-nature cooled both of us off; I jumped back into bed, and she went upstairs- not for milk, just water. As she walked upstairs, I heard Lush say, "JEEE-ZUS! Colleen, are you ok?"

"I'm great!" she said, "But I'm never doing that again."

There it is.

I won't sell my Indiana Jones Hat

Never meet your idols. I was a huge Tim Flowers' mark when I was a kid and he appeared on the local TV wrestling show and I was stoked to wrestle for him in 2001. However, 9-11 had just happened, making our trip across the border two hours longer than planned. Never trust the real world to make wrestling easy. We had to get a boost for Willis' car as we waited in line. Not Sketchy at all. When Flowers called to see where we were, Lush yelled out the ridiculous gimmick names of his wrestlers in the background while Willis talked to him.

"MEAN MIKE! THE CHEF! MOOSE WINOSKI! SLOTH! TEENAGE DIRTBAG!"

Flowers knew he was being ribbed, blew a gasket into the phone, and hung up.

"Bomber, Flowers is pissed at you."

"ME? WHY ME?"

"He thinks you were making fun of his guys."

"I was only laughing. That was Lush! Aww fuck…"

Thankfully the car didn't blow a gasket as well; we made it to Seattle. Flowers got mad at us, specifically me before and after the show. I called him on some bullshit; nobody likes that.

"Tim, you paid us $25 each and didn't pay Willis anything. We drove six hours. What is this?"

"Nobody's in this biz to make money, and who are you, his fucking agent?" He sneered, then spat out, "Fuckin Mad-fuckin-Bomber, god-dammed primadonna. Mike Willis's fuckin agent."

"You're not going to pay us anymore?"

"Fuck, you're lucky you were on the show."

"Did you hear our match? See you tomorrow, Tim."

"Sheeet, Mad-fuckin'-Bomber."

I walked out and we saddled up, ignoring the idiot asking us to help tear down the ring. We drove home to rest up for the next wonderful night of working for ICW. The next morning brought even more excitement; a phone call.

"Hello?"

"Mad-fuckin-Bomber."

"Hey Tim."

"You coming to the show tonight?"

"Well, I agreed to before, didn't I?"

Thankfully, this one was just in Cloverdale and didn't require a long drive. It was a match, no money, but a match. Bookings and matches were difficult to get with all three local promotions being in a petty war over venues and wrestlers.

"Well, you didn't seem too happy last night with your P-O" said Tim.

"I wasn't, but I already agreed to work the dates, so I guess it's my bad for not knowing what we were getting paid."

"All right. See you at 4. Don't be fuckin' late." Click.

We showed up at 6 p.m. Tim gave us instructions for our match in record time saying, "Lush goes over, get it done in four minutes."

"Ha, we'd planned a 30 minute broadway, Tim" said Lush. Tim looked at him and sneered.

"I don't wanna hear no five minute announcement; you guys get it done in 4, including entrances, or I'm hitting the ring with a chair."

"No improv battle royal?"

"Shit... you fuckin' primadonnas. Make it Three."

Three minutes to get to the ring, be announced, build some sort of a reaction with a crowd that had never seen us before, and finish our match. It was nigh impossible and pretty much pointless. This is what indy wrestling is like though. You offend promoters by sticking up for yourself but have to take their insults and desperately low wages or you never wrestle. Tim paid about $25 a night, maybe fifty if he liked you. He was the norm, but the three minute time limit under threat of assault was not.

The crowd was a bomb scare, with around 75 people in a building that could easily hold five hundred. It was no mystery why people didn't pay to watch it.

Most of his wrestlers were barely trained (some only were two weeks into school) didn't have proper ring gear, and looked bloody awful. A skinny or fat kid would walk out in sweatpants, runners, and a t-shirt and expect to be taken seriously as a wrestler. This, like the PO's (pay) was typical of a lot of promotions. And it was no mystery why he didn't want Lush and I to do a proper match. I figured he either felt bad about ripping us off on our PO's or just didn't want Lush and I to make his guys look bad by working a full match again.

At the time, I was 6'1, 240lbs and thickly muscular. I studied a lot of Dean Malenko and ECW tapes; I did springboards, good mat wrestling, and knew my craft. Not the best, but good, maybe even very good. Lush was as charismatic a guy as the territory had. Flowers's guys sucked, and he knew it, which is why he invented the improvised battle royal. I hoped we'd see one. Mike Willis had been blessed enough to witness one. He loved sharing this story.

* * *

Everybody Out

"Ugh." Tim groans, looking out from the back curtain. We hear the silence of the crowd, the one thing a wrestler doesn't want, and a few people yell out, "this sucks!" I think it was Sloth versus Sex Ed. This was his ICW BC and Washington, not to be confused with ICW Ontario. Another few seconds of "wrestling" go by, Tim staring out the curtain. Some mark yells, "What was that supposed to be?" and a chorus of "boooooooos!" and Flowers spits on the ground, scuffing it with his foot. "Feck..."

"My god, you're awful!" yells a fan and that's it. Tim shuts the curtain, "FUCK!" and turns to the boys in the back. "THAT'S it! Improv battle royal, everybody out, I'm going over!"

"What?" The boys look around, half have never heard of such a thing, the other half have been through it before and hope he isn't serious; they know just how bad improve battle royals are.

"Did I fuckin' STUTTER? IMMM-PROVVV BAT-ULLLLLL ROYAL, EVERYONE ONE OF YOU FUCKIN MARKS OUT THERE, I'M GOING OVER!"

"Do we have to, Tim?" asks Teenage Dirtbag.

"You stay back here, you better be gone when I get back." Threatens Tim, pointing menacingly at him.

Scared to death of Tim, the locker room empties out of the back and into the ring in a dizzying display of shitty on-the-fly booking and terrible wrestling. Guys stiff each other and make up their own finishes (exits) from the ring as the fans stand by, baffled, sometimes cheering to see a wrestler they actually like, but generally more confused than before, deriding the incomprehensible spectacle of ICW wrestling.

We get to the back, and I ask Tim if that means I get double the pay; he says, "Fuck, go ahead and double nothing, see if I care," yells, "No more shit Matches!" and the show continues.

* * *

I really wished I'd seen one, and wanted to make one happen, but figured there was no point in putting in any more time in Tim's ring than necessary. In under 3 minutes, in one match of about 12 on the show, Lush pinned me, we got our $25 each, and that was the end of my career with ICW and Tim Flowers. I couldn't get out of there fast enough.

Knowing Tim like I do know, the whole thing is hilarious and Tim is one of the few guys who will tell you to fuck off right to your face; we actually laugh at it now and don't mind each other. At the time, we couldn't be in the same town. At least I still had college. It sucked.

I was bored out of my mind, had fizzled out with a few girls and had a few odd relationships that made me question the point of being in BC at all. The boys in Ontario called me regularly when they were drunk. After a few calls, we planned a road trip. I used a student loan to buy a flight into Toronto and out of Winnipeg. Stylin' Bryan had arranged a tour of 3 shows with Ernie Todd.

The trip there was a miracle of good times. And it was a miracle we made it to Winnipeg at all.

In a blizzard we drove 24 hours straight and then wrestled three nights of matches, banking our PO's for each show to save up for a grand lump sum at the end of the tour. Bryan had worked for Ernie Todd before and assured us we would be well taken care of. It made sense we would; we were all working hard. Believe none of what you hear in wrestling.

JC Owens and I won the NWA Canadian Tag Team Titles on our first night there. The match was good, but I got caught with an elbow by an opponent accidentally and burst my ear drum. The second night, we wrestled a couple of kids in pajamas who combined totaled maybe 300 pounds. JC and I together were 700 pounds, but we still had to make them look good.

The final show saw us lose the tag titles back to Ernie Todd, who had thrown himself into a tag team last minute, and then get sent into a barbed-wire ropes, fans bring the weapons, hardcore battle royal. As JC and eye looked at the run sheet for entrances, another wrestler came up and asked us when we planned on getting colour (bleeding).

"Uhh, never" I said, looking like I'd smelled a fart.

"But it's a hardcore battle royal. Everyone has to get color" he said, as though he should be teaching us something. I looked at the guy, let's call him Baldy Oldshits, and looked at his forehead covered in blade marks from cutting himself.

Baldy Oldshits was wearing the trusty outfit of sweatpants, runners, and a tank-top, and holding a kendo stick. Judging from his build he had never seen the inside of a gym. JC did his duckface as baldy stressed the importance of colour to make the match good. Clearly this guy thought getting color was the only thing there was to wrestling, and his IQ probably hovered around the single digits. JC and I made eye contact, then both disdainfully scowled at Baldy Oldshits, who then left.

We decided then and there to no-sell everything and not let a single idiot hit us with anything. We were entries number 8 and 11 in the battle royal of 20 combatants. We could watch out for each other.

When we got in there, JC grabbed a traffic director's stop sign and I grabbed a golf club. Everyone who came in was met with a stiff shot to the head, then they went down and sold, gigging themselves with razorblades while JC and I ignored all their offense. We weren't going to let a single idiot touch us or bleed on us. The only people we didn't stiff were our friends or one or two locals who got the biz enough to leave the weapons alone and catch us with headlocks and punches. JC laughed gleefully, even at one point singing to his stop sign.

As the final combatant entered, JC looked at me, then at the soles of his boots covered in blood and thumbtacks.

"Bomber, throw me out."

"What? We're partners! That makes no sense."

"Yeah, but I don't trust any of these guys. Give me a shitty punch and send me to the ropes with no wires on them."

I assessed his assessment of the situation as he pointed to the ropes he meant. Blood was everywhere. It was just a matter of time until one of us got caught by something, at least accidentally. He was 100% right.

"Hussaw!" I yelled, punching him with a terrible haymaker and dropping my golf club. JC twirled his arms, selling, and then clumsily stumbled into and over the ropes all by himself, artfully avoiding as much barbed wire as possible. I followed suit, jumping out for no reason to save my skin. What a night.

Sore and tired, we waited to grab our PO's and say goodbye to Ernie Todd. He was beaming as he held onto his new belt and handed us a wad of crumpled money in a semi-secretive handshake. He reached over, palm down in a fist, then handed opened his hand into our waiting palms. As soon as I got mine, I turned around and opened it. At first I was excited; it was thick and the outside bill was a twenty. Then I realized it was just folded over multiple times. I deflated as I unrolled my whopping PO of $50.

"There'll be more next time" he hollered. $50 for 3 matches. What an unappreciative dick. I had learned another lesson in wrestling; never trust a promoter to do the right thing, especially if you haven't personally agreed to anything. Bryan, to his credit, had been taken care of properly on previous shows with Ernie. He was shocked at the PO too, but none of us wanted to confront Ernie Todd in case we actually did want to work for him again. We drank our asses off after we got our PO's (payoffs) to make sure nothing with the stink of Winnipeg would follow with us, including the $50. The next morning, I flew home and the boys drove back to Ontario.

The Cambridge Connection 2001. Back row right to left: Myself, some ref, Jer, TJ Harley, and JC Owens. Front: Romeo Adams, Stylin' Bryan, and The Hacker. Note the future PO of $50 for 3 shows.

"I'll see you in a few months," I said to Jer, "I gotta do something. Winnipeg is hopeless and BC is killing me." I meant it.

"We've got room for you on the couch, Bomb" he said. We hugged goodbye and I set my sights on a plan to get the hell out of BC. In the few months between, I got enough drunken phone calls to confirm the decision was a good one.

Drunken phone calls mean something; it's a tradition amongst the boys. If you're out, drunk, and one of your brothers in tights is missing, you give him a call to make him part of the action. I have been gleefully awoken at 3:00 a.m. plenty of times to hear Romeo or TJ or Jer yell, "Yeahhh, Bombaa! Fuck you asshole! AH-he-he" (in a Hotdog Laugh) and then hang up. It always puts a smile on my face as I fall back asleep, warm in drunken wrestler love. I got enough calls 2000-2002 to realize it was time to head back to where I belonged. One day I finally said, "Lush, this fuckin sucks. I'm going out east, you should come."

Lush, for his part, was pissed off enough at the biz to leave it altogether for about 5 years. He stayed a few more months in Vancouver, then left to Edmonton and started a kick ass band, Daggermouth. Going back to ECCW wasn't even a consideration for me. They had, in order to take advantage of Easter, decided to do a crucifixion angle at a show. This offended pretty much everybody in the business and a great number of fans at the show. It was easy to see why.

Moondog Manson or another wrestler was tied to a cross in the ring while someone else read the whole crucifixion story directly from the bible over the microphone. WWE had done something vaguely similar with The Undertaker, but steered as clear from religious mockery as possible. Say what you will about religion, but there's no reason to intentionally offend fans who come to see your show, many of whom came from some type of Christian background. The business decision was a poor one. Sadly, it was just a sign of the times.

With hardcore wrestling dying, ECCW was desperate to shock fans into wanting to come to a show. All Star Wrestling ran once every two months. ECCW was offensive. ICW had nobody safe to wrestle and no opportunity to improve my craft. All of the wrestling options in BC were terrible.

One April morning, after much discussion, The Gnarly Hippy showed up at my door, bags in hand, ready to do some wrestling on a road trip back to Ontario. We went and got piss drunk my old bar, The Roxy. While there we argued with Mattias Ohlund of the Vancouver Canucks that Hippy's Indiana Jones hat was worth more than the $60 Ohlund was offering for it. Hippy emphatically stated, "I'm not going to sell out!" as we left the bar. We slept for a few hours, piled into my car, then began the drive to Ontario. As we left, I said "Next stop, some bar in Nelson, BC."

"I probably won't be able to get in there," said Hippy, "I'm only 18."

I looked at him and shook my head; he hadn't told me, and I could have been permanently banned from the Roxy. Whatever. He still would be helpful.

"Well then you can drive."

"Ok, but I lost my license somewhere on the way out here. I can drive, but happens if we get pulled over." Ugh.

"My insurance won't cover us if you don't have it. How did you lose it? Where's your wallet?"

"I'm keeping my money in this." He showed me a brown muffin bag he had taken from Delaney's. What the hell. I looked at him, looked at his "wallet", and with a "Well, there it is" started the car. For security, Hippy stashed his money above the passenger side visor. It was 48 hours of driving home, not including rests or sleep. Jeremy had bought a house with Marco, a duplex dubbed "Shade Street Manor", and there was room for me on the floor or couch. It was time to escape again. Almost weekly, my drunken wrestling brothers were calling. Dreams were calling. Ontario was calling. We wanted to get there in time for the Animal Olympics. We stopped to do a few shows in Winnipeg with a very generous Beautiful Bobby Jay, and then booked it to Ontario. Forget day to day struggles and terrible wrestling promotions that drove us as mad as scorned lovers; we were going to be Barnyard Cocks.

Romeo Adams

Romeo and Jer. Note the awesome shirt on Jer and awesome no shirt on Romeo.

You're Gonna Hurt Yourself

Once in a lifetime you meet a person who defies description. You meet someone who truly is unbelievable, not through notoriety or celebrity, but simply through their "qua" essence of being. You think you understand them, you think you have them pegged neatly into a category, but then they surprise you.

This isn't by them doing something unexpected; in fact, it's the opposite. They continue to surprise you by how much of themselves they continue to be. Just when you think they couldn't be any more of themselves, they go further. For me, and for a lot of people, nobody personifies this more than Romeo Adams.

Romeo is amazing; not a single person I know ever said anything bad about his character. In fact, he's the most loving, warm, genuine guy of our wrestling crew. We all love him for who he is and he loves pretty much everybody in return without reservation. But Romeo, bless his soul for making us laugh so much, is a piece of work.

Romeo never ate a vegetable. Never. Jer lived with him for 5 years and never saw him eat one. When I lived with him, we talked him into eating broccoli once and he spat it out. The closest he got was eating mushrooms on his pizza, which technically aren't a vegetable but a fungus. Why he ate mushrooms but not vegetables made no sense. But eating no vegetables was simple; they tasted gross.

Throughout these stories, as I describe Romeo, keep in mind that he was 4 years older than me. He was a 27 year old man who wouldn't eat a vegetable.

Romeo loves life with a unique zest. He just wants everyone to have a good time and doesn't judge anyone. He is passionate about having a good time and loves to laugh. Loudly. He particularly loved *Whose Line Is It Anyway?* And he made sure to tape (much harder than PVR-ing) episodes so he could enjoy them on Saturday mornings. The whole household of Shade Street Manor was routinely shaken from sleep and a hard night of drinking by the belting full-belly "Ehhh hehhh hehhhh cough" wheezing of Romeo Adams at 9 a.m. every Saturday. Why was Romeo up before the rest of us? Because he went so hard early on that his pacing was completely off. This happened over and over and over.

"Come on guys, fuckin drink already" he taunted.

"Romeo, it's 4 in the afternoon. We've got the whole night ahead of us, don't worry" Jer replied.

"Fuckin weak, let's party, haha I'm going to smoke a doob."

He would smoke, come back in, and we'd start playing a game of Ueker or Kings to get our drunk on. We'd order Pizza from Two Pies, and then battle out a few video games or something else while we waited for the bar to get busy. During this daze, someone would ask, "Where's Romeo?"

After a search of shouts, we'd realize he had ditched us, not unlike Romeo in *Romeo and Juliet*. However, instead of being off pursuing love (well, he could have been doing so alone) Romeo was asleep in his bed. His no sheets, exposed springs, stained, single mattress, covered only with an old sleeping bag, bed.

"Come on Romeo, we're going to the bar."

"Fuck off."

"Romeo, come on, it's the weekend, we've been waiting all week to go down to Fiddler's Green… Jer's dating the manager, we'll get in for free." Pleaded Mike. He only half wanted Romeo to come. Waking Romeo up was almost worth him not coming along for the trip.

"Fuck off, Mike. I'm tired" was the reply. Then Mike would start to build up some hype about him coming out. Wild energy from Mike electrified the crowd standing outside Romeo's bedroom.

"Romeo. Ro-me-o. Row-Mee-Oh! ROW MEE OHH! ROWW-MEEE-OWWW! YEAH ROMEO! YEAH! AWWW, BOOOOOOOOO!"

Romeo had awoken to the chants, faked joining us and coming out his door, then slammed it shut. We heard his dresser being pushed behind his door so he wouldn't have to worry about us breaking in when we returned. "BOOOOO! YOU SUCK ROMEO" yelled Hippy.

"Fuck off."

Fair enough. It wasn't going to get much better anyways. The entertainment at Shade Street Manor hit new heights

153

with Romeo Adams, but really the key to it was Romeo
snoring and Romeo the grumpy bear when he gets woken up.
Both of these awesome things started a few years before at
the actual wrestling school. As for Romeo in his room, well,
we knew we'd get back to him, as will this segment; you
can't leave a good idea alone.

Not Enough Pictures or Words

Angelina Love once described Romeo Adams' build as
"like Mr. Potato Head." Most of us agreed, but to really
visualize it, you have to picture the Mr. Potato Head upside
down. Romeo had topgut. That is exactly what it sounds
like; he didn't have a droopy belly that hung over his belt, he
had a wide, paunchy gut that was high up near his chest. It
was the damndest thing, not really fat, but wide and it gave
him the look of being fatter than he was, or not as fat as he
was, it was really hard to decide.

Also like Mr. Potato Head, Romeo had almost comically
yet surprisingly strong skinny arms and legs. I saw him
bodyslam JC Owens no less than twice, and JC was a good
350lbs+. Even accounting for JC being able to post on his
opponents' leg with incredible skill, that's an impressive feat.

And again like Mr. Potato Head upside down, Romeo had
no ass. If you drew a straight line down from his shoulders,
you actually would have to curve the line in to hit his ass. He
was a unique specimen.

And then the hair. Romeo had sweet, crimped, flowing,
dark brown locks. They were about shoulder length, not
quite long enough for a pony tail, but formed a poufy mop
that bounced when he walked. He would bathe his locks
immaculately with the best shampoo he could buy at Giant
Tiger (basically a dollar store), then join us for Monday Night
Raw. He would smell of perfume while running a brush
through his muff, anticipating pepperoni and mushroom
pizza.

Romeo in a housecoat, brushing his hair and fingering his
handlebar moustache gave us all the creeps in a funny way.
[Brief interjection: Romeo's status update on facebook as I

write this section. "Come on leafs you really got to prove yourself tonight if u wanna make the playoffs go leafs go." – Romeo Adams' facebook status January 14, 2014 at 7:30 pm]

After describing him, it once again strikes me that he was pretty much a skinnier version of Ron Jeremy, only not as well hung (who is?). He hardly seems like an athlete, but Romeo could go in the ring.

I don't think he ever got blown up, he bumped as smoothly as anyone I ever saw in the ring, and his frog splashes and hurricanrana's were perfect. He sold well, people were always entertained, and I don't recall him ever having or hearing of him being in a bad match. In the ring, Romeo was great. Outside of the ring was where his traits did him little service.

Often what makes you a great wrestler makes you a terrible fit anywhere else in society. Case in point, a guy who looks like a sleazy Ron-Jeremy styled Mr. Potato Head wasn't high on the list of a lot of women. In Cambridge, not many guys were, or so it seemed. At 17 either a girl got pregnant or left town, at least that's what we figured.

Perhaps because it was such a shame seeing his amazing in ring ability and gimmick unappreciated out of context, we never called him by his real name, Adam. We always called him Romeo and still do.   Most of us just called each other gimmick names around the house or school; I was Bomber, Bryan was Stylin, Mike was TJ and later TK or Jewboy, Stefan was Hippie, JC was JC and never Jason, Curtis was Wayne but not always, Marco was Chico then Marco again and permanently, and Ball was just Ball. His real name was Aaron, but he was always Ball. And his brother Romeo was always Romeo, maybe Adam once or twice to Joe AKA Ike Shaw, but hardly ever Adam to anyone who knew him.

His gimmick name has lasted far longer than his career because to us, in fact to anyone who knew him in the business, he was always Romeo and nothing else could outweigh that. You couldn't improve the gimmick God himself had given him. It is legendary.

Unbeknownst to him, Romeo has been the headliner on more road trips and boozy reunions than anyone I've ever known. We've had more laughs talking about Romeo and his

Romeo-ness than any other subject. His legend is loved and, well, legendary.

In the conclusion of Spider-man, (the original with Toby Mcguire and not the poorly done remake featuring awful dialogue and miserably inconsistent storytelling), there is a touching scene between Peter Parker and Mary Jane Watson.

This is a cold, bleak scene in a graveyard, a somber moment where Peter has just helped to bury his best friend's father, a mentor and father figure who Peter had to kill in self-defense. It doesn't get much darker or heavier.

As we watched in silence, the emotional fog was palpable in the theater. Mary Jane Watson finally admits that, after all his effort, she truly loves Peter. But because he cannot endanger what he loves most, he refuses her love without telling her why. As Peter shares the immortal lines, "With great power comes great responsibility," the entire theatre was treated to an even more immortal line of, "Bullshit! Come on, bend her over the tombstone one time for daddy" yelled by Romeo Adams. Nobody laughed… except us.

An equally touching moment was when Stephanie McMahon revealed her pregnancy to Hunter Hearst Helmsley on Monday Night Raw. Before the magnitude of this announcement could really sink in, before we could hear our own thoughts about it, we heard "You're not pregnant you bitch, now get over here and suck some dick." We died laughing. Romeo had struck again. Romeo wasn't saying these things to be funny; Romeo was just thinking aloud.

Most of Romeo's beautiful moments came at Shade Street Manor, the house we lived in after we had all left the ICW school in Cambridge (after I had given up on BC and drove across Canada with The Gnarly Hippy). We rented Mario Party for N64 and spent a couple nights using it as a drinking game. When no one else wanted to play, Romeo made it his mission to finish it all by himself, even though it was a multiplayer game. None of us had the time.

One Sunday and with no new Who's Line episodes to watch, Romeo went on a mission to finish it, playing from 9a.m. until 4p.m. Jer and I were downstairs; I was trying to rearrange my bed of blankets and carpets on the floor, when a piercing "NOOOOOOOOO!!!!!" echoed downstairs. We found ourselves immersed in total darkness. Lights flickered back on and Romeo's curses echoed throughout the house; Romeo had been playing Mario Party so passionately that he had not once bothered to save the game.

"Well, there's the whole day wasted" said Jer. Even Romeo couldn't rally back from that one, but it's inspiring how he was so in the moment for 9 hours that he never bothered to save his game. Who else goes through life with that kind of enjoyment? His enjoyment, his lack of self-consciousness, defined the joy and misery he brought us over the years, starting at the wrestling school. (Yeah leafs win back to back and in regulation good job guys that was an awsome game- Romeo Adams' Facebook update January 14, 2014 9:00 pm. I write slowly.)

There it is.

Romeo Asleep

"What? What?!?"

"What the fuck do you think? I wake you up three times a night every fuckin night. You're snoring. Sleep on your side." Jer had amazing patience with Romeo.

"Fuck off, I don't snore."

"You snore like a fucking banshee. Sleep on your stomach."

"No, you'll kick me in the balls" groaned Romeo.

"I won't kick you because you won't fuckin snore."

"Fine. I want the bottom bunk tomorrow."

"Fuck off. I'm not getting out of bed to wake you up in the middle of the night. Just sleep on your stomach or side for fuck's sake."

"Fine. Fuck."

Every night for 3 months Romeo and Jer had this conversation while living at the ICW school. Romeo snored. Like a chainsaw. He came from a long line of snorers. Rumour had it that once, his family went camping. After three nights of campers losing sleep and complaining about a bear being on the campsite, his family was shamefully ejected; it wasn't a bear, it was his grandmother snoring. If you don't appreciate that sentence, please read it again. That really happened.

Romeo being asleep and Romeo being a grump when he's rudely awoken lead to an exciting discovery which seems entirely obvious now; it was fun, (and probably still would be fun) to violently wake Romeo up from a deep sleep. ("Went and watched Wolf of Wall Street that whole movie is boobs and drugs lol it's messed up" taken from Facebook Monday, January 13, 2014, posted on January 12. I didn't write these memories in order). The reason why Romeo had to be woken up one morning is a little foggy; I think we were going to the buffet and tired of Romeo sleeping in. Maybe we were just going out. Either way Romeo was dragging his ass out of his bunk bed, so it must have been at Ronny's place.

"Get up Romeo" snarled Mike.

"Grumble"

"For fuck's sake, Adam, get up."

Mike was serious because he called him Adam.

"Fuck off, Mike."

Romeo swore at Mike a lot. I'd spice up the language, but the reality is better. Romeo kept it simple and to the point.

"You said you were coming. We're not coming back to get you. Get up."

"Grumble."

"Ohh—K" conceded Mike, aka, TJ when angry.

And with that, TJ walked up to the bed, grabbed the sheets and blankets, and in one fell swoop, yanked them and their contents to the floor, the contents being Romeo. His eyes burst into white plates as he gasped in horror- who wouldn't? Romeo landed on his side on the floor with a big "OOOFFF" but somehow didn't hurt himself. From then on, it became TJ's duty to wake up Romeo whenever he could. He relished it. There were a few classic wake-ups that Mike pulled off. All of them at Shade Street Manor after we'd been at the bar.

A few snores wafted out of Romeo's room, mixing with farts. He was clearly in a deep sleep, dreaming about whatever Romeo's dream about. Mike prowled in gently on hand and knees, sneaking like a panther. When he was about

3 feet away from Romeo's bed (the single bunk now, not a top bunk bed anymore) a mighty "YAAAAA!!" burst out as he leapt high into the hair. Romeo awoke with a terrified "AHHHHHHH!" screaming his heart out just in time for TJ to land on him. Violently thrusting, TJ then sodomized Romeo through his sleeping bag, pummeling his ass with his groin. After about a minute of this, Romeo was finally pissed off enough to do something.

"Fuck off!" Thrust.

"Fuck off Mike!" Thrust, Thrust.

"Fuck off! AAA!" Romeo bucked violently, like a bronco in a ring, with us as the terrified, bloodthirsty crowd. TJ was thrown into the air, thudding back onto Romeo. Romeo then dished out his shitty version of an ass whooping. A flurry of terrible elbows got TJ off of his back and TJ scrambled to flee, but he was too slow and weak from laughing to escape. He collapsed at the doorway and Romeo punished him with a series of punches to the back and ass. TJ couldn't do anything but laugh and yelp as Romeo, in an ironic turn of events, pummeled *his* ass. With a climactic huff from Romeo and yelp from TJ, Romeo scowled at the collection of insensitive jerks.

"Aww Romeo, don't be mad" said Hippy, "here, have some chips."

"Fuck you guys." He seethed at us angrily. We tensed not knowing what was coming next. Nobody breathed. Romeo scowled, huffing and puffing, his fists clenched and ready; he stepped forward, and we yelped, cowering against the walls, shielding our groins and faces. Then Romeo grabbed a handful of chips. When we heard the click of his door and knew it was safe, we all opened our eyes and yelled, "Romeo! YEAH! Ro-me-oh! Ro-me-oh!" We left for the bar. Elated. Sad. We knew the night couldn't get any better.

Romeo was no fool. His instincts for self-preservation became finely tuned and honed by repeated awakenings. TJ attacked weeks later, and Romeo was ready; he hadn't prepared, but he was ready. Mike went for the leaping-yelling-dive attack, but his yell undid his plans. Instead of screaming in terror, Romeo kept his mouth shut, but his body responded violently with a fist straight to Mike's guts. It was incredible; he had gone from completely asleep to vicious, self-defense expert between the split second of TJ jumping and yelling in the air and TJ landing on him. He socked TJ before he even landed!

TJ was not ready for this and immediately scrambled onto the floor, crawling to the door, laughing, yelping, and crying out in agony as Romeo repeatedly caught him with punches to the back and well-placed kicks to the ass. Somehow TJ pushed himself upright against the wall. As he got closer to the door, the bizarre spectacle of a skinny Ron Jeremy-esque Romeo in faded, rotten, purple jockey underwear, teeth clenched in anger, kicking a groaning TJ (who looked almost exactly like Mikey Whipwreck) in the ass was too much for us. We all doubled over, screaming in peals of laughter. Of course none of us jackasses went to TJ's rescue, but to our credit, we were incapacitated by laughter. TJ knew something extra special was happening, and turning to face his attacker, he completely gave up any system of defense and surrendered to laughter as Romeo kept Kung-Fu kicking him in the thighs and gut.

Dangling between Romeo's legs, through the massive hole in his crotch-less from rotting underwear, were Romeo's twin prunes, his mangy hairy, wrinkled, testicles. As we laughed, he kicked harder, and as he kicked harder, his balls swung around more and more, and we laughed harder and harder, a vicious cycle of beats, laughs, and balls. Poor TJ paid the price, cringing and groaning. Romeo went for one final high-axe kick smash on TJ's thigh, giving us all a spectacular view of his balls; we collapsed, dead from laughter and exhaustion. With a "Mike, fuck off!" Romeo turned to leave. In a poetic moment of serenity, his underwear billowed behind him as he farted, then Romeo went to bed.

Yay the Buffet

There was an epic Chinese buffet about a 20 minute drive from the Shade Street Manor; donuts, chicken, chow mein, ice cream, spare ribs, sweet and sour chicken balls--

everything a person could want at a buffet. The impressive spread had at least 30 items plus a salad bar; Romeo ate only 3 items; French Fries, fried chicken, and onion rings. He never went near the salad bar. In all fairness, "You don't win friends with salad" (*Lisa the Vegetarian*).

On another typical Sunday we had all arrived gleefully hung over and hankering for some grease. We gorged at a round table, stuffing our faces with everything possible; TJ, Romeo, Jer, TJ's girlfriend Jana, and maybe JC, I'm not quite sure. In the middle of the table sat a pitcher of water because a) most of us didn't want to pay the extra $2 for unlimited pop and b) the waitress was tired of clearing our dishes let alone bringing us water. (One of my teeth really hurt been holding ice pack on my face for a while feels little better teeth pain is the worst- Facebook January 15, 2014 accessed at 3:07pm). About 45 minutes into the buffet-o-caust, Romeo looked at us and with a, "Whoa, gotta take a dump" left.

A minute later, TJ woefully said, "God, I gotta go in there too, hope Romeo doesn't stink me to death."

We continued the meal as usual; prawns, fried rice, vegetable chop suey, chicken satay all joined the pile up in our guts. I too had to use the facilities. I got ready to go in, but as I don't really like public toilets, I delayed.

A few minutes later I was still hesitating when Romeo rejoined the group. Not more than a minute behind him came TJ with a grin on his face and a look in his eye suggesting he had seen something. For the next few minutes, he ate quietly and kept half an eye on Romeo. Eventually, Romeo pushed back his seat and said, "Gotta get my money's worth. Time for more," and walked up to the buffet.

"What?" we all asked in a hush.

"Romeo was groaning and puffing and took a nasty, greasy dump. Then he got up and walked out without washing his hands," TJ Whispered.

"No."

"YES."

"NO!"

"YES!"

We all peeked over at him. "Don't say anything," said TJ, "let's see what happens." What happened was we all unintentionally smiled joyfully at Romeo as he sat down- our disgusting, stupid, pet, Romeo. We couldn't make eye contact with each other or we'd start laughing.

"Too strange to live, too rare to die" said Jer. We all choked. Jokes of this sort are infectious, but are also the sort of joke where you don't want to ruin the joke by laughing too soon. (Can the leafs do the unthinkable and win 3 in a row only time will tell go leafs go. Accessed from Facebook January 15, 2014 4:10pm)

"What?" said Romeo. He saw the glances and strange looks on our faces.

"Nothing" said Jer, "we just like you."

A few chuckles broke the silence. My bladder was swelling and it hurt because of the pressure of holding in my laughs and all the food I kept stuffing in, but I couldn't miss this. We all stared at Romeo and were trying to be nonchalant by eating our food. Of course it was hard; he's eating chicken wings, onion rings, and French fries, all of them without a fork. I looked down and tried not to laugh or make eye contact with anyone; Jana's face was bright red and getting brighter by the second. TJ had the smuggest look on his face, a look of love and disgust combined with the pure awe of witnessing Romeo at his finest.

"What?" asked an agitated Romeo. "What?"

We chuckled a bit, and Romeo wiped his face with a napkin and then licked his fingers.

"Ahh!" said TJ as we all laughed, looking at Romeo with gleeful disgust.

"Nooo!- aahha ha…. Ah Romeo!" someone laughed.

"What? What? Fuck you guys!" The finger licking continued and we all burst, staring at Romeo as he continued what we felt must have been a performance for our benefit. But it wasn't, it was just Romeo, eating greasy food with his dirty, possibly shit covered fingers, and licking them because he thought we were laughing at how dirty his fingers were— irony to the fullest.

"Whatever. Huh-huh-huh, look at Romeo eating. You guys eat too. Fuck off, I could stare at you guys eating if I wanted to be a dick" he cured. Then, he gave his fingers one final lick and reached for the water pitcher; why use the handle? His four greasy, probably shit-covered fingers splashed into the spout of the pitcher, snarled inside the top rim, and a grimy thumb curled around its edge.

"Ahh, it's infected!" yelled Jer.

"What? FUCK! WHAT?"

"Romeo," said a stern TJ, "you just took a dump and didn't wash your hands."

"What's wrong with you?" asked Jer. Any man would be embarrassed or ashamed; not Romeo. He responded with the only thing he could.

"Fuck off."

Mustering all the dignity he could, he solemnly stood up and turned away from the table. Marching with dignity, he went back to the buffet...without washing his hands.

A Typical Day for Romeo

Romeo had 4 responsibilities in life. A typical day for most of us was really a typical day for him, yet Romeo had a knack for changing the outcome along the way.

His first responsibility was get to work on time, and he almost always woke up late. His alarm clock would go off, and he'd be too asleep or snoring too loudly to hear it. It would ring, he'd miss it, and there would be a pounding on the door of Shade Street Manor. "AH!" Romeo would yell, awake, then run out the door, half the time missing an essential piece of clothing like socks or underwear. First responsibility for the day attained, though barely. He did a passing job at work, but when you learn about what his workplace was like, you realize that passing success there didn't mean much. The rush in the morning was a regular enough occurrence. Which is a logical reason for why his second responsibility, not losing his key, was a regular failure.

Walking home from the gym, coming up the steps.

"Hey Bomber."

"Romeo, what are you doing?"

"I lost my keys again."

"Haha, what? That's the third time this month."

"Fuck, I dunno what happened to them."

"Romeo, not losing your keys is all you have to do."

"Fuck, I dunno where they are."

"'Let's get you inside and out of those clothes, you poor unfortunate man.'" (*Homer Loves Flanders*).

"Fuck off Bomb…"

"Yeah, Romeo!"

This was in Ontario, so it was either really cold or really hot out. The cold was worse because Romeo's run out the door in the morning meant no jacket or too thin a jacket. The summer wasn't so bad. But it made his third responsibility in life difficult to enjoy. Romeo had a tough time staying alive.

The flies were Romeo's main foe in the summer. I guess they came from the pizza boxes that were stacked in the house, but it could have been the industrial-sized garbage can in the kitchen that was open and had everything from house scraps to smelly tuna cans in it. Regardless of how they got there, flies were a noticeable presence. I would go on a rampage sometimes, or TJ would, and we would kill them off, but it didn't last long. One shining achievement of mine was hurling a magazine directly at the ceiling once and killing a fly with it. The best part was that when I threw the magazine it levitated straight up. I think we may have killed as many as 4 at once, but they were elusive and stayed out of reach. We didn't have a fly swatter because it was either in Marco's room or we had broken it in rage after someone had smacked someone else with it. Those things sting!

The flies were always there, safe for the most part but annoying as hell. Funnily, they never seemed to number more than 6, and seldom less than 6. There were always 6 flies buzzing around in the TV room, which doubled as my bedroom for a few months. They were always buzzing around Romeo's head as he sat on the couch, which, combined with a coffee table, doubled as my bed for a few months. Maybe the flies actually came from me now that I think about it.

Disirregardlessly, flies were there and would circle around, come down to steal food, then fly back up to the ceiling and lick themselves clean while we raged and debated whether or not to eat what they had just landed on or not. At one point we thought about just sacrificing a piece of pizza and leaving it out on top of the TV, but they didn't take to it or nobody wanted to give up a slice. Considering how much pizza we wasted every day, and how many boxes littered the house, it shouldn't have been such a big deal. At one point we counted no less than forty old boxes of pizza stacked on top our three fridges, counters, fish tank, and kitchen table. This was hardly surprising.

"Two pies!" Jer would yell into his phone.

"Can you repeat the number?" said the phone in a Stephen-Hawking's wife voice.

"Two PIES!" Jer would yell. The auto dial would work about 50% of the time, prolonging our getting pizza by precious seconds, but Jer would never dial the first 3 times. He had maybe 5 numbers programmed into his phone for voice dial, and "Two Pies" was one of them. He loved springing his phone open, holding it in front of his face, yelling "two pies!" and then gleefully listening to the phone respond with either, "Can you repeat the number?" or confirming the number saying, "dialing" which was met by cheers. Two pies was an unbelievable deal; two extra-large, 3 topping pizzas for twenty dollars, including tip. \

Once, our order was being placed, sometime around September, and the voice on the other end said, "Hold on a minute." This was weird. We'd never had to wait for pizza ordering before; why now? We hung on wondering if we'd pissed them off. Marco had recently complained about a pizza, but it was totally justified; they had sent him pretty much a chunk of dough with nothing but sauce.

"Yep, it's official."

"What is?" asked Jer.

"That's a record. The most pizza anyone has ever ordered in a year."

"Yeah! Hahahaha" Jer told us the news and we were all proud of ourselves, and pretty surprised; we had no idea they actually kept track of those things. It was hardly a mystery why we had a fly farm at Shade Street Manor, but mysterious why only 6 at a time. And those six really liked Romeo.

Romeo's second responsibility, staying alive, was done enthusiastically but ineffectively, much like his eating. He would sit there, greasy and stoned, hardly moving, but giving off warmth and smelling like food, or shit if he had just gotten home from work. Usually he showered immediately when he got home and smelled like Pantene Pro-V- only the best for his luscious locks. Romeo would seem not to notice the flies. He would sit on the couch, stoned, tired, and full from eating his dinner of microwave popcorn and cream soda, and space out as he watched raw. The flies would buzz.

"Buzzzzzzz." Circling him, but his mop of hair hung around his ears and shoulders, so he didn't seem too bothered.

"Buzzzzzz- wzzzzzz," Two flies twirled past him, spiraling like dog fighters before King Kong.

"Welcome to Monday Night Raw!" Jim Ross would yell out from the TV. Only Romeo probably would hear, "Welcome to Mzonday BUZZZt Rawzz!"

We'd watch, the pies would arrive, and we would each tear into our pizza while the flies continued their dance. Most of us would employ a constant fanning motion or spot the flies on their way to the food and block them early. Romeo didn't seem to notice them as they continued to circle his plate, sometimes landing on it, sometimes getting close to his face and pizza covered 'stache. After he had eaten enough pepperoni-mushroom-salami mess and put his pizza away for the time being, he would resume the position on the couch. Raw would continue and finally then...

"FUCK OFF YOU FUCKING FLIES!!!!" exploded Romeo; he kicked his feet and shook his hands through his hair, mussing up his lovely locks with pizza grease and sauce. This explosion lasted no more than three seconds and then he would resume his position once more. His day consisted of pretty much nothing but sitting on the couch from four p.m. till ten p.m. Amazingly, there were only about three such explosions a night, but boy were they exciting! Then Romeo would settle, pretending to be Zen or being Zen and not seeing the flies. Only once did I see him go on a mission and try to kill them; usually he bore the annoyance until he exploded in a passion that could tear any man to rags. He would rage and resolve nothing, but he would be at peace. After seeing his explosion and laughing, we were too. His responsibilities fulfilled, he was content being himself-enthusiastic, alive, and doing just fine by Romeo standards. And he was ready for his final responsibility, work.

A Typical Work Day for Romeo

Romeo worked at some factory in Cambridge. It was either rubber or plastics, I'm pretty sure rubber. It involved basic manual labor skills but paid pretty well. The guys would roll out rubber or roll up rubber or squeegee rubber into mats or recycle rubber mats, something like that. At the time, Romeo made about $16 an hour, if I remember correctly. It must have been close because Jer was making $12 and change per hour and always bitched about Romeo being broke despite making more than he did. That was baffling and annoying, in that order. Romeo didn't have a lot of stuff.

He didn't own a car, he had no debts, he almost never bought new clothes, and he didn't go out on a lot of dates. His rent was about $500 a month, which wasn't particularly high for the year 2001. He also had health care and dental care at work, although he seemed to have a phobia of both. He never went to the dentist, even though he paid for it and his teeth could have used it. Whenever he was sick, he refused going to the doctor.

He sat around the house sick for days, not going in to work, but not wanting to get better either. He would sit on the couch, coughing and barking, then would run to the kitchen sink and hock a loogy in it, which he would sometimes rinse down. When Jer asked him why he didn't go to the doctor, Romeo had no reason other than he just didn't want to be bothered.

One work highlight was when Mike sat home, relaxing and watching TV, getting ready for the gym and his night shift at African Lion Safari. All of a sudden Romeo walked in at 10:30 a.m.. Romeo stunk particularly like burnt rubber.

"I was at work and I was doing some grinding today with a sander. I don't know why, but this guy starts waving at me, so I wave back. Then he starts pointing at me. I can't hear anything cause of the machines and the grinder, so I point back and wave and nod. Then he keeps pointing and waving his hands more and more and I can see that he's yelling something, but I can't hear him or anything, so I just wave back and start working again. Then he runs up and tackles me and starts hitting me. I yell 'What the fuck?' and then look down. My pants were on fire!"

TJ looked at Romeo; his black sweat pants were completely torched. The front thighs of them were gaping holes with charred edges; he hadn't noticed because the pants had left a black residue all over Romeo's pasty white thighs. Mike died laughing; Romeo went up to his room, changed, then came down and sat next to him.

"Romeo, aren't you going to bathe?"

"Why? I didn't get sweaty, I hardly worked today."

"You stink like burnt clothes."

"Fuck off, Mike."

Romeo was deservedly proud of his wrestling ability, so when people at work said it was fake, he'd get pissed. He was working at Cambridge flour or something when a guy started bugging him. Mr. Potato Head in sweat pants, construction boots and greasy hair didn't want to have his career of choice tarnished. He told the guy he could show him a hold if he wanted. The guy kind of chuckled, and said, "Sure, do that" so Romeo did.

Romeo got behind the guy and told him he was going to put a sleeper hold on him. He warned, saying he would pass out but he would be careful when he set him down. Whoever it was laughed and said something to the effect of "OK buddy." Romeo Adams with his twig arms went behind the guy, loosely put the hold on him, and then said, "Ok, here we go" and choked him out in about three seconds! True to his word, he put the guy down gently, and when the guy came to, Romeo said, "Told ya." And that was that; Romeo was deified as a god at work from then on out.

Romeo Makes Tacos

TJ was exhausted; another day of mindless and meaningless labour for a paycheque. Somehow it still didn't seem worth it.

"Bwahahaha HUUUUUUUUH!"

"Good episode of 'Whose Line?' Romeo?"

"Fuck, these guys are hilarious. They're walking on mouse traps, doesn't that hurt?"

"Attaboy, Romes."

Maybe it was the three beers he'd had during work, or the heat of the rubber factory, or the general boredom that sucks you in when you sit around Shade Street Manor and do nothing for weeks on end. Most likely it was because he had just got his paycheque. Romeo, in contrast to TJ, was excited *and* motivated. He had deposited his cheque for real this time instead of just putting an empty envelope into the ATM and laughing that he was paying himself with nothing. That money had been paid back because the bank threatened to take Romeo to court. Now free and clear, food and rent were his only responsibilities. Weed he had, and on this rare occasion, real food as well. He had made the trip down to Food Basics and bought not just a family pack of tacos but also a family sized 3 pounds of ground beef (regular 35% fat, not lean) and a block of marble cheddar cheese(27% fat). Glee! TJ walked upstairs to the bathroom; Romeo had gotten to it first.

"For fuck's sake... ROMEO!"

"What?"

"GET YOUR ASS UP HERE!"

"WHY?"

"YOU KNOW WHY! FUCK!" Stomp, stomp, stomp, stomp, grumble, grumble, stomp, stomp.

"What now, Mike?" Angry.

"You see that disgusting grease ring in the tub? I'm not bathing in that shit. Clean it up."

"It's a bathtub. It gets dirty."

"Look at that filthy ring of grease and shit on the tub. It's like someone made gravy. People don't bathe in that.

There's cleaner and a scrub brush over there. Clean your fucking mess so I can bathe."

One downfall of the shade street manor was the shower situation. There were no showers, only tubs. There was a shower nozzle, but nobody had been motivated to install a shower curtain, so for a while everybody just showered sitting in the tub to avoid mopping up. When the nozzle stopped working altogether, it was replaced with a four litre jug. Bath time was kind of fun, sitting there, scrubbing like a little kid, then dunking a tub of water over your head. Peeing in the tub was a little grosser than before. I still did it.

The other catch to the bathrooms was that they didn't lock. You had to be quick when you were getting ready to leave the tub, or someone would kick open the door and splash you with a bucket of whatever could be found. It started with cold water, but graduated to spaghetti sauce, ketchup, mustard, BBQ sauce, Kool-Aid, and eventually A5-35 lotion. I was the victim of that last one and didn't think anything of it at first.

"Eh, so I'll smell nice. At least it's not in my eyes" I thought to myself. I should have remembered my experience with pepper spray. The burning! I cursed Jer and then figured I should make him feel my agony, so I got out of the tub, chased him around his room and up the stairs completely naked. He bailed out the front door and collapsed, laughing, on the sidewalk.

"I just pictured you tackling me naked out on the street and couldn't breathe," he confided. I didn't want to get arrested or dirtier, so I stopped at the front door fully nude.

"Ha- Nice!" said Marco, barely looking up from his dinner. I don't think a day went by when we didn't see at least one other person's penis. 5 guys lived in the house. Jer once said, "Bomber, I think I've seen your dick more than mine in the past week." It was barely an exaggeration. We hardly ever saw Romeo's though because he always got home and bathed first, and we didn't want to get him dirty because he might not bother to get clean again. It would, after all, be our fault. For now, Mike just wanted to bathe.

"Fuck, Romeo, I'm tired of this shit. Every day you leave a ring on the tub and a swamp on the floor and stink up the bathroom polluting everything while getting clean. Look at that soap, its brown! How is that possible? It's white soap! Look at your toothbrush, is it alive? FUCK!"

The tirade from TJ went on and on. He later made a set of rules for the bathroom, starting with, "I will clean up my shit properly from the rim of the toilet," and progressing from there. Other great entries included, "I will clean up after I pee on the floor", "Shaving stubble is not decoration for the sink", and "My dirty wet toothbrush does not belong on Mike's shelf." For now, Romeo did as he was told, de-scummed the ring around the tub, and went back downstairs.

For Mike (TJ) the tub still required a good ten minute pre-rinse before he could sit in it without feeling contaminated.

He zoned out and smelled the clean perfume of his shampoo, conditioner, and body wash. As he left the pristine tub, he walked out into the surprisingly fresh aroma of Romeo's beef wafting up from the kitchen. After he got dressed he looked at the spaghetti sauce boiling on the stove.

"Romeo, I thought you were making tacos."

"I am. That's the meat."

"Didn't you drain it?"

"Drain what?"

"Oh god…. Hahaa, yeah Romeo!"

The beef stewed and simmered in a pool of grease and water combined with the package of taco seasoning that Mr. El Paso had decided was the genuine ethnic thing. Mike blasted a duo of pizza slices in the microwave and went into the living room, settling in to watch Monday Night Raw. Jer was home.

"Deyp" said Mike.

"Yo."

"What's the main tonight?"

"Triple H and 'Taker."

"Not Angle?"

"No, changed. You wanna order pizza?"

"I'm eating pizza."

"I can see that. What are you eating for lunch tomorrow?"

"…." Mike responded with a shift of his eyes.

"Yeahhhh," Jer purred as he picked up his phone, yelling, "TWO PIES!"

"Can you repeat the number you wish to call?" said Mrs. Hawkings.

"TWO PIIES!"

"Dialing" said the Robot voice.

"YAY! Such an awesome phone!"

"Fuck Mike, move over."

"Jesus…" The phone dropped to Jer's side, eyes wide, "Romeo, what are you doing?"

"Eating dinner" he said with a thud.

Romeo sat down to the coffee table with 3 paper plates delicately balanced. One was covered in cheese, one covered in heated up taco shells that were clamming shut; the third was 2 paper plates doubled up yet sagging under a mound of unstrained taco meat.

"Romeo, didn't you drain the meat?" asked Jer.

"Fuck, stop bugging me."

"Romeo, that's disgusting!   You're going to give yourself a heart attack. How do you not have one vegetable—oh hold on. I'll get pepperoni, sausage, and beef. And on the other one"- Jer smothered the phone against his chest, "Mike, whaddya want?"

"Ham, Pineapple, and Chicken. Tell them not to skimp on the meat either."

"Ham, pineapple, chicken, don't skimp on the pineapple"

"NO! FUCK YOU!"

"K, 30 minutes? Sounds good."

"You son of a bitch."

"Don't worry, I'll buy."

Romeo began his grease-feast, glad the guys had something else to argue about. Greasy meat went into a taco shell, on went cheese, and the taco died in his greasy mouth. He wished he had packed over another plate to stop dripping grease on himself, but his shirt was dirty anyways. He wiped his hands on it, on his greasy handlebar moustache, and on the corners of the couch. A family pack has 18 tacos. Romeo gleefully munched away as Jeremy and Mike tried not to look or hear the noises.

"Fuck Romeo, you eating is making me sick. Breathe through your nose."

"Fuck off Jer."

"Look at you, you're disgusting. You're filthy, you're dropping shit all over the couch and floor. It's fuckin gross."

"Whatever. Tacos rock."

"The Taco's aren't the problem."

Slurps, crunches, and sucking noises peppered with belches and stomps, Romeo cheered on the wrestlers on TV, laughing, almost choking at one point, and raping the tacos on his plate. The two pies arrived, Jer paid. He and TJ stopped eating after about 4 slices.

"UGHHH, I ATE THEM ALLLLL!" groaned Romeo.

"Ha, Yeah Romeo!" It was easy to picture the shards of taco shells, greasy meat, and stewed cheese floating around in Romeos topgut, but better not to.

"Romeo, that was a family pack," chastised Mike, "that's not healthy."

"Jeeebus Romeo, look at that pool of grease on your plates. Imagine how much you ate," said Jer.

"Fuck, I know, it was so good though. God I'm stuffed. BUUUURP! I need a beer to wash it down. Hahaha."

Everyone smiled and chuckled. The main event was starting. As Triple H and the Undertaker battled it out, Romeo continued to burp, and a few smacks and slaps echoed as the excitement built in the match. There was an odd slurping, the sound of Romeo putting back an Old Milwaukee beer. Even drinking a beer sounded disgusting when Romeo did it. Let Romeo suck his fingers, Mike thought; he was used to tunin this out. However, he couldn't tune out Jer's fearful and dumbstruck clawing at him.

"Ow. Fuck. OW! Stop hitting me."
Mike finally turned to Jer, "What the--- oohh Jesus! NO!"

Mike dove over the coffee table, and with a desperate slap of his hand, a wave of juice and grease splattered all over the wall and couch.

"Fuck Mike, WHAT! FUCK OFF!"

"NO! BAD ROMEO! YOU DON'T DRINK TACO GREASE! NOW CLEAN THAT MESS UP."

"Romeo, how are you still alive?" asked Jer, "Fuckin mongrel."

Romeo is still alive and thank god for that. He made day to life interesting and I've never met a nicer guy. Life was somewhat eventful and semi-fulfilling when I returned to Ontario.   Living in a house with 4 other guys, training, practicing wrestling at Jer's school, and feeling accepted. Joe's school had yet to fold or be shut down, and the promotions were still hard to convince I should be booked. They would ask for footage; mine was limited, so only the guys they knew got booked. But at least we had an escape. For one weekend, for one glorious weekend, we managed to go beyond being poor young men or failed dreamers or struggling wrestlers. We were Barnyard cocks.

The Animal Olympics

Our award plaque from the Animal Olympics. Note the Epicness.

"**B**omber, you have no idea. It's not like anything on this earth."

Sure Romeo.

"Bomb, you need more booze. You drink 24-7."

Whatever Ball. I've got 3 bottles of sherry wine- the cheapest booze around; it'll get me totally drunk for a total of $12 for the whole weekend. What else do I need?

"Bomboid, you're going to need more clothes."

This coming from Jer, the guy who had gotten so drunk that one year he lost his clothes, diarrhead all over the side of his car and fell in it, walked back to his tent naked, and nobody batted an eye. Clothes. Pfft. As far as I was concerned, I was set. I had a change of clothes, a blanket, Ball was going to share a tent with me, and I had enough booze for 3 nights of typical drinking with the boys. What could go wrong... what possibly... what...the...hell...

It all starts with the name; this weekend, forget being human. At the Animal Olympics, I'm a Barnyard Cock.

"Bomber, you got your weens?" asked Jer.

"Yeah, of course." Weens (wrestling trunks) are a tradition at a wrestling get together, appropriate or not.

"Sweet. It's going to be classic. Bring a sweater."

Bring my skimpy wrestling underwear and a sweater? This was odd advice; it was May in Ontario, it was already 20 degrees Celsius. I was pretty sure may long weekend would be about 25 Celsius, plus with all the fun and partying, who would notice?

"No glass allowed beyond this point. If you got glass, you gotta dump it."

"Absolutely, forgive my friend here, it's his first time."

Dan, TJ's older brother, or Hog as we called him, looked at me and winked. "I got it." He grabbed my bottle, pretended to twist off the cap, and then pretended to pour it into a plastic 7-Up bottle inside of the cooler. The guy who was going to drive us to our campsite was already drunk or high, so in about 15 seconds, Dan yelled, "all done" and pretended to toss the glass bottle into the back of a car. 2 bottles of Sherry were all secure in the bottom of a cooler, under my 2 packs of hotdogs, some buns and chips-- all the food I needed for the whole weekend. Pigger, the other captain, tucked the last bottle in his coat; I offered him some as exchange for his help. He looked at it, asked what it was, then said, "No fuckin thanks."

I went to the animal Olympics twice; I can't say which thing happened which time with absolute certainty. Between both I spent a total of 6 days completely ruined out of my mind, having out of body experiences, drinking all day, and never really understanding the greatness of everything happening. I'd like to say I'd live it all again, but there are a few parts I really wish I could leave out. Disirregardless, it happened and I'm glad it did.

Bonding and Bonging

The first night was the night for settling in; not for us. To kick of the campaign in a big way, it began with a beer bonging competition. Eehah (I have no idea how to spell it) vs Jer vs Stumble vs Slim. What a great idea. Beer bonging is a great way to kick off a night of drinking; amazingly, everyone had their own bong. As I looked around, I realized that everyone here is pretty damn prepared. It's not solely speed bonging these guys are going for either; this is about endurance.

Everyone loads a beer into their bong and passes the buck onto the next guy to drink after he's slammed his. Rounds 1, 2, and 3 take all of 3 minutes and my jaw starts to drop; these guys can drink! Rounds 4, 5 and 6 all take about 4 minutes together. That means that each of these guys has had 6 beers in 7 minutes. The empties get tossed into the general direction of the recycling pile that we are planning on making, which will later serve as both a recycling pile, open-air urinal, and later a splash zone for 1 unlucky person.

At round 8, which took 20 minutes, Stumble succumbs to wisdom. He's got 3 more nights of this; eight beers are a good showing and he's out. He is now referee. Eehah, a large, cushy Winnie-The-Pooh, is in fine form; he's still standing, laughing, and guzzling down the beers. Jer goes for a 9th, but just can't do it and pukes a bit on the ground beside the campfire. Nobody cares about the puke, but Hog is visibly upset that Jer is out so soon "I had money on you, Fritz!" he yells. It comes down to Eehah and Slim. Despite being outweighed by at least 150lbs, slim holds his own battling a walking version of Jabba-the-Hut. At this point, it is clear that the booze is taking its toll.

Slim is fiery, pretty sure he's capable of going for a dozen more, and for his benefit, Stumble has decided to start holding the bong for him as he slams down the beers. This is great because Stumble is at least a foot taller than slim, who's the epitome of the wiry little man full of spite. He's more than willing to do his part as Stumble puts the end of the bong into his mouth, props Slim up against the tree, and on Slim's thumbs-up signal, which is more like a 3 year old making a fist, forces the tub of the bong up in the air and the booze down Slim's throat. It is beautiful how guys can work together; we all choke back tears and Slim chokes down the booze, pushes off the tree and pounds his chest. "That's TEN mother-fucker!"

Eehah somehow is still standing and bonging on his own. Number eleven down! He pounds his chest too, yelling "One MORE!" It's hard to believe these guys are teammates, but they are, and everybody relishes this great boost in team morale. A good crowd of about 7 of us are soaking up the future misery of these partiers. Any rational person would step up, tell both guys to stop the madness, and book a stomach pump at a hospital. Not us. Not The Barnyard Cocks. We just yell, "One More Beer! One More Beer! One More Beer!" Slim steps up to the plate.

His eyes are shaky, crossing, and rolling around his head like a googley-eyed sticker. There is no way he should do a beer, but there is a will; teamwork, which is what this is all about, makes up the gap. He hands the bong to Stumble, who starts loading up another beer, but Eehah is protesting, or mumbling and pointing.

"He's right," says Jer, "He's gotta slam the beer himself. This isn't a team competition."

Never mind the decorum of society that we've ignored all day by stepping into this place; this isn't 'Nam and there are rules. Stumble looks at his friend; Slim is in no state of mind

178

to drink and is dangerously close to being dead in the morning. He does the only thing he can do, hands him the bong, yells at him as loudly as he can, "DRINK THIS!" and steps back. Slim is lucky; he falls back into the tree, puts one end of his bong into his mouth, and through some supreme human effort, raises the other end triumphantly into the air.

Up until this point, the beers have been slammed down with no breathing; things have changed. Slim chokes, and chokes, and chokes, but finally chokes down his beer, raises his bong into the air, and then slides off of the tree and onto his back then, through the grace of god, rolls onto his face and starts puking. Right next to someone's tent.

"YEAHHHHH!" the cheer echoes. Eehah is non-plussed, but somehow makes a valid point through pointing, grunting, and mumbling.

"He's right," says Jer, "Slim had help with his last one. If Eehah can put this one down even with help, he's the winner." Reason has spoken.

Another can of Old Milwaukee goes into his bong. The bubbling land mass stands to his feet, and some guy holds up him on one side, Stumble on the other. Fair is fair; we are, after all, part of the same team. With a nudge and a sudden snap, Eehah pops the bong up into the air, inhales the beer, flexes like Hulk Hogan, yells, "YEAAHHHHH!!!" towards Slim, and then collapses backwards into his camping chair. Instantly drool starts pooling on his shoulder.

Slim for his part responds with a fist pump from the pool of puke he's pouring; he didn't see the last drink go down, he just heard Eehah yelling and figured out what happened, and cheered from his catatonic state, the epitome of sportsmanship. What a team.

The rest of us soak in the beauty of the spectacle. Just as disappointment and sorrow begins to soak in, a loud gurgling noise floods out. Eehah, head on his shoulder, starts

Eehah's final bong. Note the future vomit.

to cough while his guts are rumbling like a cow. With some
quick thinking, redheaded guy goes over and pushes him ever
so slightly over in his chair; Eehah can puke safely, and puke
he does! It comes in waves of three- one huge watery
belch waterfall of beer, one dry-heave, and a smaller
aftershock of puke-beer that looks like water. Then comes
the long pause, and as we all see the heaving start again,

"YEAHHH!" erupts from the crowd of us seven idiots.
Another huge watery puke, a dry-heave, and an aftershock. It
seems that each puke is about a beers worth of vomit, and
Eehah doesn't seem to be enjoying it nearly as much as us; in
fact, he's not doing much of anything, and if it were not for
the constant waves of vomit that keep flowing out of him,

we'd probably be worried he was dead. He's clearly way too drunk and suffering from alcohol poisoning, but he's not dead; dying, maybe. Dead, no.

"YEAHHHHH!" another wave.

It occurs to us all that Eehah is puking exactly where we are going to be spending the majority of our time over the next few days, about a few feet away from the campfire, but nobody wants to risk moving him; redheaded guy makes it clear that he's already done his part, and nobody else is offering. The only guy who might make sense to move him is Slim since he's already covered in puke, and for a brief moment he actually manages to right himself and sit up with his back against the tree. This is met with a rousing cheer of encouragement from us assholes.

Slim gives us a fist pump, pukes all over himself, then falls back over onto his side, his face down in the pool of beer he has been vomiting up for the last ten minutes. That is meet by another cheer, and an even louder "YEAHHHH!" when Eehah treats us to puke wave number 12 or so.

The scene looks tragic, a horror picture or torture scene from a B-grade movie. But it makes us proud. It makes us happy. And as the puke waves continue well into the moring, with Eehah puking more than any human I have ever seen, it does something great for The Barnyard Cocks. It makes us a team. Sleep. Morning came to soon.

"Bomber, what happened?" Jer. 8:30 a.m.

"Whare we... huh? No." The world shakes.

"Jesus, look at that mess. Why is Romeo's tent down like that?" Not that it mattered.

"Ball... Ball's idea. Was good idea. Dead?"

"I'm not driving to the hospital again," a far-off voice yells.

"Romeo! You alive in there?" Romeo wasn't the yeller; we had to check. Grumbling and with a little shuffling as the collapsed tent, more really of one big wet sleeping bag, breathed and heaved up on Romeo's gut, then sunk down.

"Fuck off."

"Romeo, we've got the bell ring in twenty minutes. We need everyone."

181

"Bhbhhe." Followed by a fart and what looked like Romeo turning onto his back. Or stomach. We couldn't tell.

"Needs his beauty sleep." Ball spoke for once.

"Romeo, what the fuck?" said Jer, and with that, we poor misfits leave for what was easily the stupidest event ever held at the animal Olympics, The Bell Ring.

The Bell Ring

On our way to the bell ring, Jer relived how Romeo had done this the year before.

"He's amazing. He stays up until 5, a drunkin' varmint completely blasted, shouting, hooting and hollerin' all alone, eating mushrooms, then sleeps for the whole next day while everyone is up. So amazing."

Through the fog the center plaza of the campsite emerged. The crowd mills, wafting booze with noise and noise with booze; the air hung with the mix of both, intoxicating us as we arrived.

"I feel terrible." I said. It was my first grammatically correct sentence of the day.

"Have some breakfast," said Jer, handing me a Kahlua Mudslide. Sobriety wouldn't help anyways.

I took a drink, retched, swallowed it, then took another swig. The booze from the night and the 9:00 a.m. bell ring time made the sludge difficult to get and keep down. The Animal Olympics last for 3 days, and in order to attend, you have to be on a team. The only rules strictly applied to the campsite and contest were no bottles, no theft, and no fights. Everything else was fair game—drugs, nudity, stupidity, debauchery, filth, etc. It was like a Burning Man festival in May in the woods of Ontario but without the damn dirty hippies, just working class partiers. People drive in with trailers, cabins, mobile homes, and trucks.

They each get their campsite and deck it out according to what they want; there are raves, Christmas lights, DJ's and dance floors, huge meshes of lights hung in trees,

The bell ring. Note the high level of safety.

speakers, costumes, people wandering sneakily selling drugs (they snuck around to avoid getting kicked out as Martin, the owner, never gave them the ok; if he actually was allowing drug sales on his property, he would be in heaps of trouble) and popping in and out of each other's campsites.

People show up, keep it legal (mostly) and party as hard as possible. So what was all the point of this? The point (not that it really needs one) is pride; it is a 3 day drinking contest where teams battle it out to see who can drink the most in the most ridiculous ways on the most ridiculous teams of 40 people. And the teams were ridiculous; there were the Chemical Cats, The Eager Beavers, The Illegal Eagles, The Pigfuckers, the Horny Goatweeds, a whole bunch more that pop in and out of my head, and of course, The Barnyard Cocks. For me, this name fit like a glove; when I was a kid, I dreamed of being a pro wrestler, and my favourite character name (at the time) was Barnyard Ben. I must admit, it's still my email address—I just can't let it go.

Of all the teams, the one to beat was the Illegal Eagles. They were champions for about 5 years in a row, a peppery mix of old bikers and their ladies who drank and drank and drank and then showed up to the drinking contests to drink much, much more. As returning champions, they knew the games and had most of the same players as the years before; they knew all the tricks.

Our team was about a quarter rookies, guys like me who were already hung over, confused, and a little skeptical about the safety procedures underway at the Bell Ring.

"Everybody has to stand around the climbers or you'll be disqualified," shouted Martin. Martin was the organizer of the whole festival.

"Climbers? What?" I got a sinking feeling.

"Bomber, you're not climbing, don't worry."

"Pigger, what is going on?"

"Bomb, it's simple; you hoist up ball and he'll hold onto the pole. Then you hoist up slim with ball standing on his shoulders. Then Stumble will stand under them and they'll ring the bell."

"What?"

"Just follow my lead."

"Ready?" asked Martin.

"YEPP! YEAH BARNYARD COCKS!" Shouted Dan.

Ball actually looked focused; I was confused, didn't remember who slim was, nor how he was going to levitate up in the air with 160 pounds on his shoulders. DING!

"Whooosh!" up went Ball, no problem. However, the delegation of who was holding him and who was holding slim was completely forgotten. I struggled to hold Ball above my head by his muddy shoes as he hung onto the pole for dear life. He apparently forgot that Slim was coming in underneath him, so he started trying to clamber up the greased pole and swing at the bell all on his own. He was about 8 feet below it but convinced he could do it; he couldn't.

Slim, appearing under Ball, tried to keep his position steady so Ball could place his feet on his shoulders. Ball was still looking up; as he tap danced on Slim's head, Pigger yelled, "Ball, stand still!" Gravity forced Ball down and he sat on Slim's head; the remaining 6 guys who weren't spotters tried to heave Slim up. He wasn't ready, so he just crumpled under the extra weight and folded in half, jamming his shoulder into the pole as balls feet slipped out onto Slim's back.

I grabbed Ball's feet again, put them on Slim's shoulders, and held them there. On Pigger's count we all grabbed Slim again and hoisted him into the air, only he slid up between ball and the pole, so Ball's ass and legs dangled out while he clung onto the greasy pole for dear life. Ball didn't have too much faith in the drunk safety spotters either.

Finally, Stumble squeezed his way underneath them; a big boy of about 250lbs, he was a sturdy oak while they got their bearings, straightened up and Ball used Slim's head and neck as a springboard to leap up. On about his fourth attempt, a very excited Ball rang the bell; an exceptionally pissed off Slim slid down on Stumbles, wiped the mud off his shoulders, and with a, "that fuckin sucked" went back to his breakfast beer. This whole disaster took about 30 seconds. Luckily for us, we got one more chance; unfortunately for us, cutting our time down to 20-odd seconds really didn't offer much improvement.

We were dismayed as the Chemical Cats, Illegal Eagles, and Sweaty Hog Nuts all destroyed our best time. In reality, we should just be happy about the fact that nobody died. I really want to impress the nonsense of what happened at that event alone. A team would try and send a person 15 feet into the air in order to ring a bell. There were no safety nets, not a single person who was sober, no plan of how to catch anyone or anything- this was not a cheerleading rehearsal- and only soft, wet gravel to break the fall. If someone actually did fall, they would s mash into someone else who wasn't looking and probably break something if not worse. The one safety measure was that the people who were watching were required to put their hands up into the air while they watched, as if this would prevent any disaster from actually happening. Unsurprisingly, The Bell Ring was pulled as a competition from The Animal Olympics.

Our team of drunk/high/hung-over idiots went up and hoisted three guys up into the air to ring a bell in order to win a one-time prize of more booze and get a shot at a 3 day grand prize of even more booze. If we survived all the events, we would still have to survive being far too drunk to know what we should or should not do in a wonderland of pixie dust, drugs, booze, and idiocy- the same problem for every team. What could possibly go wrong? Our time didn't get better.

After 3 more teams beat our time handily, we shuffled back to camp, a little broken and very hung over; Romeo was all smiles eating breakfast hot dog.

"How'd it go?" he asked.

"Fuck, we needed you Romeo." chastised Jer. Romeo just smiled.

Romeo was the only person on the team who ate better than usual at the Animal Olympics. Instead of just chips, popcorn, weed, and beer, he added the valuable protein from hotdogs, the vitamins found in ketchup (not mustard, mustard is gross according to Romeo), the essentials nutrients of Sunny D, and the rainbow of vitamins found in magic mushrooms to his diet. He was happy and healthier than ever.

I was now in a weird state, one that I would encounter and have to power through many times in the upcoming weekend. If I went back to bed, I would wake up midday tired and more hung over, and then have to get exceedingly drunk in order to not feel so terrible, which would make the next day the same dilemma only it would be much, much worse. If that happened a second time, the whole weekend would make me feel about a hundred times worse than it should. As it was, I would suffer through a week-long recovery no matter what.

If I went back to bed, I would awake begging for death and a shower. I looked at Romeo eating his hot dog and all-dressed Lays. It was cool outside, but not cold, sunny, but not bright, and the fire looked inviting, but not for long. My one blanket wasn't really warm enough to keep me in bed anyways, so I did the logical thing. I grabbed a bottle of sherry wine. I would hermit by the fire to think over my problem of how drunk to get and by when. Life could be very tough at the Animal Olympics, and I was less than 24 hours in.

As I sat there, Pigger or somebody posted a schedule they had drawn on the back of a cereal box; it had the weekend's events written on it. There were huge chunks of "nothing" written onto it, but between the nothings were the real challenges. Every day there were 3 drinking events we had to attend if we wanted the grand prize 4 kegs of Ambassador beer plus a bottle of Whiskey. The events had to be attended by at least 20 members to maintain eligibility or, in our eyes, the whole weekend was a bust.

I looked over the events; Tricycle Race, Ski Race, Tug-of-War, Pussy Stampede, Ice Block, Obstacle Course and Change Race. On both Saturday and Sunday, the first event happened at 9:00 am, the next at 12:00pm, the Next at 3:00 pm, and one at night on Sunday at around 7 or so. Next up was the tricycle race, a classic bit of exercise and fun made much more adult by the two responsibilities of every team. First, each was required to bring their own working tricycle; second, each team had to drink. Hard.

I Want to Ride My Tricycle

The year before I competed, Ball and Jer had dominated the tricycle race. Naturally, this year they were the guys for the job again. The only problem was Ball had broken his ankle earlier in the year, so he didn't have the flexibility to actually ride the trike. However, after his astounding performance the year before, and his drunken guarantees that he would do awesome, he was given the starting position. The problem that became apparent very quickly was that despite the great intentions of the riders, the tricycle sucked.

The course for the tricycle race couldn't have been simpler. Instead of building some ambitious, disastrous, expensive track, Martin just had the teams ride in circles around his Gazebo. It was an eye-pleasing 4 feet high, so every spectator could watch as teams cheered their trynamic duos. 12:00 noon; time for mayhem.

The game is simple. Two competitors from each team take turns hustling around the gazebo on their own tricycle. One partner sits while the rides, each partner has to do three laps. What makes it more challenging is that every time a lap is completed, the seated partner and the tricycle rider have to slam two large cups of delicious Ambassador Beer, with 3 of the 12 beers spiked with 151 proof or tequila. It didn't matter which partner drank, so long as the beers disappeared into someone before the next lap was started.

As I watched the players secretively discussing their plans, I started to think a whole lot more was going on than a bunch of idiots getting loaded. Some teams had the first rider drink all the first 6 so the next guy could ride sober, some teams split the beers 50-50, some 75-25 so that the first rider drank slightly less his way around, etc. The first competitor did all 3 of this laps then switched until all 6 laps were done and 12 beers were gone. The big catch that kept more than a few teams from winning was that nobody was allowed to puke; if you did, you were disqualified. This really raised the stakes, which, ironically or fittingly, lead to more puking.

Jer sat and Ball tested the trike; honestly, it did not look good. Ball looked uncomfortable, but Jer readied his two beers in his hands. Jer stands, to this day, as the fastest beer drinker I've ever seen. I tried, oh lord how I tried, (*The Otto Show*) to beat him drinking out of bongs, out of cups, out of bottles; I couldn't.

I wasn't so much a big drinker as a big consumer, used to eating and drinking large amounts, but I learned quickly the key to slamming down beer was to just open up your throat and let it go down without actually swallowing. You have to just inhale the beer. Jer taught me that, but I could never quite beat the master, so it made sense that he would slam the first two beers then Ball would be mostly sober to ride, and Jer (we imagined) could recover in the three minutes before he rode. It seemed like a great idea at the time. The competitors lined up, somehow aware enough to listen to the start gun in Martin's hand; "BANG!"

Chaos.

Lap # 1.

There isn't enough room for riders easily pass without collisions. People try and one person falls off of the gazebo. Despite falling four feet, he gets up and continues the race, even though he is now disqualified. Jer slams two beers.

Lap #2

Ball is clearly wincing as he pedals around the pillars and really starts to wince when his foot slips and another racer crashes into him. He sucks it up, makes it to Jer, who slams a beer and hands him the other, saying "It'll make your foot better." We all believe it.

Lap #3

The booze is now starting to take effect; the circle is tight, and the competitors dizzy. I'm feeling dizzy because somebody gave me a couple of swigs of Snake Bite to drink while I was standing there in a haze. I look up at the sky and realize that while it's not particularly cold, it's not very warm either. In a surreal moment of peace I look at the large clouds drifting overhead, pause to consider god and the meaning of alcohol and drugs, then look back as Ball finishes lap #3 and slams both beers himself. There are in about fifth place. Now it's up to Jer.

Lap #4

Jer, a burly 220lbs, doesn't fit very well onto a children's tricycle. How we ended up with a tiny trike despite having a whole year to plan this is starting to become a bit of a concern. Some teams have full sized adult rides to tear and cut corners in. Why do we have a kid's tricycle? Because we failed to plan. As hard as he tries, Jeremy makes the trike do more waddling than moving. While he pedals like a madman, he's stuck by his super thick quads not fitting under the handlebars. As he huffs and grunts, his taint and balls are the only things touching the seat. It looks painful and Fritzy is not enjoying himself, but givin' 'er while we cheer. Competitors are not allowed to move forward if their feet are touching the ground. A few teams get away with it momentarily, but Jer keeps to the rules, his legs blurring dynamos. Confusion compounds with each lap. A few players have already disqualified themselves, one for pushing with his feet, one for falling off the gazebo, and one more for busting the wheel on his tricycle. Jer coasts in then slams a beer with Ball. Round four done.

Lap #5

Each competitor has had at least 3 beers in about 3 minutes, some a good deal more. Jer has had 5 in 3 minutes but holds it all together in fine form as he continues to waddle-pedal his ass around the pillars and competitors. Halfway through his lap, an expected obstacle finally appears--puke. A Pie-Eyed Platypus pukes immediately after slamming a beer. Now pretty much every player is going pedal through it, smearing the slick sickness into a sheet of ice. This is bad. Worse is the trickle-down effect. Since one person has puked on the course, it really isn't an issue of taboo anymore. Inhibitions gone, the puke begins to spew, partially because of the nauseating effect of smelling and seeing splats of puke on the course, and partially because this is lap 5. People are feeling downright sick. The move of the day comes when, as one of the Chemical Kats is about to pass an Seaty Hog Nut, the hog turns his head and blasts out a stream of watery-beer-puke towards the outside edge of the gazebo. The Chemical Kat tries to power through but takes the blast full on his legs and the front wheel of his trike, making his tire start to spin since all the torque is on the front wheel now painted with slimy vomit. He gets stuck spinning there for a half second and then blasted with a second wave of puke as he pedals as fast as he can- he will not get disqualified for putting his feet down!- and creeps slowly through the cascade of vomit washing over his legs. His tires spin madly. It seems an eternity of puke as both players, the puke maker and the puke catcher, are disgusted but happy at what is happening, each trying to avoid it in their own way; while the Chemical Kat starts to dry heave and the Sweaty Hog Nut finishes puking, one of the Illegal Eagles rides up behind them both. Making a quick assessment, he swerves to the left, avoiding both the puke and the players, and then rides into his pit stop for his last beer. Fritzy is not far behind, and now the Chemical Kats and Sweaty Hog Nuts are both disqualified, although neither abandons the course.

Lap #6

Lap 6 is all about speed; Ball is starting to dry heave and yawns up at the sky, avoiding the sight and smell of the swamp of vomit now on deck. He just has to hold it until Jer finishes, then he can puke all he wants. Jer spins as fast as he can through the obstacles of mud, puke, spilled beer, someone's sandal, and rain. He can't gain on the Illegal Eagle, but pulls in and powers down a last beer with Ball before they stand triumphant. Second place. We're all impressed, and happy, though Ball's ankle is throbbing. If we can dominate a few other events, we're sure to do well. And one event we feel confident about is the Tug-O-War.

Between the tug-o-war and the tricycle race we sat and drank. There's nothing else I remember, unless that was when I ate the mushrooms. I'm not sure.

Pulling for Freedom

The Tug-O-War was the only contest that didn't involve booze, so it was a bit of a let-down in one regard, but in every other way it was awesome.

Our team consisted of a bunch of pro wrestlers, a few big monsters like Stumble and Eehah, and a gang of scraggly drinkers who would fight you even if they had no hope in hell of winning. Ten tuggers per team was the rule for player numbers and, given our pounds per person, this was a big advantage. The whole contest was simple; each team pulled and battled until the final two met. It was like a final four tournament for the NCAA basketball, only instead of basketballs there was a rope, and instead of highly trained athletes at the top of their game there were highly drunk non-athletes scraping the bottom of sobriety. Both competitions are all heart though, and the accompanying party probably about equal. I can't say this for sure, but after winning the national championships in Rugby 3 times, I know how hard athletes party, particularly Rugby guys. In the immortal words of a buddy, they pre-drink harder than most people drink. That is true. I've seen it and been it. I don't think basketball players party quite as hard as that, but The Barnyard Cocks come close. I feel comfortable saying The Animal Olympics crews were good at celebrating.

In the Tug- O-War, our advantage was that we had a few guys on our team who actually gave a fig about being in shape and others who were some very large boys. I was about 230lbs Jer 220, Dan a solid 235, Stumble close to 300, as was Eeha, and to top it off, we had JC Owens, who was 400lbs + by himself. There really wasn't a way to get more weight on our side of the rope, and we also had a secret weapon; a coordinated pull.

Usually, tug-o-wars are just a bunch of random people pulling without any coordination or thought put into it. We decided to have a cadence of one-two-three, pulling on three.

All we had to do was dig in our heels, lean back, count, and then pull on three. Our leaning back was enough to take the strain of most teams pulling on the rope, especially the Chemical Kats who, as their name might imply, were a bunch of ravers and young partiers.

They were cool and set up one of the best tents/raves at the whole event, but as far as the contest goes, we steamrolled them, as well as a couple other teams. We beat one team so badly that we all ended up running into the fence a good twenty feet behind our last man, JC. We sandwiched him into it, jumping around, hollering and hooting like we'd won the world cup or something.

To keep us inspired for the next round, Slim passed around a bottle of whiskey. We all took long pulls then yelled as we yanked down our pants and waved our privates at anyone nearby. It was strange. We reflected between

You're Gonna Hurt Yourself

The Tug-O-War. Note the supreme effort. Pictured: Slim leaning in yelling, JC on the rear of the rope, Jer in the Viking Hat, me up front.

rounds, huddling with our drinks. I kept running to the front of the mound, which I thought was a great idea but Jer didn't.

"Bomb, you gotta stop running up front like that. Stay with the pack" he slurred.

I didn't even know what he was talking about, like when I was in grade 5 playing ukulele and my friends told me to stop dancing around while playing. I had no idea I was doing it, but I was swaying back and forth to the music, jamming out the songs and singing my heart out.

Only after my dad said something to me about how enthusiastic I was did I recall actually nudging up to Scott Morrier with my shoulder, bumping into him and singing away, looking at him like I expected him to join in some sort of improvised ukulele rock-out moment. He stood there, shaking his head and mouthed, "What the hell?" It was the same lack of awareness in the tug-o-war.

I looked at Jer with his plastic Viking helmet complete with horns and his Billy Cosby-esque blue wool sweater, complete red and white stripe. "K" I confirmed.

As soon as the next round began, of course I ran right up to the mound when the pull started. I got to lean back more and the mound made it less about traction, more about doing a squat/seated row. I didn't even realize I was doing it this time either, but the strategy was sound. Drugs make you very wise.

Our final two challenges were tough. Our first battle was against The Sweaty Hog Nuts. As their name implies, they were a bunch of farmer types from somewhere in Ontario, or at least a bunch of big guys who knew a thing or two about drinking and pulling a rope. As we waited tensely for Martin to sound the starting gun, it was more than a little surreal and very much like the scene from Braveheart where the Scottish first fight the English.

We were lined up and they were lined up, tensed and ready, then, "FREEDOM!" burst out from someone in our line, and we all yelled "YEAHHH!" and barely heard the starting gun, which put us at an immediate disadvantage. We slipped in the mud, dancing and trying to recover our footing so we could start our one-two-three count. Of course I ran up to the mound and heaved with all my might, and as I was there, I could distinctly hear something that was not yelling; the bastards were counting as well!

"One-Two, One-Two, One-Two!" They chanted, trying to outdo us with quicker version of our strategy. Adding further insult to injury, and to me in particular, the captain of their team had stolen my gimmick and was way up front holding tight onto the line with *his* feet dug into the mound. It was building for a humiliating defeat. Things looked dire. Then, hope flickered.

"Fuck these guys, they stole our gimmick!" yelled Slim from the sideline. Everybody got pissed off, and quickly hoisting our pride, we dug in our heels, leaned back, and took the strain of another massive hog-tug. Dan ran up to the front of the line, also digging his heels into the slope, yelling "On me, boys!" We all groaned as one more massive yank from The Sweaty Hog Nuts wrenched our backs and burned our hands. But, we held fast.

We slid but a few inches in the mud, then Dan yelled, "One, Two, THREE!" We pulled for our lives, like we were pulling our families out of a fire, like we had to pull or die, like it was our only shot at immortality.

Warrior poets eat your hearts out, The Barnyard Cocks came together, a pack of beasts tied to the same yoke of desperation and craving for the adventures GI Joe, He-Man, and Transformers promised us when we were young. When drugs, booze, and pride get involved, the miracle of modern man compounds with the resolve of primitive man into a genuine god or savage. If we couldn't be great like gods, we would pull like beasts.

We took the strain again, snorting and cursing. Then, we slowly turned the tide. Three! We stopped sliding. Panting. Three! We moved an inch back, someone yelled into our ears. Three! Two inches was our gain. Three! Our pride swelled, our pace picked up, and then the "Three!" came quicker and quicker. We burned with elation. We started hauling back towards the fence we knew we could bulldoze over, rushing as the rope floated in our hands, our feet and souls weightless.   Not to die without a fight, the captain of the nuts held tight onto the rope until the last possible second, surrendering with a dramatic flip into the pond. All the onlookers cheered, including us. He had been sacrificed, and we all were saved.

After that, The Illegal Eagles were our final competition. Despite looking like a biker gang, they could not cut the mustard and their captain threw out his back trying to hang on. Victorious, crossed around the pond to see if he was ok; he fired up, took a shot of Slim's whiskey, downed a couple Advils, (a great idea considering his blood was at least half alcohol by this time), and winked, "I'll get you bastards tomorrow!" We all cheered, patted backs, and headed back to our fires.

Later that night we sat around, shooting the shit, smoking weed, and drinking booze in Slim's trailer. I had eaten some mushrooms sometime, gently tripping out through the night.

I stood watching a joint being passed around. We were not a bunch of guys; we were a team. Our voices were the effects of communication, not the cause of it. Oneness. Team. I wanted my beer. It was on the table. I put my hand over it. I concentrated. The force was strong around us.

"Ben…" I concentrated. I relaxed. I focused, closing my eyes, letting myself feel the energy of all living things that surround us in the universe, the force that joins us all together. "Ben…" The voices dulled to a breezy hum. Surely, if ever, now I could do it. Now I could use the force. Now I could make that beer can float up into my hand. "Do or do not; there is no try." I breathed deeply, slowly, and peacefully felt the air, the warmth of the trailer, and sensed the cool of the beer can that was on the table a foot below my hand. I looked deep inside my soul, felt a change in the air. I relaxed into the Zen of being one with all. I didn't think. I didn't try. I was. "Bomber…" And suddenly the beer can was in my hand!

"Bomber…"

I couldn't believe it; I didn't want to look, and didn't need to look- the beer was in my hand!

"Bomber… here, dammit."

Awakened, I opened my eyes; Dan looked at me in a funny, knowing way, cradling the bottom of the beer until I closed my fingers around it. I looked at him, puzzled. His answer came before my question.

"The force doesn't work, buddy. We've all tried."

The Pussy Stampede

That same evening we saw the pussy stampede; guys and girls dress in their underwear, just one couple from each team, and drink and run around. I don't remember it at all. I wasn't in it. It was starting to get cold out. The menacing clouds decided to take off at night time, which would seem like a good thing, except this being Ontario in May, they were keeping the heat in, or at least that's what the meteorologists tell us.

The pussy stampede. Note the integrity.

I shivered awake in bed a few hours after my experiment using the force. I had only one blanket, no mattress, no pillow, and barely any clothes. My jeans were tight and wet after the tug-o-war and all the other nonsense; my second-hand jacket came down only to my forearms. Wearing all the clothes I had, I was still freezing and shivering. Ball, with a proper sleeping bag, was barely any better.

"I'm going to my car" I grunted, and Ball decided to tag along. I walked out, ignored the security guard trying to keep us away from the cars (once there you couldn't leave so there were no drunk drivers), went to my car, revved the engine to get some heat going, and slept the night like that.

The number of nights I have slept in that pink salmon-mobile Toyota Tercel of mine is far too many. It was

197

freezing, but way warmer with the heat turned to max. When the sun came out, it wasn't long before the car was boiling and we made our way back to the campsite, dirty, tired, hungry, and still a little drunk. Sunday Morning. Time for purification.

The Ski Race

9:00 a.m. The same ski race you did for outdoor day in elementary school, only everyone is hung over and each team has to chug down two liters of nasty mixed booze. And only two people from each team are allowed to drink. I don't think I was really awake for this one. I remember that all 12 of us had a hell of a time walking on the skis. Not that we had practiced, but it was amazing that none of us had become any more coordinated since we had done this as pre-teens.

Ball and Slim were our drinkers, slamming down the booze to give us a reasonably good time, definitely top 5. Sobriety, my enemy, jabbed at me before and after each round of drinking. I had to defeat it; a break in booze would set up me up for rational thought, the straight right hand that would put me down, out, and into a ride home to forgo the rest of the competition. JC and Mike and I fought against it with a game of kings, an Ontario favourite drinking game.

We yelled at passersby's, taunting them as we downed bongs of booze and beers at 10:00 am. Despite our noise, people kept passing us twice, both times happy to see us. After a deep sniff of the air, I realized why. We were stationed next to the canteen. Food. Hamburgers. Fried eggs. Sausages. Pancakes. Bacon. Toast. I eat like a shark when I have the munchies. I hadn't come prepared.

I had brought all of $20 with me to the Animal Olympics; I spent half of it on a breakfast of fries, eggs, and a hotdog disguised as a sausage, which I heaped ketchup, mustard, and relish onto, maximizing my fullness. That kept the hunger pangs at bay until we started the Obstacle Course.

The Obstacle Course

The obstacle course was a beautiful disaster. You'd think it would be something simple, and the first stage made it seem so; all we had to do was hold up a pole and toss a tire onto it, like a giant cup-in-ball game. Then the obstacle course started inflicting its misery.

There were 6 of us; Romeo, one girl, myself, Slim, and I don't remember who else. I was still reeling from the last two nights and a morning beer didn't make me feel any better. I thought it was nice of Slim to give it to me, but not when I saw the first drinking obstacle of seven beers and seven shots. There were only six of us, so I threw my shot into my beer, chugged it, then did the deed again. Ugh.

We ran through, well, slogged through the muddy pond from the tug-o-war and got good and soaked (did I mention I only brought one set of clothes?) and then went to the second table; there were 14 more drinks- seven beers and seven shots- waiting for us. This was starting to feel like a drinking game in a hurry. As with the other games, no puking or excessive spilling; if you did, you had to redo the drink. I did one beer with a shot in it, felt like I was going to puke but somehow didn't, then split one of the beers with Romeo. UGH.

Panicked for time and miserable from cold, we ran through a huddle of tires football style, the next stage of the course. We weren't drunk enough for it to be a problem, but explosions welled in our stomachs. Somehow our misfit army made it through to the second to last table. There we met our old friends, seven Ambassador Beers, which we spiked with our seven shots of whiskey and/or tequila. UGHHHHHHH. Slim stepped up and drank two, saving me from certain puking. Grimacing, we sized up the only obstacle that really mattered; the chicken wire.

About 2 feet high, the chicken wire was a simple enough obstacle. We had to slide beneath it on our bellies as quickly as possible. At the far end of it waited obligatory beers and shots. And attached to the ends of the chicken wire were a pair of car batteries. That's right, the chicken wire was electrified.

I looked at it and figured, "No problem. I've got like two feet of space. I'm not going to even get close to it." Freezing and drunk, I wasn't thinking clearly.

First went Slim, and this was good, not just because he was short and quick, but because he had done this before. He knew to reach in under the wire and grab the next person as soon as they got near the end, saving precious seconds.

Next went the girl on the team, I have no idea who she is or what her name is, I'll just call her Janelle (after the Teen Mom superstar). Janelle slid through no problem. Romeo dove in and he was amazing. On a few occasions, Romeo has baffled me with his grace and athleticism.

Once was during our long swim contests at Grand Bend, Ontario. Another time was at the chicken wire. Romeo stepped back a few feet, dashed forward, and splashed in head first, arms pinned to his sides, sliding along his belly and paddling his feet like a Penguin. His poise blew my mind. Inspired, I rushed in.

I dove headfirst Romeo style and was making pretty good progress into the wire until some idiot smacked into me. There was a buzz in my neck and I was pretty sure I'd gotten a stinger or compressed vertebrae; I turned backwards to curse out whoever it was. I was baffled. Nobody was there. Could it be? One more errant movement confirmed that yes indeed I had stupidly bumped into the wire and yes being electrocuted bloody hurt.

In my adult life, I haven't had too many other electrical shocks, but this one was up there.

Another one was when I was in Tanzania taking a shower. The showers there don't have heated water tanks; instead, they have electrical elements on the top of the shower head itself. The element is boiling hot, heating the water running through it. I was tired and out of it; I wondered to myself, "Is this thing grounded?" and for some inconceivable purpose tested this by putting my hand on top of the element.

Clearly the best place and best way to test if something could potentially electrocute you is to put your hand on it in a running shower when you are soaking wet, all alone, and in a country where you don't speak the language, by far my brightest moment.

A split second later I realized I was still standing in the shower, soaking wet mind you, and that I had indeed just given myself a shock of 120 volts (according to the stamp on the showerhead). Thirty minutes later the numbness in the whole left side of my body, including my left testicle, subsided enough so that I could walk down the stairs without fear of falling. The chicken wire wasn't as bad, but only by a few jolts; as I was the first one to hit the wires, they were well charged.

Jumping like a cat near a firecracker, I shimmied and slid towards the end as fast as I could while Romeo laughed his ass off. Thankfully Slim yanked me and pulled me through the last few feet; we ran back to the starting point, slammed another beer and shot each, threw the tire over the pole again, and rang the bell. We had beaten The Illegal Eagles, but not the Chemical Kats. Our standing was good going into the change race.

Getting Back my Strength

I had a serious problem. I was out of food. I had eaten it all in about a day and a half and had been subsiding on hand-outs of chips, burnt food, and my meal at the food shack. But now I was out of money. I was bored, starved, but still very drunk when we decided it was time for a walk. In a scene that reminded me of something from a Nazi death camp, Hog, Pigger, Ball, and I went strolling through the frozen campground.

It wasn't all frozen; when you were in the sun it was comfortable, almost toasty. Once you stepped into a shadow though, it was bloody awful, and this at 11:00 a.m. in the morning. We were like fish sticks made by Lisa Simpson; "They're burned on the outside but frozen in the middle so it balances out" (*The Last Tempation of Homer*). It might work for fish sticks, but does not work for people. It was impossible to really warm up unless we went for a run, which none of us were going to do. As we strolled along in a daze,

Hog (Dan) was talking, words floating in one of my ears and out the other. Suddenly, I thought I heard something important. My ears pricked up.

"What was that? What happened?"

"I said this is about where those guys dropped those burgers" answered Dan.

"Burgers?"

"Yeah, a whole box of them. They fell out of their truck and they just left them. Right there. Ha, idiots."

Dan kicked the box lying on the side of the road, skidding it along with us. It had been run over at least once. I noticed it was still sealed shut. Intact. Very squished though. I felt like I was missing something important, but what? It was my "Lisa needs Braces" (*Last Exit to Springfield*) moment.

"Ha, Bomb, you said you were out of food right? Want some burgers?" Dan said before giving it a final kick into the ditch, laughing, "So dirty, ha."

A light went on! Before he had finished saying, "So dirty" I was in the ditch fishing out the burgers that had been laying in the sun/cold, getting run over and stepped on for the better part of two days. Shaking like a heroin addict I opened the box; I was drunk and high, but smart enough to know that actually eating burgers that had been warm for a few days would be suicidal, especially at the Animal Olympics. There was hope though. Christmas hadn't been this exciting for me in years, and I tore into the prize with glee.

"Bomber, what the fuck are you doing?" asked Dan.

"Burgers. Ho. Hold on."

"Bomb, you can't eat those. They've been there for two days."

"Frozen though. If they're still cold, they're all mine."

"Fuckin' rights they're all yours. Nobody's going to eat those, don't, for the love of god, just leave them."

"Bomber, you're going to die or get the shits or both," Hog added. Probably true.

I peeled back the wax paper and looked at the burgers. No signs of decay yet; they were still properly formed, well, a little mushed to one side because the box had been on its side when it was run over, but they looked mostly edible; no, I lie, they looked delicious. These were the all fat burgers too- 25 grams of fat and 21 grams of protein each. And I was cradling 24 of the beauties all for me. It was by far my happiest moment at the Olympics. I was even happier when, sticking a finger in one, I found it cool to the touch. Good enough!

"Fuck, dude leave those."

I loaded the case under my arm.

"Which way to camp? I gotta cook" I demanded.

"Right there."

The heavens opened; the campsite was only twenty yards away. We had focus and walked.

"How was the walk through the wasteland?" asked Jer.

"WE GOT BURGERS!" I yelled.

"What the fuck are you talking about?"

"Remember that box of burgers I saw fall off that truck a couple of days ago?" said Hog, "we found them. Bomber's going to eat them."

"No… Bomber, you'll die or get the shits."

"Don't worry about it" I said, which was the best response possible. I don't care who you are or what the argument is; when someone breaks out the, "Don't worry about it" they've got you beat. If you carry on, you seem like a whiny bitch making a big deal out of nothing or you've just been outmanned because the person who should worry about it, namely the person you're talking to, doesn't.

Seriously, what do you say to "Don't worry about it"t? I am going to worry about it? You should worry about it? You're too drunk to drive? In almost every situation, don't worry about it trumps worry. Jer knew this and quieted down, but I quickly deflated when I realized I had nothing to cook the burgers with. In a rash decision I threw one onto a stone at the edge of the fire. Despite immediately sizzling, the shortcomings of my action were obvious. There was no way to keep the sizzling burger from sticking to the rock.

"Jesus bomb, use this already" said Slim, handing me a blackened sandwich press attached to two handles.

"What is this?"

"For grilled cheese or hot sandwiches. It'll work for burgers."

I kicked someone off of their seat and sat and grilled and ate and ate and ate. I licked my fingers and my lips constantly to keep them from burning, but just ended up wincing and yelping. It didn't work and I didn't care. The burgers hissed, popped, wafted deliciousness into the air and fried in their own fat; the sandwich maker kept in all the extra nutrition of pure beef fat. It was my "64 Slices of American Cheese" moment (*Rosebud*). Even Romeo found it nauseating, and after two hours, he walked away. I didn't move nor did I want to.

All I cared about was making sure the burgers were done and that I ate them. I went from frying one at a time to mushing two patties into the press simultaneously, frying them for a few minutes, licking my fingers and flipping them so that the burnt outer part of the patty swapped place with the still mushy wet inside of the double patty, and then hooting, puffing, reverse blowing and ho-ing while I stuffed another burger into my mouth. It was worse than Romeo and his tacos. At hour three, stuffed and satisfied, I felt like I should not drink or eat anymore.

"Bomb, time for the change race" said Dan.

"What?"

"You're doing it. We volunteered you."

"Oh."

"You feel sick?"

"A little. I can't drink anymore."

"You think you'll puke?"

"Probably" I said, nodding. I wanted sleep.

"Well…"

"Well what?"

"Well don't worry about it!" laughed Dan.

Fuck.

Testicles as Spectacles

The change race is a pretty simple concept. A guy and a girl from the same team skip or pogo ball jump across a big open field, slam 2 liters of disgusting mixed booze, switch clothes, then run back to the start line. Each team does it separately to maximize the nudity, giving the crowd the best viewing opportunity possible. The crowd is understandably large. Given the cold air, genitals sometimes are not. Still, it is the best attended event at The Animal Olympics.

"Before I begin, I'd just like to say it's cold out" I told my partner. Who she was I don't remember. I think it was Slim's girlfriend, I'm not sure. She was a trooper though. She'd partied for 2 days straight and had put up with a bunch of Neanderthal idiots without ever seeming tired of us. She also was focused on winning.

"K, get rid of your underwear beforehand. I'm not wearing any so we'll be quicker." Good advice, not sure if she had prepared specifically for the event or was always prepared. Like I said, she was a trooper.

Bang! I pogo hopped, she skipped across to the end of the field, and we started slamming the booze. It was awful. Fermented orange juice mixed with nail varnish mixed with mouthwash mixed with cola. After taking a pull on it for about 15 seconds I handed it to Trooper. The crowd booed. Trooped flipped them all the bird, and took a pull off of it for a good 30 seconds, putting a noticeable dent in it. The crowd cheered. Half the bottle gone. 1 liter left. I wanted to puke but had to man up.

I took a deep breath and a good 30 second pull, just imagining that I was actually warm and it was summer and I was hot and needed to drink and that the juice would balance out the saltiness/grease of the burgers. The crowd cheered. She finished it off, we held hands, and ran back to the halfway point, two innocent babes in toyland.

Then I whipped off my shirt, shorts, and handed them to her and started helicoptering my dick in my hand. Trooper would not be outdone; already naked, she simultaneously twirled both of her nipple rings around while sticking out her tongue. The crowd erupted. I looked at a particularly appreciative section and was readying to yell at them, when Slim belted out, "Bomber, it's a race!"

Oh yeah. We jumped into our clothes, bolted to the line, and high fived the team. First place. One team later passed us by literally milliseconds. If we hadn't done our dance, we would have been a lock for first. The time moved us ever closer to first place and the enviable prize of more booze.

Perfect Form

It takes skill to ruin a friendship; Mike and Jer had been best buds since forever. They started backyard wrestling in a converted trampoline a good ten years before they trained at a wrestling school. Ball and Romeo, brothers, were also part of this backyarding troop, but Jer and Mike stood apart. Their bond was strong and deep; shared dreams and hours spent together paying dues early in wrestling forged it with steel. It's fitting that it was almost undone by just one wrestling move. One move executed with perfect form.

For three days we had been peeing at the edge of our campsite. Forget walking the 15 meters to the washroom, we were men. There were 40 people, 38 male, on our team. Taking an average of 5 pees a day, and each pee being close to 500ml, that's 5 X 500ml X 38 X 2.5 days, so close to 300 liters of pee flooding the grass beside the recycling bin for empty cans. If you consider that we had all been drinking excessively for those days, it probably makes more pee. Many times more. Disirregardless, there was a swamp of pee at the edge of the campsite. Nobody was quite sure where it began. The marker was a blue recycling bin, and if you weren't near it, the boys all yelled at you. We had our standards.

Mike (TJ) went home for a day and re-arrived late Saturday. He had boyfriend duties to fulfill, and this was an offense to the male bonding of the Animal Olympics. He knew this and power drank as much as he could when he returned. He caught up quickly. But he had deserted us for showers and cleanliness, albeit briefly. To take him down a notch, we made sure he peed where he was supposed to… kind of.

"Not by the blue bin, just past it!" someone yelled.

"Fuck, this is gross. My feet are already soaking up piss!" Mike yelled back.

You're Gonna Hurt Yourself

"No, no, just a bit further, don't pee there, we've all been standing there. You're flooding out the camp."

Mike was not happy, but not sure if we were being completely dishonest. He grumbled, shuffling a step further, his dick already in his hands, trying not to pee on himself as he trudged on. We snickered. Mike heard us.

"You guys are the worst" he cussed, still peeing. Jer whispered, "Shhhhhhh" wearing the most devilish look on his face I have ever seen. Mike's back was to us, with him staring up at the stars, tranquil in nature. He'd been holding his pee for a while. Relief.

Hunching over, like Elmer Fudd prowling Bugs Bunny, Jer snuck towards Mike. Then he started to Jog... then, he sprinted. Mike sensed something was wrong. The noise of camp had died. Everyone was holding their breath. The only noise was Jer's thudding feet. Mike turned his head sideways just in time to catch a peripheral view of Jeremy sailing through the air in a perfect cross-body block. "Wha--" then "THWOCK" Jer hit mike high on his shoulders and back, followed by "SPLUDSH!" A perfect cross body! Given the context, this was the most devastating move possible.

All of Jer's considerable girth, 220lbs, smacked into Tj's back. TJ hadn't seen it coming enough to do anything. His arms were pinned under him, no chance of slowing his fall, and his face dug into the puree of pee, soil, and spit. There is a right way to take a cross body block- face your opponent, catch him with your arms, and roll back or bump back if you feel like being a trooper. This was the complete opposite.

No cushioning roll, no use of the arms, no planned landing. It was a totally graceless dump into the swamp, taking the full brunt on his shoulders and chest, hands pinned to his groin. The only grace was he had turned his head sideways.

"FUCK! FUCK FUCK GET THE FUCK OFF OF ME!" Mike yelled, his face buried in the muck, like a swimmer breathing mid-stroke. His arms were completely trapped! He was completely at the mercy of Jer!

"Ahhahaha,aaaaaa!" Laughed everyone, Jer loudest.

"FUCK YOU GET THE FUCK OFF ME!" Mike's voice was muffled by the sludge of pee filling his mouth and our laughter, with Romeo laughing the loudest. We all soaked up the fuming, kicking legs, arms pinned at his sides, probably still peeing, yelling "GET THE FUCK OFF ME YOU PIECE OF SHIT," Mike.

"No, you're going to hit me!"

"GET THE FUCK.... AGH!" Mike had a whole body convulsion as his face was pushed back into the mud by Jer's hand. Jer had to get into position to flee; Mike's face made the best starter's block to post on. Jer got poised, then flicked himself off of TJ and ran away, legitimately afraid.

TJ got up. Wiped the mud/pee off his face. Walked over to the washrooms. Came back with his hands and face clean. The air sizzled around him. Not a word.

"HAHA, love you TJ!" said Jer.

TJ said nothing. He walked past us, out of the campsite, and to his car. Then he drove home. He was mad. He's still mad. And they're best Friends. Still.

Doink vs The Wolf

After the crossbody block into the piss, I lost track of everything. We drank and drank and goofed around and went to the awards ceremony. Two things stand for this night. First, Doink the clown made an appearance. Second, a wolf appeared.

If you've never seen Doink the Clown, you've missed out on one of wrestling's finest and worst moments. Doink the clown was originally played by Matt Borne, son of Tough Tony Borne. Matt is a legend in the Pacific Northwest territory of Washington, Oregon, and BC. It was a brilliant gimmick because Doink was originally a bad guy, taking a cartoonish character and using the innocence of it to add creepiness, like a possessed baby.

As a legitimately tough guy, Borne brought a haunting fear to Doink, a clown who played pranks and terrorized people. His promos were great, improved by his insane laugh, intense eyes, and his overall work. The character went well beyond its potential. Borne was so good at being creepy that eventually the fans bought into the power of his performance and realized they were witnessing something artistic. Doink became a babyface, but shortly after that, he was gone from the WWF. One of wrestling's finest, at least at for the times, disappeared. Then it became one of wrestling's worst.

The gimmick was too easy to replicate and soon there were at least a dozen "Doink the Clown" wrestlers across the US and Canada. Borne kept doing the gimmick and people loved it- I witnessed a great show with him vs Michelle Starr in Victoria. But the others were, for the most part, a bunch of guys trying to find a spot on a card or promoters trying to book a star without actually having to pay one. Sometimes it was just guys who happened to be at a show fighting for a spot on a card getting thrust into a costume. This was what happened to me months before the Animal Olympics.

"He looks like Doink-a da Clown" said Scott 2.

Scott 2 was the right-hand man of Scott D'amore, one of the biggest promoters in Canada and later a success with TNA wrestling. He ran proper, well attended shows and everyone wanted to be a part of Border City Wrestling. I was trying to get onto the shows, but I missed Scott 2's drift. Scott 2 explained.

"D'amore wants you to be Doink the clown. Doink didn't show."

"I don't look like Doink" I countered.

"You want to be on shows, right? Don't worry about it."

Fuck. Preparations began as I pondered Doink, hoping to channel him. In a team locker room, somewhere in an Ontario university, I donned the tight while Scott 2 began applying the makeup as best he could. I had no mirror and was dying to see what was happening.

"K, now smile." I did. The face paint was almost complete, but I knew it was terrible because Scott 2 kept chuckling, saying, "We gonna give them Donk-a da clown." I realize now he was saying it that way because the costume had come from Winnipeg, not Matt Borne. It was mailed by Tony Condello, a legendary Italian promoter who probably said Doink just as Scott 2 was imitating. Tony had a great accent. In contrast, this Doink, had awful makeup.

"Oh jeez, dis Doink-a da clown is great. HA!" said Scott 2. I looked in the mirror. Ugh.

The suit was designed for a man of 260-300 pounds with a huge melon head. I was about 220lbs at the time, having been working hard to get abs. Abs were great when I was walking around on the beach, awful when being Doink the clown. The suit drooped and sagged, particularly between my legs, well, Doink's legs, looking like a diaper full of poop. It also hung too far back, exposing my shoulders.

The hair of the wig rested on the back of my neck because my head was too small, so Doink was bald with a nest of green hair on his neck. And the make-up was done with a tiny picture from a magazine as the example; Scott 2 was no artist, and had nothing to work with. It looked awful. I couldn't keep a straight face, which was fine for Doink since he was a clown. But nobody else could either, which was a problem. I snuck up on Showtime in full gimmick, squatting like an ape, and then laughed, "Hoo hoo hoo, hee hee hee, wwwhoooooo" behind him. He turned, saw me, and fell over. Tyson Dux almost had a heart attack.

"Bomber, did you dye your teeth?" asked Angel Williams.

Sadly, no. They were just really yellow, accented by the blaring white of the paint. If I'd yawned, traffic would have slowed down (thanks Phyllis Diller for that one.) The whole locker room died laughing at Doink, particularly at my droopy underpants. It was bloody awful. The only person I did fool was the other star on the show, King Kong Bundy.

"Hey Buddy, how are you?" Bundy. Engulfing a chair. A case of beers next to him, a dozen empties on the floor.

"Great Bundy, how, how are you?" He had no idea who I was, or so I thought, although I kind of had no idea about how to respond, and I had no idea what to do or what to say. Lots of no ideas were coming into play.

"Good, you're not working for Vince, huh?" I think he thought I was Borne.

"No. Uhh, no, no I'm not." Bundy was the biggest heel for years, a huge star from the 80's. I was star-struck.

"Well, those guys are still there. Maybe we'll get there again someday, huh?" Wink.

"Yeah, that'd be great. Big crowds."

What would you do? It's embarrassing for him to make such a mistake, and embarrassing as a fan to explain it to him. I just hoped he'd think I was Doink a little longer and say nothing else so I could leave.

"Well, have fun out there Bundy" I mustered.

"You too pal." I turned to leave.

"Hey!" yelled Bundy.

I turned back.

"Uhh, yeah?" I said as he looked at me quizzically.

"Good show, brother. Good show" he nodded to me.

"Ok. Good show." I nodded back. And then I left. I realize now he was ribbing me the whole time. Fuck.

It was a good show, but not because of Doink the clown, a rendition that I feel safe in saying, was probably the worst Doink ever. Other than one girl who kept yelling, "Yeah Doink, you're awesome!" I think everyone was unimpressed by Doink's performance, which was thankfully short.

It consisted of me squirting my opponent with a water gun over my shoulder, drawing on him with face paint, and then getting pinned. Nobody bought it. Even the girl cheering me probably didn't buy it. But I enjoyed it, and for weeks afterwards, I would employ the "Hoooo hooo, heee heee, hahaha whooooo" laugh of Doink the clown, particularly when I was drunk. So, of course, it came out when I was at The Animal Olympics. But with exquisitely bad timing.

At the change race, I had locked onto a girl I called Wolf Eyes because she had, wait for it, eyes like a wolf. She was cute, smallish but curvy, and I was high and out of it. She was one of only ten girls at the whole event. I was transfixed. I chatted with her, got a few laughs, then went back and power drank for the afternoon.

Jer kept beating me at beer bonging, and I was getting annoyed. To improve my chances, I drank more. This didn't help. After about 6 beer races, it was obvious I had no chance of winning and little chance of surviving the night. We headed to the awards ceremony, beer bong around us, stumbling and dreaming. Dreaming of wrestling, of victory at the Animal Olympics, and of Doink the Clown.

"Hoooo, hoooo, heee heee, hahahaha, whoooooooo!"

The crowd gathered; Martin held aloft the magic cup and said, "The Winners of the 17th annual Animal Olympics.... The Barnyard COCKS!!!

We exploded, jumping up and down. Slim, Hog, and Pigger accepted the cup. We all poured in bits of booze and took triumphant draughts from the cup. Our award was 3 kegs of delicious Ambassador beer. Ugh. The same dreadful brew that had been spiked with raw eggs, 151 proof, Tequila, and lord knows what else during the drinking contests. It seemed like a challenge.

What could we do? 3 kegs is a lot of booze, and as only about 12 of us had made it to the celebration, and maybe 100 people from all the teams together (the drop off rate for the games is understandably high), we left the kegs out in the courtyard. Let people have at them. "Hoooo, hoooo, heee heee, hahahaha I'm Doink the Clown, have a beer!" I kept saying. Or thought. We were high on life - hard work does pay off!- and a multitude of other things. I still wanted my revenge on Jer.

"Jer, bong."

"Bomb, no. We've only got one, and I've just puked in it."

Hippy had puked earlier. Chunks. Big, meaty chunks of hot dog. You could still see teeth marks on some of them. A puke hot-dog stew by the fire.

"Fuck, someone should eat one of those. What a waste of food," I'd said.

Hippy stooped, picked one, blew the dirt off it, and ate it, followed by a cheer of disgust/respect. That set the bar. By comparison, Jer's puke was just water.

"Fuck, rinse it out." He poured out the puke, rinsed the bong with some fine Ambassador Beer, poured it out again, swished some more delicious Ambassador beer into it, poured that out, then gave it to me, and I filled it with exquisite, princely, supremely delicious, noble, Ambassador Beer. CHEERS!

"Ho, ho, heee heee, hahahaha, whoooooo!" Doink revved. My seventh bonged beer in about two hours, as well as the other stuff I'd been drinking to be a good citizen. It went down. "Ho, ho, heee heee, hahahaha" up and out came my

The Barnyard Cocks celebrating our victory. Left to right: Myself, Hippy, Idunno in front, and a haggard Romeo.

voice. Then an inebriated Doink siren went off, "Whoooo, I've got piss. Whoooo!"

I looked around for the blue bin we'd been next to for the last three days. Too far from our campsite. Even further to the washrooms. But there was open space. And a picnic table for a marker. Now fully Doink, I staggered to it. "Ho, ho, heee heee, hahahaha" Doink whipped out his penis, "whooooo!" and laughed, and as Doink laughed, I peed, and I laughed doing my best rendition of how a clown pees. The funniest thing in the world at the time was my peeing between the seat and surface of the picnic table.

"Hoooo, hoooo, heee heee, hahahaha, whooooo!" it was quite a ride! Doink laughed, resting his beer on top of the table, and putting up one hand like a cowboy in a rodeo, waving his hips from side to side, a human pee-sprinkler. Doink and I belted, "HO, HO HEEE HEE HEEEEE HAHAHAAHAHA WHOOOO—peeing forcefully through the gap of the picnic table- OOOOO!" and then I saw wolf - eyes. Staring directly at me. With her two friends, marching up to the courtyard and specifically the picnic table I was using for pee target practice. My member in my hands, pee streaming out, laughing like an idiot, Doink the Clown met Wolf Eyes. She blew my cover. Even in my state I realized how embarrassing it was. For anyone. And everyone. Particularly for me. I spun and finished peeing, grabbed my beer, and marched to the gravel dance floor of the courtyard. If it hadn't been Doink doing it, I would have died. No ordinary person could live this down. Jer was there. I smiled. Then laughed. Then began gasping for air. I had to tell him, but once I realized how awesome, how terribly embarrassing it was, I couldn't get the words out.

"Jeeeez-us Bomber, you all right?"

While dying from laughter, I got the story out in pieces, and he put them together. He looked at me and looked at her across the dance floor. Then he laughed for 10 minutes straight. Tears rolled down our cheeks as we craned our necks back laughing, dying, breathing, leaning on each other, and loving life. When he finally could speak, he grabbed me and said, "Bomb, I don't know why, but Wolf Eyes keeps looking over here."

"What? Really?"

"Fuck, don't look, but she is."

Immediately I looked.

"Ho, well, what the hell."

"Go git 'er!"

Drunk, stinking like campsite, BO, booze, foul beyond description, pee definitely still on my hands, I stumbled over, grabbed her clean hand, and dragged her onto the dance floor. I'm an awful dancer. All I did was cling on and pretend to be smooth. It worked surprisingly well and I felt great. To top it off, out of the corner of my eye, I could still see Jer.

I repeatedly saw him repeat the story every time another of the boys came up, then they'd die laughing for a few minutes with Jer. Then he'd point to me and her. The newcomers would cock their head to a side, look at us, nod as if to say, "All right, I'm impressed." and then stand there having a delicious, invigorating, heavenly draught of Ambassador Beer, watching me at work. My magic consisted of nothing, just grabbing and leaning, then getting her phone number, and passing out in my tent with Ball, no Wolf Eyes in sight.

"The best part," said Jer the next morning, "was the guy with her. He was so pissed, he was probably her boyfriend or something, but all he could do was sit there fuming. Awesome work Bomb." No human could overcome that situation, but Doink could. Sometimes a gimmick *can* help you in life.

When we left the Animal Olympics, we headed into a McDonald's for our first civilized meal in three days. Romeo screwed up his face at the cashier and sniffed.

"Something stinks" squealed the cashier.

"Can I take your order, please?"

"Yeah, I smell it too. What is that?" I asked.

"Can I take your order please sir?" Impatient.

"It smells like a dead monkey's ass. Gross." Romeo was offended. High class.

"If you're not going to order, please step aside or outside."

"No hold on, what the hell is that stench? That's disgusting." Romeo wouldn't let it die.

A light went off in Jer's head.

"Romeo, just order."

"Ewww, no, gross. You guys go ahead, I'm not going to eat in this filth."

"Romeo trust me, just order" hushed Jer.

"Not until I know what smells."

"Romeo... it's us."

Romeo breathed in deeply near us, took a step away, and took a deep breath by the cashier. French Fries and Burgers-delicious. A step to us and another deep breath. Romeo dry heaved. We ordered our meals to go.

At home, it indeed took us a whole week to recover. Romeo had a few beers the first night to get ready for the week. Amazingly, the tub was less filthy than usual when he got out of it. That week, we trained and wrestled, albeit a bit lazily. Our minds and bodies had a lot of healing to do. This was in May. About a month later, summer actually started. The temperature was a constant 32 degrees Centigrade in the house and outside. Muggy. Hot. Sweaty. Romeo glowed with beads of sweat.

We would run to the Wrestleplex just up the road, Jeremy's school, to train just about every night of the week. We'd stop to mop the pools of sweat between spots. In the day we'd go to work and sweat more. It was miserably busy and sweaty, and we all dropped weight, enjoying our summer of living fraternity. Jer and I were lucky enough to do the tour of Nova Scotia, New Brunswick, and Prince Edward Island for a few weeks (the Road to Nowhere Section), then I took a brief trip home to see my brothers before they took off to Utah for school and France for a mission, both very different from my path.

A booking came up, and I flew back to get picked up at the Toronto airport for a road trip to Montreal. Our tight crew of friends all worked the show and had a great time. And in a rarity at the time, things didn't go back to stagnantly waiting for a booking.

Fortune called; a full time tour in the Maritimes. In the early 80's, there were plenty of full time territories for wrestlers to make a living. By the mid 90's, almost all had dried up, but Atlantic Canada still had one, at least for the summer. This was a once in a lifetime opportunity and I took it. I've never regretted that decision.

Road to Nowhere

The Mad Bomber touring the Maritimes. Nothing to note.

Brothers

Ribs are jokes wrestlers play on each other. Usually they're cruel with a hint of love attached to them, but often they're just cruel. You don't mind the ribs after you realize guys are doing it because they're bored and see you as able to take it. This, of course, is after you've proven yourself and been ribbed as a rookie for a long time. It's the guys who are the best or worst natured about being ribbed that get it the most. Ribbing is first meant to see if a guy can handle the business. It slowly turns into acceptance mixed with the torturous love of a big brother. Painful love is the calling card of a professional wrestler.

The more time you spend with people, the more comfortable you are with them, and the more comfortable you are with them, the more sinister the ribs become. Just as matches are often stiffest (hardest hitting) with a wrestler you are comfortable with, ribs are often stiffest with the wrestlers you are closest to.

(A thought occurs to me as I think about this stuff; I've never heard of a female wrestler ribbing another female. Ever. I have no idea why. It could probably be a master's thesis. Or because girls are more mature, or that guys don't understand the ribs girls pull on each other.) Dissirregardlessly, in Cambridge, at the wrestling school, most of the ribs weren't that good. We were all new, didn't know each other, and only knew we wanted no Keith (Nerdly) around. He was ribbed poorly and clumsily. Two years later, on a tour in The Maritimes, the ribs were better for everyone.

We ribbed each other constantly on the road. Not just in the ring, but in the van, the hotel, the mall, the gym, on the beach, at dinner—everywhere we were together except at the nightclubs. I'm a touchy asshole nowadays, but back in 2002 in Halifax with Nick (Sinn Bodhi), Jer (Eric Young), JT Playa, Elvis Elliot, Street Fighter Jason Bates, and Kingman (Brody Steele), we were all up for ribbing each other and enjoyed it… mostly. The ribs flowed and, if you can't rib back or take a rib, you're done for. There was too much time to kill.

We sat for 8 hours a day, sometimes more, driving to venues. When I fell asleep in the front seat of Jer's car, "SPLASH" I woke up with a cup of water on my face. I turned and saw a lineup of purely innocent bastards smiling at me. I knew what they were thinking. If I started a rib war with three guys, two of whom were not quite innocent but not completely responsible, I would be constantly uneasy. I muttered "You bastards" and let it go; I had to.

The forum for ribs grew as we grew closer. Kingman wrote "PS I love you" under Streetfighter's name at every autograph session; I threw stones at Eric Young; Elvis pretended to fart every time he got in the van and his ass was near your face; Nick once wrestled me for an hour while I moaned the whole time about the heat, just wanting to be left alone; Jer pounded the mat when he sold a chinlock, bashing Sneaky Martin's toes; Kingman threw beer bottles at us as we drove from town to town, etc. You get the picture. And there were the usual ribs of food getting hidden (one I never found funny) or sat on (even less funny), gear bags getting thrown into people's faces, mock battles in the backseat of Nick's Van, and of course turning into a dead fish in the middle of a match. JT Playa got it the worst though.

JT was the blackest man on tour because he was the only black man on tour. He was only half black, but he was good and dark and grew one hell of an afro. He was a character, a dynamo, a lightning rod for great reactions. I've never met a more animated storyteller; put him on a street corner and tell him to preach about paint drying. In five minutes he'd have a crowd at his feet hanging on his every word. He was a classic; somewhat hot tempered, most often at my bullshit, but generally testy when nonsense was involved. He would mock something, laugh, and hate on it in all the same tone. Humor was his way. One of my favourite memories of him is us parading around Shediak beach in Moncton. Moncton had beautiful beaches. They made the tour there a treasure, whether or not the money was good. The sand is smooth, surprising in Canada, and the sun powerfully bright, especially in July. This day was another beauty on the East

Coast. JT and I, both a little homesick, pondered life and wrestling, wading through dancing water under a bursting sun. "Street Fighter" Jason Bates briefly pondered joining us.

"You guys sure there aren't sharks in them waters?" he asked in his middle-America twang.

"Yeah, it's fine." I said.

"You sure, Bomber? I've never swam in the ocean."

"There's like 'eighty-hundred' (*Marge Gets a Job*) people here. If there is a shark, what're the odds it'll get you?"

He paused and looked at us, then out at the waves. His eyes scrunched together, sizing up what I had just said. It could be true; it could be a rib. Would I dare rib a man-beast with a black belt and bowling balls for fists? He looked quizzically at us again.

"I'm just going to chill on the beach, thanks."

Surprised my reasoning didn't work, JT and I walked, then swam out to five feet of water. JT was talking about his past matches and how much he'd liked working Japanese Strong Style Wrestling or a few years, but then realized how dumb it was and how he didn't need to. He explained how he had done all sorts of stupid and crazy stuff, like a reverse hurricanrana off the top rope.

"What? What the hell is a reverse hurricanrana?" I scoffed.

"You just get up on the buckle, facing away from the guy, and he does a Hurricanrana."

"How the hell does that work? How do you bump?"

"You do a backflip and land on your stomach. It's not that hard, Bomber."

I paused for a second as we waded through the water. I really had no idea about sharks off the coast of New Brunswick or anywhere in Canada for that matter. It was probably best to keep moving.

"Jess, I don't get it. Why would you do that? You moonsault from his legs being around your head? How do you not land on your head in a backwards piledriver?"

"Fuck Bomber, you just go with it. You hang onto his legs and do a backflip."

"Off the mat or off the top?"

"Fuck, either one!" he yelled.

You're Gonna Hurt Yourself

When JT was getting mad, the pitch in his voice began changing so it sounded more like his gimmick and less like his shoot (real) day to day voice. He predated auto-tune, but his gimmick voice had a robot-gravelly resonance a bit like Tone-Loc or Bobcat Braithwaite. He was close to full on character-promo voice.

"So you can do a backflip?" I had to ask.

Something in my tone really pissed him off. I didn't mean to insult him, but his jiggly belly and general lack of athletic wrestling because he was a gimmick wrestler made me doubt him.

"HAHAHA, RRRRR! Yes, you FUCK I can do a backflip. They're not hard. You just jump up and throw your feet over your head. Hhuh, huh, huh, you know bomber sometimes I want to punch your face so much… FUCK!"

I may have egged him more, I may not have. I often got people into situations, myself included, without meaning to. Often these situations lead to a painful experience for someone involved, myself included. Half the time I was ribbing myself without knowing it. For whatever reason, and however it came to be, JT decided that he was going to do a backflip in the water right then and there to show me. I had a quick clarification to share. I wasn't sure why, but I had to speak up.

"Anyone can do a backwards tuck in the water, JT. It's not the same as doing a leaping backflip."

"OH fuck, really? Huhuhuh, fine. Come here. I'm going to backflip and then you can shut up. Genius."

First we tried standing with him on my shoulders in five feet of water. That didn't work because he was 240lbs and his feet killed my collarbones as he stood up there, grinding his heels into me, trying to get his balance. I wondered if this was a clever rib by him… but he seemed so genuine. After a few failed attempts and few more expletives, he changed tactics. We waded into water a little shallower, maybe two feet deep or so. I had a big grin on my face and JT must have seen it. It pushed his rage close to boiling.

"Yeah, that's it you fuck, keep smiling. Don't jinx me and let me do a couple warm up jumps."

Which he did. I cocked my head sideways watching him. I was impressed.

I don't know if he could have dunked a basketball, but he had pretty decent hops in spite of all the tour and poutine weight he had gained. He had thick legs and a proportionately built butt, so it made sense that he could jump. JT had some of the best genetics for wrestling and muscles I've ever seen. If he'd been a serious saucer, he had the frame to be a thick 260+ with perfect symmetry. He chopped me and I tuned back in to him.

"Ok, I'm ready. Watch this."

Anyone could tell you that it would be a hell of a lot harder to backflip in the shallow water, but I didn't see why I should. He'd just chopped me. And since there was only he and I there, nobody did tell him. The extra weight and suction of water pulled on both legs and swimsuit. But that was just a detail. JT was determined; I was excited, waiting for the punch line. Grinning. He noticed, and after a quick "Fuck you, Bomber" he leapt up, and it was more or less like he said. He jumped, went mostly vertically straight up, and swung his legs over his head. The only difference was he swung his legs back just enough to get completely upside down and then land fully on his afro with a splashing thud. His trunks and legs splayed out in wobbly V for a split second before he completely crumpled into a heap, knees in his face. It was sort of three motions that should have been one- leap till upside down, lawn spike into the water, and crumple over in a toppling V shape. I burst into laughter; he came up with fury, snorting out water, spitting and more pissed off than ever, "FUCK YOU BOMBER!" and then, just as he predicted, he punched me as I dived away for safety.

"Goddamit you fuck. I hate you, huhhuh, Fuck!"

At least he had a fro to cushion the fall. His fro was good for other things, too. A favourite game of Showtime, Fabian Stokes and I was, "How long will it stay?" Whenever JT sat in the front seat, we would each try to foist a penny, a straw, or a piece of paper into his hair while he told stories or rapped to us.

JT actually wrote a couple of pretty sweet rap songs, one called "Brainbusta" that was awesome. I remember being serenaded by it as we drove through a thundershower in the middle of nowhere between shows. It brought surreal reality to our situation and hopes for the future. I think we all emerged from that drive with newfound respect for JT Playa. But, on a day to day basis, he was just the guy with the fro, and we dropped shit into his hair.

It was great when we went into a gas station and JT bought something. What made it better was that people in New Brunswick were frank enough to ask what the hell was going on. And there weren't a lot of black people in New Brunswick either, so their stares were often confused for being racially inspired.

I was lucky enough to witness a beautiful exchange at an Irving gas station. JT and I got out of the car, went in to buy some food, and JT plunked a Snickers bar and a water down on the counter. Standing there, bits of paper, fast food straws, metal wrapping from candy bars decorating his beautiful afro, and a big friendly smile on his face, JT had no clue. I stood behind him, biting my lip.

The cashier gave him a funny look before he started ringing in the purchase. Some tension started sparkling in the air, like the sparkling garbage in the hair of JT who, for his part, tried to play it cool. He knew he was being eyed, though; the background chatter in the store had died. I saw his back stiffen up as he took a deep breath.

"Err, what's the crack with that there hair, mate?" asked the cashier.

"Huh?"

"You're hair. Looks funny, don't it though?"

We couldn't blame the young guy at the gas station, living and working between the middle of bumfuck and nowhere. He had never seen a spectacle like JT before and questions had to be asked.

"Yeah, it's an afro" spat JT.

"Is it, erhm, natural- like?"

"Yeah, my hair is natural. It's an afro! I was born with it!" Anger level and gimmick voice almost achieved.

"Hmm, all that stuff too?" he peeped, pointing his finger.

"Huh? Aww dammit…"

Fingers flew through hair, litter rained down on the counter, JT paid, fumed, stormed out, and then threw ice at the responsible parties in the back seat of the car, spitting, "Goddammit I hate you all, especially you Bomber!"

"Yeahhh, JT, hahahah!" laughed Jer. We all laughed, even JT. It kept the rest of the world at bay and us closer together to be ribbing each other on the road.

At one arena, we were all especially tired after a night out and a long drive. It was the same arena where the referee asked Showtime which way was east. Showtime guessed, pointed, then left the room in a stupor of respect as the ref, a skinny white guy from Antigonish, Nova Scotia, or somewhere else rolled out a prayer rug and started doing his Muslim daily prayers. In 2001, none of us had encountered Islam in life yet. Befuddled, Jer told us what happened as he sat down with JT and I.

Our eyes were stinging with booze and exhaustion, our minds confused. On days like this, putting together a match and getting warmed up enough to bump safely was painful. The labour of doing it twice this night was especially painful for me. Showtime groaned how it had gotten harder to lace up his boots because of all the poutine he'd been eating. I ached all over from the ring, Kingman's choke slam finish every night, and more particularly, being crammed into a car for 8 hours per day. JT seemed broken and was bleeding out words of agony at Satan's ring and our cramped room. We were all slipping over the edge.

Silence blanketed us as we dreamed for a break from living the dream for a day. But fate stepped in. JT sat down, leaning over to start lacing up his boots in the dread silence. A gentle thud sprinkled into the room as we looked in starry eyed wonder as a penny spun magically around on the floor.

"What the fuck?" spat JT.

We all looked at the penny, our exhausted minds chugging along to put the pieces together. Huh. JT figured it out quickest of all; no warm up, all rage.

"Goddamn you guys, leave my fucking hair alone!"

We burst, laughing; none of us even remembered putting the penny into his spongy afro. It had been there for hours.

"Every time… every fuckin' time I'm in the front you guys do this shit…hahaha, I hate you all! You especially Bomber!" he shot, leaping up and hurling a kneepad at me.

We just laughed harder. He had a fro, we had time, what else were we supposed to do? He sighed, plunking on the bench, laughing and cursing.

"Yeah, haha. Fuck you guys, I'm going home!" chimed JT. We looked at him. We smiled. He shook his head and gave up. He smiled. The ribs would keep coming, as would the threats, potatoes, hang overs, aches, pains, laughs, and wonderful misery of the mystifying journey to anywhere away from reality, to nowhere. This was the road we all loved.

"Damn fucks anyways. AHHHHH FUCK!" he yelled at no one in particular. We all knew the truth. Only professional wrestling made it possible to mix love, hate, pain, and pleasure together with your best friends who are your worst enemies. In our phony feuds we were all winners. Damning and saving us all was the knowledge that JT's threat of going home was transparently empty; this was home.

Working (Stiffly) Through Life

Forearms to the back are stiff. They hurt for real, or they look too phony to do. That's wrestling- what doesn't look like it should hurt does, and what does, doesn't. Any wrestler worth his salt will forearm stiffly but safely. We got the point of forearming each other or punching each other randomly. I'm pretty sure that it actually began with the bag packing that we did in the van, but can't remember precisely.

It makes sense that it began there, so since this is Professional Wrestling (yes, in capital letters), that is probably not how it happened. Whatever the source, the result was the same and the rules of the game were not set whatsoever. Basically, any chance you had, you would stiff somebody. The more ludicrous or out of place the context, the funnier. The stiffer and more painful, the funnier. And if it took advantage of something that was particularly bad already, like a sunburn, funnier yet.

I had two memorable gifts of being ribbed this way. After the bag hurling and face stuffing had begun, I really had gotten a good head start. I was always late and always the last one to get into the van, so I had the job of passing the bags to the other workers and did a resoundingly bad job of it as often as I could, especially with my bag.

Once most of them were in place on the lap of the person on the back seat, I would toss the remaining ones quicker and quicker so that it was impossible to actually handle them properly. The last one would hit the bag holder in the face; he had no defense because his hands were tied down by all the other bags. It was annoying but funny as hell, especially if Elvis added a fake face fart to the injury afterwards.

Once, by some fluke or on purpose because the boys were tired of my shit, I ended up in the back. I didn't think anything of it. And then the bags started flying in and I didn't think anything of it- this was all part of being on the road. Then a bunch of punches followed, which I mostly blocked with the bags.

"Haha, that wasn't so ba— WHAM! Showtime gleefully punched me in the face, barely pulling back. I yelped, saw stars, got super pissed off, and then realized that I fully deserved it and couldn't get out from the bags anyways. I was starting to push them off of my lap when Nick yelled, "We gotta go, sit down."

A bruise started growing on my cheek- Showtime had decked me right in the middle point of my right cheek bone. Cheek swelling, ears steaming with anger, I had no recourse as the sliding door slammed shut and Jer chuckled, "Ha, I just punched Bomber legit in the face. Ha."

Someone mumbled something, then he added, "Love you Bomber." I don't know if I was on one of my non-swearing phases or not, but I probably cursed him anyways. We then sat there for 5 more minutes with me plotting more and more revenge but not being able to get up and do anything and wishing I could get out from the back seat.

"No, stay in the van!" Nick kept yelling. Maybe he was in on it. Usually, we just stiffed each other with forearms to the back or shoved a guy from behind as he stood at a urinal- one of Sinn's favourites. Needless to say, I remembered the punch to the face.

When we finally got to the next arena, we had driven for a while and were all glad to get out. Showtime rode with Sneaky Martin and the ring crew that day, so we didn't actually see each other until arrival. I hopped out, stewing on revenge.

Nothing unique or interesting presented itself as we walked through the gravel parking lot. I had to pee, so I wandered off, then saw a rock the size of a softball. Showtime was walking towards the ring truck, and I pondered throwing the rock at him through the truck window. Then I remembered a time Stylin' Bryan had done something similar in Cambridge.

I had just flown in from BC to do some shows for Ernie Todd in Winnipeg, and the 2 days before were spent eating, boozing, and crooning at Karaoke. I was sitting at the end of a string of tables, talking to someone and having a beer when suddenly something tapped me on the chest, and then smashed on the floor. I looked down to see an empty, shattered beer bottle, then looked up to see Stylin' laughing to himself. Everybody at the table looked at him in disgust- even Romeo kind of sneered and shook his head - then Bryan looked at us, stopped laughing, and with an "Aw, I guess that wasn't as funny as I thought it was," sheepishly went to get a broom.

Remembering that, I couldn't really justify hurling a stone at the ring truck. But I was in luck; Showtime turned, walked back towards Nick's van, and then turned to walk back to the ring truck. I knew he had hurt his ankle a while before, so from about 30 feet away, I viciously lobbed the rock – at least 3 pounds- with an underhand toss at his feet, like Fred Flintstone tossing a bowling ball; in exquisite timing, it passed directly between his legs as he obliviously marched back to the van. He hadn't even noticed. I was disappointed, but Kingman had a laugh.

"You shoulda seen the look on ol' Sneaky Martin's face, he just about had a heart attack when you launched that boulder at Showtime. It just missed him by an inch."

I was unavenged but more opportunities would come. After the show, the boys all headed to a local pub to indulge in our two favourite treats of the Maritimes - local beer and super fattening Poutine. If you haven't had poutine, you're missing out. Showtime liked it so well he packed on 10 pounds in 21 days. Poutine; fat mistress of the Maritimes.

"Bomber, you go first" offered Showtime.

"No man, you go ahead."

"Fuck off, you're not getting me now. I'm sore, Kingman said he bruised his forearm on my back during our match, and that stiff as shit ring is killing me. No more forearms to the back. Fuck off."

I felt a little of his pain, but forearms were the standard rib currency. His back was messed up from the ring as most of ours were; if he was complaining, it must have hurt, so it would be funnier to stiff him than usual.

"Fine" I said, walking in.

We entered. JT, Kingman, Duke McIsaac and I paused, reading the menu. I was the last one in front of Showtime. As the waitress asked, "Table for 5?" a stroke of genius hit me; I turned and forearmed Showtime in the temple as hard as I could. Brilliantly effective. Eyes crossed, cheeks puffing like Jim Neidhart in a comeback, he crumpled onto the stack of menus at the front door, spilling them on the floor and groaning loudly. To her credit, the waitress didn't even bat an eye, just said, "Follow me" and we all casually walked to our table and sat down.

Two minutes later, Showtime picked up the menus off the floor and joined us. Dinner was surprisingly friendly.

At the two week mark of the 3 week tour, I cut an interview for a fan out in Halifax or Moncton backstage at a show. He was filming a lot of us, asking questions about training and the road, good typical mark stuff that was fun to answer and kind of exposed a bit of the biz but highlighted the sacrifice and talent of it all. As I stood there talking, a log fell out of the ceiling and smashed me on the back. I stumbled forward about 4 feet, said, "Holy fuck" and then looked up to see a laughing Kingman.

I've never been so happy about a stiff forearm; at 6'8, 320 pounds, the strongman competitor/ comedian considered me strong enough to take a stiff, unexpected forearm from him. I was the biggest and most muscular I had ever been at 6'1", 245lbs, but still, taking such a shot would crumple anyone. I did crumple, but I got up, bewildered, and as Kingman laughed saying, "You're it" I realized we were into something special.

We were all the boys- a great mix of respect, tough love, and shared misery kept us all together and all level headed. No egos prevailed, no attitudes hung around, the boys were the boys enjoying the road as the ride in never-never land it is supposed to be.   Unfortunately for Kingman, God had a big rib planned for him that I don't think any of us who ever heard of it will ever forget.

Morning Routine

"What's going on? "

"I can't tell you over the phone, we'll talk about it when we get there."

"How long do you figure?"

"Probably 20 minutes, not sure. We'll be there in a bit."

"Alright man, see you." Jer hung up. 11:30. Pick up for us was 10, especially when we had a longer trip to the show. Today was about a 5 hour drive each way today, Moncton to Nova Scotia.

Minutes lingered and left, the usual for a day when you really didn't have to do anything but felt you needed to. We'd be on time for the show and if we weren't it wouldn't matter anyways. The fans would wait; they were respectful and patient in the Maritimes, and probably didn't have any more to do than we did. Some minutes flew by when we threw rocks at each other or told stories. When I told JT Playa how I'd like to be a millionaire so I could always wear a new pair of socks each day, that took up about 3 minutes because he was so pissed off at the idea.

"Fuck Bomber, when you say shit like that I want to fight you." Grumbly, gravelly, sour but still funny.

"Why do you care if I want new socks every day? I'll give the old ones to charity."

"Fuck, because, hun hun hun," he laughed, "it's such a waste of money. Hahaha, bomber and his brilliant idea of wasting money on socks. Shut up, you're making me hot."

"I'm making you hot because you don't want me to waste my millionaire money? Go cut your hair."

Three more minutes passed by in quiet stupor, 5 went by when I decided to go to the bathroom and we argued about whether or not I'd be back before Nick and Kingman got back. I wasn't, but if we hadn't argued about it for so long, I would have been. But that wasn't a problem for me. I was the last guy in, JT was the first, so he was at the back and had to hold the bags. I started pushing one in, handing it to him.

"K bomber, just a sec."
I handed him another one, just slightly ahead of him being ready.

"Fuck, hold on just a sec."
The next two came in rapid fire succession, the first hitting his face, "Fuck!" the second hitting the bag that was already pressing against his face, and he shouted out,

"Bomber, fuck, hold on." For good measure I double fist punched the last bag nice and hard into his face.

"Goddamit bomber what the fuck? What's wrong with you? That's my gear." Punch! I smiled.

"Fuck bomber, I hope we're working tonight, I'm gonna be so fucken stiff...hahaha! YOU'RE FUCKING DEAD! HA!" and away we went.

I laughed because after a week on the road, wrestling in a ring with thin carpet for padding and absolutely no give, with a sawhorse underneath it to keep the boards from bending at all, stiff didn't exist for any of us. In the words of JT, the ring was "Hand crafted by Satan" and he gleefully jumped around barring his teeth imitating monkey-devils, laughing maniacally, pretending to saw at the stiff boards. He was an asset of pure entertainment on the road. Regardless of how much we all liked him, I didn't have any bags on me. JT did and was hot, both emotionally pissed and physically hot, because there was no AC and a lot of heat in Nick's Van. The Maritimes in the summer can melt anybody, especially a bunch of hung over wrestlers each carrying a few extra pounds from too much poutine and booze. Other than the occasional fart, we rode in silence. We met Kingman at the restaurant; he refused to talk until he got a coffee and some food.

"This is fuckin' moronic," was all he muttered, then elbowing Nick, "you tell 'em, I'll get too pissed off."

"All right," Nick said as he stirred his coffee, then fiddled artistically with the pen in his hand. "let me paint it this way."

* * *

Magnus Meets The Wall

So last night we were all drinking at the bar; Magnus kept drinking and drinking and I didn't think anything of it. He kept saying, "One more beer, one more beer" showing off to some strangers and pounding beer back like crazy, but who cares? It's just beer and he's huge. I left and curled up in my sleeping bag on Kingman's floor, passed out, and figured that was it.

"Open up I gotta go!" Huh? Nobody made a sound.

"Open up, I gotta go NOW!"

What is buddy yelling about? I don't get what the hell is going on. All I know is it's barely light out, Magnus is yelling at Kingman's Sister in law, and he's only wearing his tighty whities. (A brief interjection here- Magnus was 6'3 and 300 + pounds;. He was huge but usually no problem.)

Kingman's wife's sister runs out of the bathroom wearing nothing but a towel, screaming and crying down the stairs. Kingman walks out (another brief interjection here- Kingman was 6'8, 320 + pounds, competed in strongman competitions, and had as sharp a wit as any. And this is his house his sister is getting yelled at in.)

As a very pissed-off Godzilla stared a hole through a very drunk King Kong, a loud rumbling began, groaning then roaring out from Magnus' stomach. Stokes and I are awake on the living room floor and fully expect the throwdown of the century; what we get is King Kong turning into Stay-Puff Marshmallow man, and then the gurgling turns into a roaring

231

fart. Magnus turns, sees Kingman, then stars erupting out of his ass with a landslide of shit as he falls backwards through the wall.

Kingman stares in disbelief and Stay-Puff sits there erupting shit through his underwear, onto the carpet, into the drywall, and all over himself.

"Get into the fuckin' bathroom."

I don't know how Kingman formed the words; I was in shock. I think his deep subconscious just stepped in and took over. Stay puff brown pants stumbles into the bathroom, falls through the glass window of the shower, and then begins shitting himself again.

He lays there flopping like a turtle on his back for a few seconds, all the while erupting out of his ass, then pulls himself up by the now broken door of the shower and finally gets his ass over the toilet for the last 3 blasts of murky yellow-brown diarrhea, which still manage to fill the bowl. He sits there for a few seconds staring off into space, dreaming about god knows what, as if the whole thing is just another day in the life of Magnus. And then I see the look, the look that says not, "I'm terrified of what I just did," but, "Oh my god, it happened again!"

But then doing the thinker pose as he sits there listening to the gentle farts of shit expelling from his ass and echoing throughout the house. His work done, he grabs a roll of toilet paper, wads some onto his ass, and gets some of the wad off his ass and into the bowl covered in blood and feces, but not all. Then he drops the roll of toilet paper into the toilet, hits the flusher. The toilet won't flush. The shit groaned when it came out of Magnus' ass, the toilet groaned when it tried to choke down on all of it, like it's complaining that this is beyond the call of duty.

Satisfied, Magnus gets up, walks out into the living room, and pulls his sleeping bag over his head. A shit bomb has gone off in the bathroom, destroyed the wall and the shower door, and sprayed shit all over the floor, onto the carpet, and into the cracks of the house and carpet.

"What the fuck are you doing?" Kingman manages to say. He walks over to Magnus, kicks him in the ass, and Magnus complains back, "What?"

"Clean your shit up!"

Confused, as though he's thinking, "What? I wanted to use the bathroom, I used it, it's your house clean up the mess of your bathroom cause this is all your fault for having a house", Magnus gets up, walks into the kitchen, and with shit still running down his leg mind you, grabs a roll of paper towel.

Clearly nobody is steering this lost train because Magnus doesn't grab any cleaner or soap or anything. He just takes the roll of paper towel, and without unrolling it, begins smearing the shit that is on the floor and bathtub around the whole bathroom. He even manages to get it on the mirror.

Then, he looks at the toilet. Even he can see it's full and clogged, so he grabs his shit brush of paper towel, walks into the kitchen, and casually tosses it into the sink. He tossed a whole roll of paper towel covered in shit into Kingman's kitchen sink. Right next to the dish rack. Once again he slugs out into the living room, looks at me and Stokes, shrugs like, "I don't know what the big deal is" and rolls up in his sleeping bag.

Kingman is steaming, much like the shit staining into the walls and carpet. The stench is overwhelming and I dry-heave while trying not to laugh or puke; Stokes is losing his mind of course, but keeps his laughs under wraps out of respect of Kingman; his eyes tell the story. I figure Magnus is about to die, but Kingman in a surprisingly quiet, calm voice just says, "Get the fuck outta my house."

"Huh?"

"Get. The fuck. Out. Of my. House."

Even Magnus realizes that his safety may be in danger; he grabs his gear bag, his sleeping bag, and with a hundred-yard stare walks out the front door wearing only his shit-stained tighty-whities, his sleeping bag dragging behind him. (And here Kingman interjects for Nick.)

"The worst fuckin part is that I've white carpets and 2 cats. One of my cats walked through the shit and over to where Magnus had been sleeping. It stopped, looking at me in disgust and crinkled up its nose, as if to say, "your friends disgust me." I looked behind it and saw a trail of shitty-kitty paw prints through my living room over my white carpets and onto my couch.

* * *

We sat there jaws drooping, dumbfounded. After our minds recovered, someone asked, "Where is he now?"

"He was in his car. If he has any sense he went somewhere, took a shower, and cleaned up. We're all supposed to meet up at the hotel 30 minutes ago."

A few days later, Magnus left the tour. A week or two after that, Jer, myself, and JT all returned home to daily drudgery of day jobs and boredom. It was tough returning to reality.

In the saddest footnote I will ever write, I put two pieces together weeks after Magnus had left. As we wrestled in St. John, New Brunswick, a guy came around backstage asking for Mark, Magnus' real name. He looked a bit like him, smaller (which was the only possibility given Magnus's size), same face, same kind of hair. I told him no, then he left.

Later, I realized it was Magnus' father whom Magnus told us he hadn't seen in years. Maybe the pressure of seeing his old man again had caused Magnus to overdo it that fateful night. Sometimes even the strongest, toughest gimmick can't shield you from yourself; maybe that just makes it worse.

Halifax and the Maritimes was one of the best summers of my life. It's pretty rare to find a fulltime tour in wrestling anywhere, and the crew that I was with was awesome. Most nights I was teaming with Fabian Stokes against "Evil" Elvis Elliot and Kingman. The matches were good and we worked well- not too much for the fans to follow, not too little for the fans to be bored. The fans mean so much to a match.

You can go out there and do a million spots, but if you're not reading the crowd and engaging with them, they really don't care. Fans at wrestling shows have come to appreciate and expect the wrestlers reacting to them personally while the matches are going on. It's what really makes professional wrestling unique in comparison to other sports. You don't see Sidney Crosby turn to the crowd mid-shot and yell "Huzzaw" or "You can't see me!" It just doesn't happen.

This territory made life fun; at $575 every week, I was actually earning a living and enjoying. Wrestling was actually my job- wake up, workout, tan, eat, drive, wrestle, party, then repeat. We were living the dream.

Why Wrestlers Should Only Wrestle

When first at the wrestling school, I had 5 months to train full time to become a solid pro wrestler - why would I swap that for $6 per hour at a towel factory or something else? I told myself that it didn't make sense, that I could take a day job somewhere, that I was better off training and focusing on that. I was kind of right. But needed to prove that I was better cut out for wrestling than anything else. Day jobs were really useful for that.

The work itself was boring; I often daydreamed or cursed my time at such places. The worst was the wafer factory. The shift was a night shift from 11 p.m. until 7:30 in the morning. The factory went 24 hours a day and the jobs were beyond mind-numbing. My first job there was supervising wafers. They came off a conveyer belt, I stacked them into tens, put plastic cutting board on top of the tenth, and then stacked up another ten on top of that.

The stacks went 100 wafers high and I filled up a cart with 10 stacks of 100, side by side. Then I went and got a new cart. If the wafers were misshapen or flawed, I threw them into a giant bin or my mouth. 7 a.m. was a weird time at that place; I was exhausted, wound up on sugar, and no good to anybody.

Sometimes the temp agencies who got the wrestlers the jobs would say you had to work at such and such a place or you wouldn't get any work, so you did. I hated it, so that particular place lead to a long stretch of not working anywhere. It was probably a favour to most of those places anyway; I was 20 and not attentive or sensible. I was philosophical, but totally useless at work.

A year of school back in BC and working 2 jobs would improve my ability to work a normal job... not.

You're Gonna Hurt Yourself

When I went to work again after leaving BC a year later, my first job in Ontario was in a warehouse doing quality control on car parts. I dreaded that job; I would arrive exactly at 8 or 1 minute after, walk in, and then spend the first 4 hours of the day across from a guy whose breathe smelled literally like dog shit. There is no other way to describe it.

I know it sounds unbelievable, but when I'm not eating enough and have only coffee in the morning, I know my breath smells the same; I've tasted it. His smelled like dog shit. The mornings were dreadful. I dreaded returning. I would go to Fast Eddies for lunch, grab some crazy fries and a burger, then arrive back 5 minutes after lunch was over. They must have been desperate to keep me around.

My crowning moment came when using pressurized hoses to blast dirt out of engine blocks. The nozzle on one of the hoses had broken and 3 guys were standing around doing nothing. I hated the total pointlessness of the situation, so I stepped up. I went to the opposite side of the warehouse, grabbed another hose, and brought it over. The end nozzle was what we wanted, but the plug at the base of the hose didn't fit the line we were next to.

Thinking quickly, I sliced open the hose with an exact-o-knife and then tried to jam in into the end of the hose from before. That didn't work, so I cut the other hose a bit shorter to make the end tighter and more likely to fit the hose. That still didn't work, so I grabbed a pair of pliers and tried prying open the end of the hose, stood on it with one foot while another guy to tried to kick the nozzle into it the hose. That still didn't work, so I grabbed some crazy glue, made a lengthwise slice down the hose, placed the socket of the nozzle into it, closed the hose around it, and then glued it while wrapping it with tape to hold it in place. Then we waited.

After 5 minutes, I turned on the air; "Thunk." Instantly, the nozzle flew out of the hose into a wall. Now it was covered with glue and dirt and the hose also was all gummed up with glue and tape. I was about to cut off another section of the old hose when the supervisor came over and put a stop to the madness. He pointed directly behind me; there was another hose hanging up there the whole time and not one of us had seen it.

At least I had managed to ruin 2 other hoses in the process. Believe it or not, I quit working there; they didn't fire me. I found something better to do. I was going to the Animal Olympics. I was going to be a Barnyard Cock.

Life as a wrestler is completely out of touch with reality; you do everything you're not supposed to do in the day to day of human existence. That's your daily life, so naturally your night life, your chance to escape from reality, is even more ridiculous. Especially with a crew of us together.

Take the Good, Take the Bad...

You live your gimmick in wrestling; you are always looking for bits to add, pieces of reality to weave into your stage persona. It is still weird how Mike was always TJ to me but always Mike to Jer. I was always Bomber to everyone, even Jer's mom, his girlfriends, and his sister. JT was always JT to me, but Jess to Jer and Mike. Rudy was always Rudy, but his real name was Greg. Stylin was always Stylin' because we all knew too many Bryans back home and he was so much more than just another Bryan. It's a strange paradox that these people you know the best of all are ones who often know nothing about you away from wrestling.

When you enter the world of wrestling, you are in a very literal sense renamed and reborn. You are new. Whatever happened before, you are now your gimmick. People know only that side of you, a side that till now has been the private fantasy of your life or your dreams. You share something that was completely private before you began wrestling. It is something true but liberating, an embarrassing confession. Fragile. Sensitive. Honest.

At some point you don't know who you are and reality loses its bite because you aren't in reality. The line begins to blur. When you really start wrestling a lot, you become more of your gimmick, less of yourself until finally you are fully your own invention. After you retire, you have to rediscover the you that lives at home with a wife, kids, day job, and finds watching other people try to entertain you fun. You have to re-learn everything, even who you are. You have to see who is going to survive- you or your gimmick. At home, it really can't be both.

For some reason Jer was always Jer. He'd spent the longest time wrestling; he formed the Florence Wrestling Federation with TJ, Romeo, and Ball when they were in grade 9. He had built the longest legacy behind his name. He was fun, he was a good wrestler, and he loved wrestling. So he wasn't Showtime or The Director, he was always Jer. But the rest of us, well, we knew each other so well that we didn't need to know each other at all.

We always fought life-- daydreams, day-jobs, and reality battled our gimmick selves on a daily basis. Maybe to combat this, we usually didn't learn each other's real name. We helped our brothers fight reality. This caused problems.

Fake Names, Real Problems

Picking me up in the airport highlighted a bit of a problem that is common in professional wrestling; none of us knew each other's real name. When they finally did track me down, Jake Fury tackled me and JT Player gave me a chop. "You stupid fuck, why didn't you tell us where you were coming from?"

"I was in BC, everyone knows that."

"Yeah well, none of us know your real name. We didn't even know the flight number! Let's go!"

"I almost got arrested trying to find you!" said Jake.

"What? Why?"

"I yelled out "BOMBER!" thinking you'd answer. Everyone turned and looked at me, terrified! (This was only 2 years after 9-11). I hightailed it to the street, ran in a few doors down, and here you are. Fuck."

We left in a hurry. It was 4 hours to Montreal. There, Jake and I had one of my favourite matches of my career at a packed bar. It was a good show, but weird as we were all paid by cheque, then went and gave the cheque back to the promoter who gave us cash plus $25 extra for it.

It was also weird because his office was in the back of the bar and surrounded by huge security guards. Nobody wanted to speak up or piss anyone off, and nobody knew why the heavy guards were there. We all had a feeling it was best to not ask questions, to just take the money and go.

From there JT, Showtime, and I headed out to Nova Scotia for ten more days of tour with Bobby Bass. When we arrived, we all got back pay from Bass that he had been holding on to for the past couple of weeks.

Today, I would never leave a territory without getting all my money. At the time, we were all young and dumb, and Bass came through. After we got our checks, we finally went back to the hotel room and got a night's sleep. As we crashed onto our beds and a rollout couch, I was a little annoyed because Bobby had hinted he might pay me double for working twice a night; once under a hood and once in a tag match. He hadn't, but I was still happy to be back. JT was extremely sullen. Uncomfortably so. A few minutes passed in silence.

"Jess, what's the matter?" asked Showtime.

"Nothing."

"No, tell us."

"Fuck look at this."

He threw over his paycheque. Across the envelope, Bobby Bass's unmistakable writing spelled out in big, magic marker letters, "TK BLAIR".

"I've been working for the guy for 3 fuckin weeks and he still doesn't know my name!"

It wasn't really too shocking, as for the last 3 weeks Bobby Bass had been doing introductions and announcing. He had yet to say JT's name right. "TK Blair... TJ Hair... MC Prayer... JT Flair." He wasn't ribbing him, either. We all started to wonder if Bobby Bass was a little slow. It could also have been that JT Playa had switched from roles so many times that it was confusing everybody. The first week, it was easy; go out and cut a heel promo.

"Looky here, looky here, looky here..." JT started, "Moncton, I just want to say I've been here for 1 week and you are the most disgusting. Putrid. UglypeopleIhaveeverseen! Shut up, I hate you all!"

"BOOOOOOOOOOOO!" yelled the fans. That was his first promo, and it worked like a charm. The next week we returned to Moncton for our weekly show, and were down a babyface because Magnus had left after Shitstorm 2002. JT had to switch. He couldn't have done it more simply.

"Looky here, looky here, looky here.." he began.

"BOOOOOOOO!" went the crowd. "Please Moncton, just listen. Last week I came out here and said I hate this town and all you stupid people. Well, Moncton, I apologize. I take it back, after a week here, this town in fantastic! You people are lovely, I love you all! YEAH!"

"YAAAAAAA!!!" Went the fans. And just like that, the crowd was on his side, breaking out in a chant of, "J-T, J-T, J-T!" Somehow, Bobby Bass still didn't learn his name.

A new babyface star was born. JT was destined for a great future as a glowing babyface in the Maritimes, and Moncton in Particular… until the next time we wrestled in Moncton. We had too many babyfaces again.

"Looky here, look-y here-ah, look. E. Hee-yuh!"

"Yaaaa, we love you JT Playa!"

The crowd was hot. JT was over.

"Moncton, how you doing? Last week, I came out here and I made amends with your lovely town and you people. I said you were fantastic!"

"YAAAAAAA!"

"Well, I just gotta say, I take back my apology. After another week here-uh, I hate you all. You disgust me. You and your no cash Bobby Bash. Tst-tst-tst (JT Suckin on his lips) 'Duhhhh, I'm no cash Babby Bath, uhhhhh, I live in Moncton, Tst-Tst-tst! I love TK Blair Tst-tst-tst!"

"BOOOOOOO! GO HOME!!! BOOOOO!"

JT was heel again, and managed to mock the promoter without getting fired. It was great and made him feel better, but Bobby still didn't know his name. The people in charge in wrestling aren't much different from in life.

As the tour went on, we meshed and milled together wonderfully as a group, but knew it was for the summer only at most. A few guys had options already planned to explore later. Renee Dupree was a mainstay at the time, an already amazingly jacked 18 year old, and he was pretty good friends with Sinn. One day we stopped by the house of his father, Emile Dupree.

Emile Calls the Finish

"Guys, welcome, let me show you something."
He lead us into the garage of his spacious rancher home.

"Guys, I want you to look at dis. This is a poster from the promotion I run here for 20 years. I sell out a lot of shows and make a tonne of money until Vince said he want in, so I let him in and stop promoting. Look at the poster."

It was about as simple a wrestling poster as you could come up with. It had huge letters saying, "WRESTLING" at the top, and four wrestlers prominently displayed above the date and location. Simple. Readable. I noticed a picture of Sailor White on the poster and wondered if he wanted his shaving gear back. There was another poster underneath which had the exact same layout only with a different group of wrestlers, different day, and different location. So clear.

"Guys, with this I drew a crowd every week in Moncton for twenty years. A crowd of minimum, minimum 400. We would even sell out. Everybody made money and I pay the boys well. They keep their merch."
I wondered why he was telling us all this. Was he going to start running again?

"When I started running again 2 years ago it was just to get Renee signed wid Vince. He's done it and leaves soon. I've already quit promoting and let Bobby run the territory, but I tell you dis. He's probably not going to last the summer."

He showed us a Bobby Bass poster; it had small lettering, including "ACW/ Atlantic Coast Wrestling" (ironic ACW since was the offshoot of ICW that Curtis, Bryan, and a few other guys had given Joe thousands of dollars for). Underneath that, there was a medium sized photo of Bobby Bass, and then small portrait circles of the rest of the wrestlers, every last name. When took two steps back, Emile's point became really clear.

"Look at that from there. Can you read it?"

"No" I bemoaned.

"Of course not. Guys, enjoy the tour and get paid cash. Mark my words, Bobby Bass is honest but bless him, he will probably be out of business by the end of the summer."

Bass was doing better than average, but... Of the crew there with ACW, 3 of us left back for Ontario at the end of the next week. It had already started to look like Emile was right, but wrestling was slow everywhere we told ourselves.

When we got home, we found out the grim details. The promotion had folded, but luckily we who left had been paid. Half the guys ended up getting cheques but figured they would bounce. Bobby Bass had cashed in his wife's RRSP's (rumour said) and Kingman had demanded Bobby Bass's ring as payment.

He got it, but was still out hundreds or thousands, even taking the ring at top value. Bobby had done his best, but the business had changed. We were all at home and then heard the news that Sinn and Stevie Lee had totaled Sinn's van just outside of Montreal. No full time wrestling was to be found anywhere else in Canada. Business was in the dumps. So was my career.

Departure

Ontario was still impossible to break into, and as September rolled in, a few things were obvious. JT couldn't get me booked with Neo Spirit Pro, his own promotion, because 4 guys were involved in doing the bookings and they wanted to push their students before any other outside talent. It made sense.

Other than my one shot with Border City Wrestling, there wasn't much from D'amore. I was shredded with abs for the first time in my life, I could do it all in the ring, and I had just gone from being "The Mad Bomber" to, "The Bomber" Nelson Creed, a better name but not by much. However, no matter my ability or look, nobody could see it because I had no footage.

I had no tapes and very little exposure that put me in the proper light. There were no internet videos to send promoters links of. No bookings. No job. Not even a bed, just some blankets and a spot on Jer's floor. It sucked and winter was coming. The long, shitty, freezing Ontario winter. The writing was on the wall.

"Boys, I think I'm going to head home."

"Bomber, you've said that a thousand times since you came out here" said TJ.

"Yeah, well, I think I mean it."

"K Bomb."

"No, I'm serious. I'm going to leave Tuesday. If I drive straight, I can get home by Thanksgiving."

It was Saturday. Last minute.

"Really? You really going to take off?"

"I can get a job at Delany's again, actually have money and work as much as I'm working out here for ASW out there." On paper, it looked a hundred times better. Paper isn't life.

"Right, well, if you do go, we'll have some beers."

"Let's do her up."

Nobody quite knew if I was serious. A phone call could change all the plans I'd made so far, but I had a feeling. So did the boys. We went out, drank at Fiddler's Green, played some video games, ate two pies, and Sunday I made a big goodbye breakfast for everyone. Monday we watched raw and ate pizza.   Tuesday, after burning some CD's and taking a lot longer to get my shit together than planned, I drove out to Mark Betollucci's place in Thunder Bay.

After crashing at his house for 6 hours, most of them spent laughing at pictures of me as Doink I popped a couple ephedrine pills and drove and drove and drove. When I started hallucinating things were running across the road, what The King of the Yukon calls "ghost-dogging", I pulled onto a side road. I followed it for 5 minutes, parked, and then read the sign above my head. "Something town Community Cemetery." Already seeing ghosts, I figured I'd better drive a bit further. Then I remembered Stylin Bryan telling me about his adventure falling asleep behind the wheel in Saskatchewan.

* * *

Bryan's Way Out

"AAAAHHH!!! AAAHHH! NOOOO!!!!" Bryan screamed. Snow all around the car. Panicking, he tried not to hyperventilate. "Whew, whew, whew, whew, NO GOOD! AHHHHH!!! " He honked the horn, stomped his foot on the brakes. The car still ran. He honked again, "PLEASE GOD NOOO!! SOMEBODY HELP! SOMEBODY!!!! OH GOD, I'M SORRY! I SWEAR I'LL....!!"

He finished the bargain in his head. Surrounded. Snow in front, snow on both sides. He stomped the gas. WHEEEEEEEEEE. The car was in neutral. Had he gone into neutral when he crashed? Was he in neutral when he fell asleep? WHEEEE he revved the engine. The tires didn't spin. What??? Bryan spat, a trick every Canadian learns for finding the direction to dig in an avalanche.

"Ugh."

The spit had landed in his face. He looked up and shook his head. Snow was falling through the sun roof. Were those stars? He was upright. His car was in neutral. He flashed the lights and pounded the ceiling. No snow on top. Hardly any on the windshield. A little inside. He checked his mirror. No snow behind. It came back to him.

"Ohh, God.... God, you can't hold me to that one. Nobody has to honor a debt sworn under false pretenses." Bryan breathed out deeply. Calm. "Fine" he muttered then backed his car out of the snow mounds he had parked between an hour earlier. He didn't want to fall asleep behind the wheel and crash. Irony.

Bryan got his life, and God got the retirement from Stylin' Bryan Silver of his attempt to be a career wrestler. It may seem sad to be swindled out of your dream by a near death experience, but it was merciful, better than dying under a wall of snow. Take it for all in all, Stylin' probably got two wins out of it.

* * *

That put a smile on my face; when I finally pulled over close to Brandon, Manitoba a few hours later, I really needed to sleep. I didn't eat. I figured it would make me sleepier, but I did finally pee. As a trick for driving, I drank so much that I had to pee, and took mass doses of ephedrine to keep awake, albeit somewhat out of it. I did the leg from Brandon to Vancouver in 18 hours. I actually did fall asleep for a few seconds behind the wheel outside of Calgary, but as the road was perfectly straight, I was ok. I reached Vancouver just in time to catch my brother and his wife at their house. We drove to the ferry, went over to Victoria for thanksgiving, and after the meal, I slept for 12 hours. Ontario, and my dream, were now both very far away.

The Heat Is On Me

In a sell-out move, I went back to work at Delany's and The Roxy. It wasn't all bad. I had a job, managed to get my own dodgy apartment, and enrolled in a college few courses that interested me.

While I was figuring out my life, I would let the government sponsor me through a couple of student loans. It wasn't the best plan, but wasn't the worst plan either; it was just a fall back plan. I had fallen back. Even back with my old girlfriend.

After about 3 weeks, I met up with Adrienne, and soon we were dating again, probably as much for security as anything else. We both needed something comfortable. My apartment, my outlook on my future, my job- they were not. We had dated for four years. She was.

I also started wrestling for All-Star Wrestling again, run now by Fabulous Fabio and Joe Crantz. Despite really enjoying a feud with Jumping Jason, the son of The Missing Link, things looked bleak. After a few more shows, I realized how bad it was. My first matchup was wrestling with Layne Fontaine. I later showed the tape to Jer and he said, "Bomber, what is he going to do? Attack you with his skinny arms or his belly? You shouldn't be selling for that guy."

He was right, but Layne was the best that ASW had to offer. His in ring work was good, but his refusal to actually give the fans a clean finish hurt the matches. Instead of just tapping and settling into a best of 5 series, he tapped weakly as though reaching for the rope, then argued the finish. I ended up working him again in some awful match that also ended unclearly. And in one of the stupidest finishes, he convinced the bookers that I should say, "Say 'I quit'" in our I-Quit match, the blowoff match, thus costing myself the match.

It was awful but I just wanted to wrestle. I was afraid of speaking up and being debooked by the last promotion in BC that seemed decent to work for. No surprise, the match, which had been good, fizzled out at the finish. He booked it, so it's more on him, but I shouldn't have gone along with it. It sucked. And that was about as good as it got back in BC.

Sure I had a job, a girlfriend, and bed to call my own, but they were all filler. There was no genuine content, and no emotional content, in my life. I've never been so bored in daily existence.

I had come back in great shape; after a few months at Delany's, being exhausted and too poor to eat proper food, only leftover muffins, my build hurt and so did my back. My bank account kept me afloat but miserable. My home kept me alive but drained. Wrestling was keeping me occupied but unhappy. Life. Sucked.

Old Time Wrestling Hope

About this time, a bright spot emerged in my wrestling career; the Cauliflower Alley Club (CAC). When I first returned to Vancouver, my brother was in film school seeking fuel for his final project.   Using my time in Ontario as an inspiration, he put together *Wrestling Dominion,* a story about a boy at a wrestling school who has mother issues and falls for/ is betrayed by a mother figure as he wrestles the head coach of the school. What? You've never heard of it? It was not a huge success, but was fun to make. While prepping the actors for it, I became friends with Eugene

Thiessen, who happened to be good friends with Don Leo Jonathan.

In 2002, Don Leo was to be inducted into the Cauliflower Alley Club Hall of Fame and Eugene was going to attend.

"Ben, you should come on down to Vegas. You'll meet some names and it might open some doors for you."

"I can't afford it and the Roxy might fire me."

"You've got to invest in yourself in this business, The Roxy will be there when you get back."

I went, and Eugene sprung for the room at The Golden Nugget. The convention was fantastic and even included a workout session with Les Thatcher. After a warmup of mountain climbers, pushups, and jumping jacks lead by one of Thatcher's boys, we got into the ring.

They assessed if we could bump then picked guys at random to do called matches. When you did the match, you first came in as the babyface, then after the finish, wrestled the next guy as the heel. I was nervous.

There was not only a huge crowd of young wrestlers there being critical of everything we did, but a huge crowd of wrestling legends watching our every move. Harley Race, Moose Morowski, Killer Kowalski, Bruce Hart and Keith, and a few others scrutinized. I got the nod. Butterflies. Show time.

My first match as a babyface had a botched spot. My partner, the heel, called, "Tackle, dropdown, switch, hiptoss." Where I had wrestled, you switched the actual hiptoss. What he had called was for a switch on the run, something I had never encountered before, so I fucked it up. I went for the hip toss right away and he wasn't ready for it.

He blocked it, then threw a closeline that I ducked; I returned the closeline he ducked, then we kind of stood there. I grabbed a headlock.   Les Thatcher then piped in with "Slow down!" the best advice I've ever heard in wrestling.

We did, the match got better, and we finished it with a leg laced pin- I don't even know what to call it, only that Malenko does it a lot and it flows smoothly out of a sunset flip. Next I did a called match with another guy, I honestly can't remember who, and it went reasonably well.

He let me call it, I gave him a few hopes, and finished it with a small package after a blocked suplex. It was much better. Another 60 matches or so happened. The legends in attendance conferred for a few minutes and then Thatcher spoke up. This was a critical moment for all of us in attendance. If the legends all agreed that they wanted to see more of you, it meant you had something.

"We're going to read out all the names of the guys who we chose to do matches tonight. If you didn't hear your name, you're not doing a match."

Hearts skipped as we waited and I had a sinking feeling. I knew I'd fucked up, but my second match was better, and I felt that I definitely looked better than a lot of the guys there. But...

Les read the names slowly. Definitively. After about 15 names I was genuinely panicked. After 20 I gave up hope. After 30, there were only four or so left and I was getting ready to be depressed for a long time. I tried optimism, thinking,

"At least I didn't get hurt." He read the last four names. Not mine. My heart sunk and my brother Paul caught it all on tape. The dejection is palpable, but I searched for gratitude, falling back on my Mormon roots.

"Well, even if I didn't get picked, I'm not going to drink tonight. I'm just happy I'm alive and not injured."

"Did you get picked?" asked one of two tall twins I had been chatting with before. They were both 6'4ish and built.

"No."

"Sorry man, I thought you deserved it" said one.

It was what you'd say to anyone in the situation, good or not, to spare their feelings. A few more guys asked, unintentionally rubbing salt into the wound in my pride.

"No."

"Maybe Next time."

"No, I didn't. Ah well..."

"Sorry Benny" said my brother Paul. What else could he say?

"Yeah, I guess that botched spot kind of hurt me."

"Weird though, I asked a few old timers and they all thought you'd get a match for sure. Harley Race said you could do anything you wanted in this business. And I overheard the twins saying to each other that they were surprised you weren't picked. Odd."

"Well, I'll just go ask Les what he thought."
Bumbling, more than a little choked up, I went to Les.

"Hey Les, thanks for the feedback and help out there. Maybe tonight I can buy you a drink and you can tell me what I should work on."

"Sure. What was your name again?"

"Ben Nelson."

"Oh yeah, the Canadian. I'll see you tonight."

"Yeah, but you'll be busy organizing the matches."

"Yeah, but so will you. I called your name."

"Uhhh... Did I miss it?"

SLAP! His wife hit him then chimed in with, "I told you that you didn't read those names."

It sounds like a lie, like I am building drama, but that's what happened. I swear on my dog. It's the truth. I think it's on tape.

"Oh, sorry... You're doing a match tonight. See you at six."

"I got a match?"

"You got a match, I'll see you tonight, be on time."
I ran to Paul with a weird smile on my face. He was intrigued.

"What?"

"Ha, let me tell you outside." We stepped out, I told him the whole thing, and the story is pretty funny. I did the match. It was good, not great, but good. It told a story. I was a bit shaky on one springboard dropkick, but other than that, it was solid.   I got a few contacts and a bit of praise afterwards, and Don Leo's wife said to Eugene that my match was the best of the night. I don't think she was just flattering me; she's seen a lot of matches, and if it wasn't good, she would have just said, "he's not bad" or something like that.

After the match, I got contact info for a few promoters and spoke with a few people about working. Harley Race told Paul that his brother (me) could, "Do anything he wanted to in this business." A few promoters even offered to fly me to shows, and the door was stated as open for me at the LA New Japan Dojo.

As I headed home from Vegas, there was still a hope that I might make it work. All I had to do was keep putting up with ASW, my annoying job, my courses at Simon Fraser University, and my dull life (due in no small part to me, I'll be honest) long enough to get out of town.

Really Breaking Into the Biz

The Situation with ASW continued to decline; Fabulous Fabio was a busy guy, with a family, two full-time jobs (one being a fire fighter) and trying to do the training as well as wrestle.

I don't know if it was on purpose or not, but I would often show up at scheduled training to find Fabio and his trainees, guys who could really benefit from some in ring time with someone experienced, just finishing. I'd ask why he hadn't told me about the change in time, and Fabio would just say he'd forgotten or dismiss it. None of his students have ever gone on to do anything in the business at all- ironic coming from me- but some are guys who never learned a proper headlock.

Fabio couldn't find time to let me work with them in the ring. It seemed I wasn't welcome to even help train his students. I was one of the smoother workers in the area at that time, yet I couldn't get booked more than once a month and couldn't find anyone to train with. It was awful.

To make matters worse, the shows frequently had me jobbing to talent that hadn't bothered to train properly or buy ring gear. If a guy can show up in sweat pants and sneakers and be considered a wrestler, the mystique and value of the whole business plummets. Matt Borne always protected the business; so did a lot of guys. But that protection started at training.

If a guy didn't train properly, they didn't get on the shows. If they couldn't handle the training, the training wasn't modified to suit their lack of ability. They were told to not come back or put into a role of ring crew or a ref until they learned. The guys in Portland, with the exception of a blatant Sabu rip-off, all knew this and had paid their dues. They knew their stuff and trained properly. They were taught to respect the business. This was something that BC was seriously lacking.

Junk filed into training, and spilled out of the ring in the form of matches. And the fans recognized it.   As much as ECCW had been doing too many garbage matches, they still had some amazing talent and high flyers working for them.   All Star Wrestling, at the time, took the business down a few notches. The bookers, Fabio and Joe, did what they could, but it was awful. I was sick of it. Kenny was still gone. The shows were painfully bad. I was at a breaking point. And then the break happened.

I showed up to train, and low and behold, three talented other guys were actually there. Excited at having a good bunch of guys to work with, I wanted to get wrestling. The ring, as always, wasn't put together properly. After ten minutes of fumbling with repairs and fixing the piece of shit, we stopped. It was passable, although there was one piece of ring that was pretty stiff to bump in.

Overall, Fabio wouldn't get his new students to pay their dues and actually fix the damn ring, and I was tired of having to fix it every single time I got in there. The students were so painfully ignorant about the business that they didn't know a proper ring from a deathtrap. Frustrated, we began training.

We got warm then began running the ropes. We started doing turnbuckles and leapfrogs and sweating hard. I did a few super leap frogs (where you jump straight to the top turnbuckle then leapfrog backwards over your opponent) and did a few top rope bumps and the ring actually felt good.

We started running a three man spot, and before we knew it, we were subbing one guy in and one guy out on the fly in an up and over, switch, baseball slide, whip, up and over repeated spot. It was a good cardio drill and a killer for coordination. We had to kick our feet high as the canvas was catching our toes because it wasn't put on properly, but we kept busting our ass through the drill and then SNAP!

My whole body ached as I looked down. On my last baseball slide, my foot caught in the Canvas and, as my body kept sliding under my opponent, my foot stopped. I looked down and saw my foot sticking out at a right angle to my leg.

Instead of my foot facing forward, it was turned 90 degrees. Imagine that looking at me straight on my foot should make letter "I", with the toes facing you. Now, instead, it was the letter "L" with my foot being the bottom of the "L". I've never felt so much pain. Thank god for endorphins. I looked at my foot and hoped that it was just a dislocation; Layne Fontaine started to dry heave and Lebaux groaned aloud. I didn't dare take off my boot and we decided to drive me to the hospital.

The big problem was the car. Somehow summoning some calm, I phoned Adrienne and explained to her what had happened, and that Kasaki, a student, would pick her up, take her to her car, and then she could meet me at the hospital. Lebaux then drove me there and I did my best not to move my leg as I hopped onto a wheelchair. I also wanted to make sure my boot didn't get cut off, and told the nurse just to cut the laces.

"I'm betting fracture-dislocation" said Lebaux, making a bet. The nurse took off my boot and picked up a phone.

"We have a fracture-dislocation," said the nurse into the phone then, "ok, we'll send him right through."

I rolled through doors. They hooked me up to an IV and few other things. The doctor looked at me, was surprised I wasn't writhing in agony, and then said, "You must have done something pretty forceful to break it like this."

I don't know what I said back; by that time, the drugs were starting to kick in. I do remember him saying they were going to try and relocate my foot, and that they would be using a bunch of drugs to calm the muscles down, similar to the time I dislocated my shoulder.

"AARRGGHHHH" I moaned as my bones burned.

"Ok, the drugs aren't working enough just yet. We'll wait a few minutes."

The doctor came back, and I'm not sure if I knew it was going to hurt, or if the drugs still didn't do their job, but the second time was only a little less painful.

"Hmmm. It looks like it's not going back in. We need more muscle relaxants."

You're Gonna Hurt Yourself

They came. I got more and more relaxed. I started seeing things, like ghosts and goblins and dead people in the walls. Things were getting really messed up. On the third try, they used a splint on one side of my leg, popped it back into place, then put the splint onto the other side to hold it in.

Why they hadn't listened to the nurse I didn't know, but they seemed to have forgotten all about the fracture of the fracture-dislocation assessment. X-rays followed, confirming the fracture of my fibula, but the foot still wasn't right. I was going to have to stay overnight in the hospital. Adrienne waited with me till 2:00 a.m., then went home and came back at 8:00 a.m. to see me into surgery. But before surgery...

"We're going to try and relocate your foot one more time before surgery. Unfortunately, since you are about to go under sedation, we can't give you any relaxants and need to cut out your pain killers."

Looking back, I don't know why they even bothered. After 3 attempts, it wasn't sticking in place. Obviously something was wrong that they couldn't see on the X-ray.

"ARRGHHHH!" I said through clamped teeth.

"Just a little more"

"MAN, what's the point? You know I have a broken leg, Right?"

"Sorry, we do, we're just trying to relocate your foot."

"IT'S NOT WORKING! TIMES 4!"

"We'll stop. It's not working."

Genius. I think he stopped because I was rearing my other foot to boot him in his face. They left, thank god, and Adrienne said something to the effect of taking it easy on the doctors. I got hot. She knew it was wrong to take their side. The doctors were wrong, too. The one that did have competence was the surgeon. That was clear instantly.

"We don't know exactly what we'll see in the surgery. I've read the report and X-rays. I believe it's going to be some soft tissue damage. We'll be able to fix it when we get in there, but you need to sign this waiver giving us the right to make repairs as we see fit and use this for future study."

"If you're asking me to give you permission to cut my foot off, I'm leaving" I said I looking at him soberly.

"I can guarantee it won't come to that."

I signed. As it turned out, he was correct. The tendons and ligaments that run around the foot to the ankle had gotten stuck in the joint. Every time they relocated my foot, it popped back out. Like jamming a door closed on a piece rubber; it never went quite back in.

I also had broken my fibula but thankfully cleanly; it was just one break requiring one metal rod and four screws or so to repair the bone. And 24 staples on both sides of my leg to hold the whole mess together. I got a cast, crutches, breakfast afterwards, and Adrienne gave me a ride to a pharmacist for some drugs and plastic bags. As we stood in the pharmacy I suddenly felt very sick. Animal Olympics sick. I stopped moving. And turned green.

"Uh-oh."

"You want to wait outside?"

I shook my head.

"You going to be sick now?"

Nod. Quick thinking girl that she was, she tore open the bag of garbage bags and handed me one. I took it and heaved out my meatloaf, pudding, and cornbread brunch. Thankfully, I didn't get any on the floor. Unthankfully, the bag was see-through plastic, inspiring a second wave of ˉ Vomit. The contents slushed around like the fat parcels in *Fight Club*; neon, chunky puke, which I spun once to close, then held in my hand as I crutched my way out of the store. Everyone got a good look, and one person almost stopped me to pay, but left me alone when they saw the bag. I got home, slept for days, and tripped out on morphine while reading *The Iliad* and playing Nintendo. I had time to think.

After 3 years in wrestling, I had almost broken my neck, had been bled on, thrown through tables, wrestled people who were drunk and high, made no money, temporarily lost my girlfriend, been separated from my family, had very little education, and had broken my leg. I had posted goodbye on the ASW website.

One fan said, "Good luck" and a few of the boys did too. A few other fans said, "Good riddance" and I'm sure some of the boys did too, but not to my face. No friends in BC, no opportunities for wrestling in Ontario. Things were grim. I paused to consider what I had seen and been through.

It Had to be Me

The Ladies Choice and I in 2001. Note the awesome trophy.

Dog Duties

Wrestling is a world-wide community that is surprisingly small. There have been more times that weird things have happened than I remember. Some of them are unforgettable. One strange coincidence doesn't seem too weird at first, but makes me think there was a higher power sending me a message when I came back to BC to wrestle.

My reasons for coming back were simple at first; I had a girlfriend, I hadn't found a day job in Ontario (definitely from a lack of trying) and I missed my family and rugby life in BC.

I hadn't realized something. In wrestling you have to be ready to sacrifice the big things for the biggest thing- your dream. It's true of any passion, and I was set on a course of small compromises that would lead to me turning away the opportunity for a WWE career when it came. At the time however, I was trying to stretch myself across the country and walk two paths. Looking back, I should have seen the signs and the weird coincidence of how my career would be shaped by the coast.

The weird coincidence was Starr. In Ontario, we had a "family" dog. In reality, she was Joe's dog, a smart, neglected border collie that needed too much stimulation for a 350 pound man provide.

"Ben, would you please take out the family dog? I think she needs to go."

Siggghhh… It was nice to get out of the school with its boarded-up-with-pink-insulation windows. And it was nice to get a break from the smoke inside the school—the common area was a smoking area, as was Joe's office, the kitchen, the bathrooms, and everything except for the bedrooms and the training room. But those were the only positives.

I hope Starr liked the walks. I should have taken her out more, but the issue wasn't with her; it was with Joe. He didn't take care of his business, namely his dog, nor his other business, namely getting us a trainer, so it was a sore point for all of us when his fat lazy ass asked us to do something

256

for him. He had good intentions and they obviously loved each other. She sat at his knee as he fed her, petting her and being genuinely sweet. Joe was very sensitive at times.

No matter what his intentions were, none of us were pleased by his laziness forcing us out into the cold in the Ontario winter. All in all, the truth was Starr, through Joe, was causing a lot of our misery and we were her bitch.

The other piece of this coincidence is that the combo for the school entrance was 0620. That's all there is to it- I don't know if Dickens could artfully drag this part out. There was a security code to the front door, and the number to it was 0620 *, or 0-6-2-0-Starr, or 0-6-2-0-bitch as we joked. The most childish of revenges made us feel so validated. Being able to say "bitch" to refer to Joe and his dog in one go made us all feel better.

The coincidence appeared when I came out to the West Coast. It was impossible to get booked, although the big issue didn't seem to be with my work or look or anything. When I brought out a camera crew and did a documentary for the local television station, I still only earned $20 for my first matches, even in my hometown where I personally brought out 15 people the first time and 50 the second time. The booker, promoter and company owner was Michelle Starr.

I'm sure he had good reasons from his perspective, and after a few months of misery, he did start to book me semi-regularly, but it was clear that my career was in the hands of Starr. I think that it was a sign about how the promotion was going to use me; I was now Starr's bitch, if you want to see it that way. I did.

The even stranger coincidence came when I was going to work a tour in BC to Quesnel, Prince George, and William's Lake. I had to get in touch with Starr, so after a show, I took down his email address and phone number.

It wasn't until I got home that I saw it; the last 4 digits of his phone number were 0620. I don't know what it means; probably nothing, but the literary student/ religion-abused former Mormon in me looks for the meaning. I take it to mean this.

Starr, once full of potential and talent was, like the dog, being abused by the business and making young wrestlers' lives' miserable. He was loveable, but ultimately his place in the business was compounded by neglect and stupidity by the powers that be in wrestling.

If I was going anywhere, I couldn't do so under the guidance of a Starr controlling my wrestling fate. God was telling me that the West Coast, maybe even all of wrestling, was ruined by apathy from many sources and to treat Starr like Joe's dog -- be decent, be a good person, do my part, but don't spend any more time with the dog or the territory than I had to.

Joe argued that walking Starr the dog was paying wrestling dues, but I knew it wouldn't pay off. I would get nothing out of it no matter what people said. It was an exercise in charity, not growth. Similarly, there wasn't a real payoff for loyalty to the promotions on the West Coast, and this turned out to be true. A totally strange, prophetic coincidence. Or just four numbers.

Streetfighter Likes 'Em Tough

Streetfighter Jason Bates is one of the nicest guys around, which is a good thing. He's the last wrestler you'd want to fight. He was 6'1, 245+ pound beast. His hands were the size of bowling balls and he was a legitimate black belt in a type of Karate. I saw him do incline bench press with barbells that were 160 or 200lbs each. He was awesome, he loved Elvis Presley, spoke with a soft semi-drawl in a slightly raspy voice, and he never had a cross word to say about anyone.

We worked many matches together in Halifax and all of them were fun; he was kind and worked with you even though he could probably knock you out with half a punch. As we cruised the windy road to Truro or somewhere else in Nova Scotia, he drove, turned up the Elvis, and belted out tunes while I fell asleep in the back of the van. What everyone else did, I don't know, but I slept. I woke up as he was mid-conversation with Sinn Bodhi and they joked about their women.

"Mine's nicknamed 'Tank'" Sinn said.

"Tank?" asked Streetfighter.

"Well, she's solid, she's a tough girl, and she's got a few tank tattoos. She could probably kick my ass."

This was coming from Sinn, another great guy and one of my favourite things in the bizness; he was (still is) an amazing artist, kind man, and a black belt in Karate. This was before MMA was huge, but the fact was and is if a guy does his Karate properly, his punches are going to have a hell of a lot of force and accuracy behind them. Nick's brother once told us he had seen Nick get tough with someone at a bar and that it wasn't a pretty sight. Nick ended it instantly. At 6'1, 235lbs, Nick had a slightly bigger lower body than Jason, and slightly smaller but still damn impressive arms and shoulders.

"I like girls with a bit of clout to them" Sinn added.

"I love it!" said Streetfighter, "my old lady back home is a solid woman too, she's dusted up a few girls at the bar when she's had to; it's a turn on when a woman is tough. If I'm going to love her, she's gotta be able to handle herself and take a punch, hahaha!"

I remembered it because it was so odd and I had just woken up. It was such a ridiculous thing to say, but we all knew tough women would fit him perfectly. If you put him and his lady in a couples "Fight it out to the doom cage match", one couple against another, Streetfighter and his girl would be pretty likely to take anyone in North America.

Weeks later I had left the Maritimes after flip-flopping over the decision for days. Curious, I called Sneaky Martin, Bobby Bass's right hand man, to see how things were going.

"Bamber, they're awful," he started, "we've run out of money, the shows haven't been drawing, and Bates is in all sorts of trouble." He explained further.

While in Northern Quebec, the boys had gone out on the town for a couple of drinks and some fun. I'm not sure what the date was, but it probably was close to Bastille Day (a nationalist day for French Canadians) and this might have made things a little hostile. Anglophones and Americans can run into trouble with Francophones on Bastille Day.

Us wrestlers, well, "We work hard and we play hard" (*Homer's Phobia*), so out the boys went. Streetfighter was doing his thing, chatting and drinking. I'd seen him drink a buttload of times, and he would have some beers, chat with a pretty lady or goof around with the wrestlers. He'd probably seen his fair share of trouble, but didn't try to find it.

This night, trouble found him in the form of a bar full of guys who picked on him for chatting to a pretty looking French gal. Streetfighter tried to avoid trouble, but sure enough some ass took a poke at him.

I don't know what the guy was thinking, but mess with Streetfighter he did. As Showtime pointed out that his father pointed out to his sister so that she would understand the point of not bugging him when he was a kid, if you mess with the bull, you get the horn. Yes, horn, not horns. Well, Streetfighter gives you the fist instead of the horn, and one is usually enough.

It turned from a problem between a guy and Streetfighter, to a problem between a bar and Streetfighter. He lived up to his name; he broke the jaw of some jackass coming at him with a bottle, booted another guy a few yards, and in the words of Sinn, "He single-handedly outnumbered them all and basically went to jail for destroying a bar full of frogs" which I can say and appreciate being half French myself.

He was then tackled from behind by a last assailant. Something cut his head open for a few stitches and then he tossed the attacker off of his back with the most basic of martial arts throws, the Ippon Seoi Nage, or drop shoulder throw. He was about to kick some serious ass- at this point he was genuinely pissed - when he saw he had just tossed Mr. Newly Broken Jaw's girlfriend four feet into the floor. She was out cold.

Everyone around him realized that this bull had some major horn and let the cops finish the problem. Streetfighter knew well enough not to mess with cops, was charged, and spent a month lingering in Canada. He had bail posted by Bobby Bass (a genuinely nice promoter) so that he could fight the charge. He was totally acquitted as it was self-defense and never had any problems, but his words rung true. He hated the dumb bitch that had jumped on his back, and it was pretty clear that she couldn't take a punch.

That's Me Trying

Another strange irony revolved around my leg and had a clear message for me. My leg, when I broke it, was a mess and hard to fix. When I went in for surgery, I had a plate screwed into the bone to hold it back together with 4 screws. It also required 11 staples on the left of my leg and 6 on the right side of my leg to repair the incisions. The incisions were made for the doctors to assess and repair my joint, and to move the tendons out from the joint between my foot and leg, a fairly unique operation. It was a mess, and a distinctive one. A friend of mine recently had the same injury; his stiches and staples were very different. It required a lot of rehab, and I would recall later that it also required a waiver before the emergency surgery.

When I had the outer cast removed, it was impossible to even go for a car ride without wanting to throw up from pain. The doctor showed me the X-rays which were taken after I got out of the cast, and it was clear my foot was messed up in a pretty major way, although it was going to heal.

The X-ray showed the plate and screws into the bone and all the staples, which would be removed another 2 weeks later. We spent a few minutes staring at the X-rays, me asking questions, and him explaining. I was on crutches for 2 months, and would be for another 2 months after having a knee surgery to repair torn cartilage in my knee. My activities were limited and I spent all day staring at my foot, trying to heal it, and playing Zelda.

When I could finally walk around, my renewed girlfriend Adrienne and I went to Science World in Vancouver for an easy date; not too much walking, kind of fun, and lots of stuff to see. As we wandered around, we saw they had a section on the human body. As we came closer, I noticed a whole section devoted to X-ray machines. They had the back screens used for lighting the X-rays and had actual X-rays with explanations. As we went through them, I got a sick feeling in my stomach, feeling how rough these people had had it. I knew the pain and grinding agony they had suffered.

There were spinal supports, braces, fractures, and a leg with a plate in it. It looked eerily familiar.

With a "Lemme see that, kid" I grabbed it and I shit you not, it was my leg. It had the same number of staples, same screws in the bones, and the same angles for X-rays; I had spent considerable time staring at my X-rays. I double checked by counting the scars on my skin against the number of staples on the X-ray. There could be no doubt. It was even from Royal Columbia Hospital in New Westminster, where I had been for surgery and follow up examinations.

"That's my leg" I said to Adrienne.

"No, it's not."

"Look at the staples, the rod, it's exactly the same."

"There's no name on it" she snarked back.

"Are you listening to me? It's the same injury, same number of staples."

"There are probably a lot of broken legs in Vancouver."

"From Royal Columbian Hospital? The same exact staples, support rod, and leg? Breaking only the Fibula and not the Tibia? No way."

"Well, what are you going to do about it?" A challenge.

"I don't know—I'm just mad."

As I should have been. I was clearly not sober when I signed the waiver at the hospital and felt pretty shitty having my medical files displayed for everyone to stare at.

"Well, nobody knows it's you."

"They're not the ones being exposed."

Today, I wouldn't hesitate. I would grab the X-ray, stuff it in my pocket, and walk out. Adrienne had little support for this train of thought.

"If you take it, you'll get arrested or something."

"Just cover for me or stuff it in your purse. How would you like a picture of you up here?"

"You signed the waiver."

"In pain, just wanting it to end! Help me out."

Today, as I said, I wouldn't hesitate. But I did. That's wrestling. And life. You get these opportunities that you have to seize on the spot. You have to think on your feet. You have to put yourself first. You have to make your own safety, emotional and physical, a top priority... if you want to succeed. I had a chance to take back something, and to remind myself of wrestling, and why I wanted to wrestle and what I had committed, a tangible record of my dream. A sign it was coming along or a sign to quit.

The break in my leg took a tonne of effort, even if the effort caused the injury. It was clear, tangible proof of my pain and pride, breaking in and breaking out of wrestling. The Slide. A chance to cling to something that would keep me out of wrestling forever, to remind me why I should never have gotten into the business or stayed committed was right there. I had put up with the pain; now the part where it would all be worth it was about to come. Time to bounce back.

"Like I said, I was high. This is pissing me off. I'm not a joke or a spectacle for people."

"How is that different from wrestling?"

Damn her reasoning; to any outsider, she was right. Study nihilism and you'll realize that everything is a joke and validation at the same time. Wrestling is idiotic but so is Opera.

"Wrestling I get to pick my exposure. That's my job."

"Just leave the X-ray and don't embarrass me." It was about her.

"You don't understand. This isn't right. It isn't what I signed up for."

"Well, everyone told you. You should have known."

"I should have never left Ontario; I should have kept at it out there, kept wrestling" I said, half to myself.

"It's not my fault you're here."

Who wants to argue in such a situation?

"Fine take the picture, use it to resurrect a stupid career or motivation in wrestling or something. You just broke your leg, you've been injured more in 2 years of wrestling than 8 years of rugby. If you do more, you're gonna hurt yourself."

"I never said I was done with wrestling," I said, thumbing the X-ray.

I looked it up and down. My guts told me. I knew. I knew I was right about the X-ray and myself. Wrestling was all I wanted. All my friends knew this too, but it was a big secret nobody publicly endorsed, a shameful secret passion that they hoped would pass. If it's not your dream, you seldom get it. Everyone knows what's best for young wrestlers, for dreamers, for kids. They forget they had dreams too.

If you're successful, hardly any of the critics apologize. If you're trying, most people hold back support until you've shown your success. If you're failing, people love to tell you it would happen that way. And if you dream big in wrestling, everyone tells you, "You're gonna to hurt yourself."

No support. Self-doubt. Nobody wanted my dream to succeed except me and a few close brothers in the biz. I thumbed the slide, fighting tears; if they weren't going to support me, they weren't going to embarrass me either.

"You're gonna hurt yourself." Even she had said it. I threw down the slide, and stormed out, fighting my limp, determined not to show it. I would do that at least, injured or not. If it was a show, I would keep my smile on while I broke on the inside. They were right; I had hurt myself. I knew I would before I started. I knew I would again.

But next time they said it, I could say with full conviction "I already have. Don't worry about it. Injuries are part of life." In life you can fail at your dream, or you can fail doing what other people tell you to do. I made my decision to be hurt and finally accepted it. I hated it, hurting sucked, scars were awful, but they were my scars from doing what I loved and nobody could take them away from me.

I could counter, "You're gonna to hurt yourself" because I had hurt myself and survived. I knew I could recover. But when I started wrestling again, the critics said something else, something worse.

As my injuries healed, as I got back in shape, as I won titles, and as I finally got my shots with the WWE, I heard it from all angles and all sorts of people. They wanted me to sell out. To quit. To surrender. And they all said it in the exact same way. Friends, family, foes; all told me, over and over again...

"You're never gonna learn."

WHO IS THIS GUY?

Ben Nelson is/was/is professional wrestler Nelson Creed. Search him on the interweb and you might find him wrestling or retired. He prefers dogs to cats, pets to people, and misadventure to plans. He also wrote "What Would Shakespeare Say?", wrestled very briefly for the WWE, and has appeared in several films and TV productions.

Made in the USA
Lexington, KY
17 March 2016